Releasing the Mother Goddess

Also by Gail Carr Feldman, Ph.D.:
Releasing the Goddess Within (with Katherine A. Gleason)
Taking Advantage of Adversity

Releasing the *Mother Goddess*

Gail Carr Feldman, Ph.D., and
Eve Adamson

ALPHA
A member of Penguin Group (USA) Inc.

With thanks, to the guiding hand of the Great Cosmic Mother

Copyright © 2003 by Amaranth

All rights reserved. No part of this book shall be reproduced, stored in a retrieval system, or transmitted by any means, electronic, mechanical, photocopying, recording, or otherwise, without written permission from the publisher. No patent liability is assumed with respect to the use of the information contained herein. Although every precaution has been taken in the preparation of this book, the publisher, book producer, and authors assume no responsibility for errors or omissions. Neither is any liability assumed for damages resulting from the use of information contained herein. For information, address Alpha Books, 201 West 103rd Street, Indianapolis, IN 46290.

International Standard Book Number: 1-59257-068-2
Library of Congress Catalog Card Number: 2003105463

05   04   03   8   7   6   5   4   3   2   1

Interpretation of the printing code: The rightmost number of the first series of numbers is the year of the book's printing; the rightmost number of the second series of numbers is the number of the book's printing. For example, a printing code of 03-1 shows that the first printing occurred in 2003.

Printed in the United States of America

Note: This publication contains the opinions and ideas of its authors. It is intended to provide helpful and informative material on the subject matter covered. It is sold with the understanding that the authors, book producer, and publisher are not engaged in rendering professional services in the book. If the reader requires personal assistance or advice, a competent professional should be consulted.

The authors, book producer, and publisher specifically disclaim any responsibility for any liability, loss, or risk, personal or otherwise, which is incurred as a consequence, directly or indirectly, of the use and application of any of the contents of this book.

Trademarks: All terms mentioned in this book that are known to be or are suspected of being trademarks or service marks have been appropriately capitalized. Alpha Books and Penguin Group (USA) Inc. cannot attest to the accuracy of this information. Use of a term in this book should not be regarded as affecting the validity of any trademark or service mark.

Most Alpha books are available at special quantity discounts for bulk purchases for sales promotions, premiums, fund-raising, or educational use. Special books, or book excerpts, can also be created to fit specific needs.

For details, write: Special Markets, Alpha Books, 375 Hudson Street, New York, NY 10014.

Publisher: Marie Butler-Knight
Product Manager: Phil Kitchel
Senior Managing Editor: Jennifer Chisholm
Senior Acquisitions Editor: Randy Ladenheim-Gil
Book Producer: Lee Ann Chearney/Amaranth
Development Editor: Lynn Northrup
Senior Production Editors: Katherin Bidwell, Christy Wagner

Copy Editor: Jan Zunkel
Cover Designers: Charis Santillie, Doug Wilkins
Book Designer: Trina Wurst
Creative Director: Robin Lasek
Indexer: Heather McNeill
Layout/Proofreading: Megan Douglass, Ayanna Lacey

Contents

Part 1: Embracing Fertile Goddess Energy 1
Chapter 1   Goddesses, the Creative Force, and You 3
Chapter 2   Celebrate the Female Cycle 27
Chapter 3   Fertility and Conception 41
Chapter 4   Embryonate: Potential Takes Hold 57

Part 2: Pregnancy: Nurturing the Goddess Expecting 71
Chapter 5   The First Trimester: Dreaming, Planning, and a Sense of Wonder 73
Chapter 6   The Second Trimester: Feeling Good ... Powerful, and Showing It 89
Chapter 7   The Third Trimester: Living Large 105
Chapter 8   Labor: Empowering the Pain of Creation 125

Part 3: Celebrating Birth and Motherhood 141
Chapter 9   Birth: Manifesting Life 143
Chapter 10   Postpartum: One Becomes Two 157
Chapter 11   New Mom Fulfilled: Nurturing New Life 175
Chapter 12   Mother and Child Reunion 193

Appendixes
A   A Who's Who of Mother Goddesses: Ancient and Contemporary 211
B   Mother Goddess Library 227

Goddess Index 233
Index 235

Introduction

You are pregnant! You are a new mother! Suddenly (it seems), one who is well educated, well traveled, and recognized as developing expertise in the world is now focusing all available energy on the vegetative skills of sleeping and eating (only what's right for growing baby or nursing baby), and propping the eyes open to read a dozen books or more to learn the skill sets necessary to take on Motherhood.

While we acknowledge the importance of "domain knowledge," our book is here to remind you that this accumulation of baby-centered info can seep right into your cells and add to the richness of the many aspects of womanhood that you embody, including your own personal creativity.

I want to open the book with my co-author Eve Adamson's wonderful poem, "What Goddesses Do." Eve's poem encourages us with the vast attributes of womanliness—physical, sexual, mental, and spiritual—and with humor says, "Don't you forget it! You are a Mother Goddess."

Too often in our time, the physical expansion that takes place while becoming a mother is matched by a slowly shrinking view of oneself in the world at large. We need to reinforce what the ancients knew about the power of the female body and spirit to bring forth and nurture new life. Learning how to care for the baby in utero, how to enhance the birth, and then how to be a loving mother and a competent homemaker should be empowering and centering, and not a diminishing or marginalizing experience of a woman in a man's world.

After raising two daughters and participating in their many life adventures, careers, loves, and now motherhood (I am a Grandmother Goddess!), I am here to declare with certainty that the patriarchy that began more than 2,000 years ago to divide up the One Great Cosmic Mother into tiny spheres of influence, hoping to disempower Her completely, has failed.

Our destiny as women compels us to discover the truth of who we really are—and that truth involves a vast capacity for expressing creativity in many forms. I believe it is also essential for our well-being to discover our spiritual relationship to the Divine Goddess, the spiritual energy that will aid us to heal all of our false, societal-taught beliefs in limitation, and facilitate our ability to grow into our fullest embodiment of Love as Mother Goddesses in our own lives.

—Gail Carr Feldman, Ph.D.

What Goddesses Do

When goddesses meander home
After a long day of lording it over,
They like to sit and sip a warm drink,
Put their feet up, listen to jazz.

A goddess might call a demi-goddess
Or two and chat about easy things.
She might decide to write a letter,
Paint, play the cello or the violin.

A goddess might spend an entire evening
Thinking about what might have been,
But only out of curiosity.
A goddess doesn't know regret.

When goddesses dress, they always wear
What complements their regal shoulders,
Their curvaceous legs, their magnificent
Hair. A goddess knows exactly what

Sets off that signature heavenly glow.
Goddesses may not always have
An accurate picture of themselves
But nevertheless, they pull it off

Every time. When goddesses eat,
It is with their wide mouths wide open,
Full of relish and delicate gusto.
Goddesses savor the pleasures of food,

The pleasures of drink and earth,
Which they symbolize and transcend.
Goddesses know how to enjoy a meal
The same way they enjoy a lover,

The shape, the taste, the presentation,
The aroma of sex, the texture, what stays
And what fades. Every goddess is a hedonist,
Doesn't feel the need to apologize.

Every goddess has Buddha nature
And can be meditative, serene,
But every goddess is always hungry,
Inhaling the nectar from the honeysuckle,

Biting the petals off the roses, insatiable.
Goddesses know the delusive nature
Of physical love, they enjoy mocking
Its entourage, making the most of it.

A goddess believes in the earth's green beauty,
Water's rhythms, instinct and fear,
Stones and creatures, lust and good grooming.
A goddess sees the big picture, embraces reason

When reason serves and when it doesn't,
Intuition is her backup plan.
Goddesses always look for more,
Knowing themselves the way they do.

Still, they hover out of reach
Clustered together, a flirtation
Of angels, a rift in the clouds
Shot with light, or gold

Along the horizon. Although
They don't like it publicized, most goddesses
Have apprehended truth, and just for the pleasure,
Carry on the quest for beauty,

Which is why they give birth—
Which is why they engulf you—
Which is why they make you beg with offerings—
Only a few may dwell in that sepulcher.

—Eve Adamson

Acknowledgments

I give first a thank you to my grandmother, "Nanna," who taught me the fine arts of homemaking: sewing, cooking, canning, gardening—all with grace and attentiveness. I thank my mother for all the years of hard work in the aircraft factory in order to support us, and for teaching me the only value of money: to provide for the basic needs and the little extras that bring joy to those we love. Thanks to my daughters, Nicole and Megan, both wondrous women, for making me a proud mother and now a Grandmother Goddess. Thanks to Lee Ann for truly birthing this book, and to Eve for her amazing creative-writing talent! And most of all, thanks to the guiding hand of the Great Cosmic Mother.

—GCF

Thank you to my mom, who taught me about unconditional love and is a Mother Goddess herself, even though she would never admit it. Thank you to my dad, for teaching me the fine art of play, and for mentoring my sons. Thank you to Gail for her knowledge, spirit, and precision, and to Lee Ann for mothering my career with such care and love. Thank you to Jim, for making me feel like a Goddess every day. Finally, thank you to my two sons, Angus and Emmett, for turning me into a real live Mother Goddess, and transforming my life from good to miraculous.

—EA

Together, with Lee Ann, our book producer at Amaranth, Gail and Eve thank the wonderful team at Alpha Books: Randy, Mother Goddess to daughter Samantha and our own New Age Muse; regal publisher and Goddess Marie; divine developmental editor and Goddess Lynn; and production editor Goddess sprite Katherin. We also thank the many women who have shared their very personal and joyous Mother Goddess experiences and their families with us in the photographs you'll see throughout *Releasing the Mother Goddess*. Thanks to Gail's daughter Niki and Gail's grandson Ethan; Eve's sons Angus and Emmett; Doris, Becky, Nana, and Frank; Leah, Bob, Shane, and Robbie; Ruth and Debbie; Ethel and Nancy; Lauren and Claire; Carolyn, Lucas, and Emerald; Heidi and Andy; Rita and Erica; Mary Kay, Maggie, Pete, and Tess; Wendy and D'arcy; Lee Ann, Stephen, and Julia; Tamara, Gary, and Sydney.

Part 1

Embracing Fertile Goddess Energy

You'll meet Mother Goddesses who draw you in and connect you to the creative force and fertile energy of the Great Mother and original Creatrix. Through the construction of an altar to the Mother Goddess and a reclaiming of Pandora's box to release the energy of wishes and dreams for you, your partner, and your baby's future together, you'll discover inroads to Mother-Goddess wisdom about the female cycle and its link with the Moon, the feminine principle of creativity linked, surprisingly, with the Sun (that star so traditionally associated with male energy), and your own fertility as you recognize, honor, and celebrate the new life taking hold in your body. The ancients believed the very heavens themselves to be a celestial womb. We Mother Goddesses have it within us to give birth to the universe!

Chapter 1

Goddesses, the Creative Force, and You

So you're having a baby, or are soon to have a baby. Motherhood is finally a part of who you are as an individual, as a woman, as a human, as a ... Goddess?

Although you might never have thought of yourself as a Goddess before, you might think of yourself as less Goddess-like than ever, as your abdomen grows, your ankles swell, and your back aches, or as you get up yet again in the middle of the night to feed the baby, wondering if you'll ever get enough sleep again.

Yet now that you are becoming or have become a mother, you have a special bond with Goddesses, real and mythical, throughout the history of the world. Motherhood, that awe-inspiring power you've harnessed, can bring forth the Goddess within you, echoing Mother Goddesses and the creative life force that have been a part of the spiritual lives, stories, myths, and beliefs of every culture all over the world since the beginning of humankind.

Whether you are a first-time mom or you've done this several times before, whether you are frightened or fearless, quavering or confident, whether you plan to birth naturally or choose to have an epidural, whether your maternity clothes are jeans and T-shirts or a froth of pink ruffles, whether you are spending pregnancy lounging on the chaise or only slightly decreasing the pace of your daily five-mile run, you … yes, you! … are a link in that magnificent chain of female energy that stretches like an armor of chain-mail all over the planet. We would like to help you forge your individual link in that chain by helping you to release the Mother Goddess inside you. Consider it our baby-shower gift to you.

Conceive the Goddess Force

How do you envision the Goddess force? Some people see "Goddess" as the female aspect of the divine, whether that comes in the form of the Virgin Mary, a Greek Goddess in a white robe and gold headband, a less specific sense of the feminine part of God, or the pagan vision of Goddess as the overriding principle of nature. Maybe you see Goddess as Mother Earth or as the inner power in every woman, or as the initial creative force that engendered the universe. Maybe you think of Goddess as encompassing power, beauty, compassion, or all of these, or maybe you aren't sure *what* to think when you hear the term *goddess*. And that's okay, too.

For the purposes of this book, we would like for you to begin looking at the Goddess within yourself as a manifestation of *all* the things we've mentioned. Many historians believe that the great Creatrix or Cosmic Mother was worshipped long before humans conceived of male gods. Just imagine living thousands and thousands of years ago, before humans had any idea that men were involved in the creation of human life. Women would become pregnant, seemingly by some mystical force. Their bellies grew, and nine months later, a baby emerged. Astonishing! A miracle!

Even today, when we know that men and women together engender life, we can still appreciate and revere a woman's ability to carry life inside her and then, at last, bring it forth into the world. It is still astonishing. It remains a miracle.

> **"** Nothing in life is to be feared; it is only to be understood.
>
> —Marie Curie (1867–1934), Polish-born physicist and chemist **"**

And that miracle has happened inside of you. What you are experiencing is the very stuff that Goddess is made of, making you no less a Goddess than anyone else who has ever given birth to a child. You can conceive your own inner Goddess to bring you courage, strength, love, compassion, and to help you realize how amazing and powerful and beautiful you are. And doesn't every child want a Goddess for a mother?

Gail with her daughter Niki, who is 33 at the time this book is published, all grown up, and herself a new mother to baby boy Ethan, now 6 months old.

Cultivating Mother Love

As you move through pregnancy and childbirth, you feel many different emotions, but perhaps none are as strong as the intense and overwhelming love for your child. Every woman we know who has given birth, even those (and there were many) who doubted they could ever really love a child the way they were "supposed" to love a child, was soon overcome by the depth and strength and power of Mother Love. It just happens ... and it is a Goddess quality.

Mother Love binds you to Mother Goddesses everywhere, and you can believe in it. Let's look at that love.

> Kwan Yin is one of the most beloved of Chinese Goddesses. Sometimes called the Chinese "Virgin Mary" and sometimes pictured with many arms, each with an eye in the palm, Kwan Yin is the subject of many different and sometimes contradictory legends, but everyone agrees that this Goddess was a *bodhisattva*, or someone who attains enlightenment but delays entrance into heaven to stay on earth and help others toward finding the truth.
>
> Although Kwan Yin is a symbol of purity, she is also depicted as sensual and earthly. A protector of mothers and children, often pictured breastfeeding a child or with a child beside her, Kwan Yin is the Goddess of both mothers and prostitutes, encompassing and embracing every woman as part of herself, leading all to the path of self-actualization.
>
> One of the most common legends about this compassionate Goddess is that she was the youngest of three daughters in a powerful Chinese family. Her parents' focus concerned wealth, and they married Kwan Yin's older sisters to rich but unkind men. Kwan Yin begged her father to allow her to enter a Buddhist convent instead of marry, and he finally agreed, but arranged for the nuns to give Kwan Yin the most difficult chores so that she would become discouraged, return home, and marry as he had hoped.
>
> Instead, against all odds and in ways that could only be described as mystical, Kwan Yin was able to do it all, and was summarily beloved by all who knew her because of her kindness and compassion for all life. At last, her father, tiring of the rumors of Kwan Yin's purity and goodness (for what financial gain can come of purity and goodness?), hired a swordsman to kill his daughter. But like the hired huntsman in *Snow White* (another Goddess who probably ended up a mother), the swordsman found himself so taken with Kwan Yin's goodness that he shattered his sword into a thousand pieces and let her live. Some say she was whisked away by spirits to an island where she could live in safety and piety.

Eventually, her father became gravely ill and a doctor told him he could be cured only by eating the ground-up flesh of the arms and eyes of someone completely free from anger, and that he knew of a nun so pure who might be willing to make the sacrifice. Indeed, Kwan Yin gladly and willingly gouged out her own eyes and cut the flesh from her arms to save her father. Cured, Kwan Yin's father traveled to thank the nun who had sacrificed for him, not knowing it was his own daughter. When he discovered it was indeed Kwan Yin, he embraced her and begged her forgiveness for his cruelty. At this moment, Kwan Yin rose into the heavens and her arms and eyes multiplied, to see and offer succor to all who suffered. Kwan Yin became a Goddess.

But the story doesn't end here. As Kwan Yin approached the gates of heaven, having achieved ultimate enlightenment, she heard a cry—the cry of a human on Earth, suffering. Kwan Yin paused at the heavenly gate and turned back toward Earth. How could she leave the earth behind if anyone still suffered? And so, Kwan Yin turned around, left heaven behind, and descended back to Earth. Some say she still wanders the earth, relieving suffering and leading people to enlightenment—especially women and children most in need. People throughout the ages, even in the twenty-first century, occasionally claim to have met her or claim that she appears to them at some crucial moment in their lives, enabling them to see the path they should take and appealing to them with her gentle beauty and ultimately earthly understanding.

Perhaps someday she will appear to you! Remember to call upon Kwan Yin if you need her. Goddess energy is always available to strengthen you.

Like all women, Kwan Yin is complex, multifaceted, and mysterious. Most important, Kwan Yin embodies the Mother Goddess because, like mothers, she suffers gladly, loves unconditionally, and devotes her life to the protection of her dependents—to Kwan Yin, the whole world is populated with her dependents, her children, those who need her guidance and compassion. Like Mother Teresa, a more recent Mother Goddess, Kwan Yin had no actual children of her own but, instead, mothered the world.

Every mother has a little Kwan Yin inside her. In the same way that Kwan Yin gave up selfish pursuits to help others, you will guide your own child through life, nurturing, teaching, encouraging, and suggesting, to help your child become the best human being she or he can be. There's a paradox here, however, because as we raise our infants and children, our children make us grow, too. Their developmental stages help us to face and resolve incomplete growth from the past. Their fragility motivates us to let our own fears dissolve in the growing capacity for strong and fierce mothering.

Some mothers embrace Kwan Yin's energy with such enthusiasm that they take on a mothering role toward their entire families, their communities, their countries, even the whole world. You, too, can be a bodhisattva-in-training, just like Kwan Yin, by digging deep within yourself to find the place where your caring and compassion overflows for others because you have let compassion for yourself fill your own heart. This can prompt you to give, offer help, or donate your resources and time for others without expecting anything in return. You do it for the joy of knowing you are helping ease the suffering of others. Your own children will benefit immensely from the love and guidance you will give them, and also from seeing your compassion overflowing to others. They, too, will learn compassion, and, ultimately, everyone benefits.

> The ultimate lesson all of us have to learn is unconditional love, which includes not only others but ourselves as well.
>
> —Elisabeth Kübler-Ross (1926–), Swiss-born psychiatrist and writer

The more in touch you become with your inner compassion, which is already flowing from you as you rest your hands on your expanding abdomen and stroke the flesh that protects your unborn child, or as you look into the eyes of your newborn baby, the more you may feel the bodhisattva urge. Tap into that compassion and see where it leads you, a little bit at a time. You might find a path for yourself that feels right, a path that was always available to you. Maybe you just never saw it before. Think of how you are now germinating and preparing to birth this new part of yourself. Honor every step along this new path.

You might start by offering to listen to a friend who needs to talk, inviting a lonely neighbor over for a cup of herbal tea, doing an errand for your grandmother and listening patiently to her stories of childbearing (imagine giving birth during the Great Depression!), or chatting with a child about that "baby in my tummy." Perhaps you could pick up a few extra groceries for a food bank the next time you are at the store, donate clothes you no longer wear to a shelter, or join a baby-sitting co-op. Tiny changes in your life can help compassion to flow freely, and the more compassion you can direct into your home, your community, and your world, the more loving kindness will flow back to you. You are a Mother Goddess, and your compassion *can* make the world a better place.

Mother Goddesses Everywhere

The world is full of Mother Goddesses, both real and mythical. Sometimes, as a new mother, you can feel like you are all alone, and even if you know that millions of women have given birth before, you may still feel isolated, as if you are disconnected from them all.

Let us assure you that you are not! Think of all the strong, powerful mothers throughout history, from Inanna, the Sumerian Queen of Heaven (3200 B.C.E.), considered to be the first all-encompassing Mother Goddess, to Mwana Waresa, the Zulu Sky Goddess whose rain brings forth the earth's fertility; from Hera, the Greek Goddess of marriage and children to Devi, the Indian Mother Goddess and creator of all life; from the Virgin Mary, mother of Jesus Christ, to Gaia, Greek Goddess of the earth and creator of all life; from Helen of Troy to Aphrodite; from Ingrid Bergman to Lucille Ball; from artist Georgia O'Keefe to U.S. Supreme Court Justice Ruth Bader Ginsburg … obviously we could go on and on!

But powerful and inspiring Mother Goddesses don't have to be famous. They don't even have to be mothers in the literal sense. Keep in mind that there is little difference between a mother and a mentor, someone who supports us and nurtures our creative inspiration. Take time to think of Goddesses in different areas of the world of work (down-to-earth Goddesses, if you will). As writers, we think of Natalie Goldberg (who wrote *Writing Down the Bones*) or Carol Bly (who wrote *The Passionate, Accurate Story*). These are women who mentor other women writers, but there are inspirational "Mother Goddesses" in every field: sports, education, acting, psychology, medicine, science. Bring the concept home to your own life and think of a woman who encourages you in a field of interest. Think of her energy as energy of the Mother Goddess.

Behind every successful woman or man, there is likely to be a loving mother or mother-influence whose guidance, though it may not be known worldwide, has influenced the world nevertheless. Consider, for example, what two of our greatest presidents have said about the mothers we know little about. George Washington once said, "I attribute all my success in life to the moral, intellectual, and physical education which I received from my mother." In turn, Abraham Lincoln is quoted as saying, "All that I am or hope to be, I owe to my angel mother. No man is poor who has a godly mother." Make that "Goddess Mother," Abe!

And what about world literature? Whether you read books daily or have dim memories of high school literature class and mostly stick to the newspaper or Internet, surely you can think of many famous Mother Goddesses throughout literary history. Mothers appear so often in works of great literature because their spirit and power rises so often from the subconscious mind. The famous psychologist, Carl Jung, popularized the concept that humans worldwide and throughout history have in common certain archetypes, or character types, that they all intuitively understand. Jung believed that the Mother archetype was a particularly prevalent one in all society. Mother archetypes aren't all the same, either. We all intuitively understand a variety of mother "types" and the world has room for them all.

The appearance of Mother archetypes in literature is further evidence that we all understand what it means to be, or to have, or at least to know, a Mother Goddess. Why not crack a book or two as you bask in the glow of pregnancy or as you sit beside your sleeping infant? Even if you can only read a few pages before falling asleep, you'll be infusing your mind with Goddess energy. What should you read? Here are a few suggestions for books we love, to get you started:

- *The Joy Luck Club* by Amy Tan
- *The Color Purple* by Alice Walker
- *A Mother and Two Daughters* by Gail Godwin
- *Dale Loves Sophie to Death* by Robb Forman Dew
- *Gift from the Sea* by Anne Morrow Lindbergh
- *No More Words: A Journal of My Mother* by Reeve Lindbergh
- *Hula* by Lisa Shea
- *The Divine Secrets of the Ya-Ya Sisterhood* by Rebecca Wells
- *Like Water for Chocolate* by Laura Esquivel
- *Operating Instructions: A Journal of My Son's First Year* by Anne Lamott
- *Picturing Will* by Ann Beattie

- *The Red Tent* by Anita Diamant
- *Where the Heart Is* by Billie Letts
- *Ladder of Years* by Anne Tyler

And remember these famous literary Goddesses, listed in the following table? While many of them have complex, difficult, even tragic lives, their power, compassion, strength, and character have made them famous and have revealed the multifaceted face of the Mother Goddess. This is just a small sampling from well-known pieces of Western literature. A more complete history of the Goddess, from both written and archeological sources, will be provided later in this chapter.

Mother Goddess	Her Story
Jocasta, mother of Oedipus in Sophocles' play *Oedipus the King*	Jocasta and her husband, Laius, were told by a prophet that they would bear a son who would murder his father. Laius takes their child and leaves him for dead, but young Oedipus lives and eventually and unknowingly murders his father and marries his mother, after which she bears his children. This story is the source of Sigmund Freud's famous "Oedipus theory" of infant development, in which children go through a stage in young toddlerhood where they become "romantically" attached to the mother.
Venus, from Ovid's *Metamorphoses*	Venus, the Roman incarnation of Aphrodite, bore many children by many different lovers. Ultimately sensual and reveling in her own beauty and sexuality, Venus was a mother who played by her own rules!
Morgan le Fay of the Arthurian legend	In direct opposition to the beautiful and ideal (if flawed) Queen Guinevere, Morgan le Fay was both a mother and a powerful

continues

continued

Mother Goddess	Her Story
	enchantress who secretly studied the dark arts. In ancient versions of the Arthurian legend, she was Arthur's foe; in some modern versions of the legend, she was Merlin's adversary. In all cases, she was strong enough to be at odds with the most powerful of men.
Queen Gertrude from Shakespeare's *Hamlet*	Queen Gertrude is mother to Hamlet. She marries her husband's brother after her husband dies, not knowing the brother himself was her husband's murderer. She watches her kingdom fall apart around her but loves Hamlet unconditionally, even as he acts like he has gone mad. She meets her end by drinking poisoned wine intended for her son in the ultimate act of sacrifice.
Nora, in Henrik Ibsen's play *A Doll's House*	Nora is a beautiful, cheerful, happy wife and mother, or so it seems. When her husband realizes she has actually been managing their difficult financial situation on her own, he considers her independence a betrayal and this recognition that their love wasn't based on equality forces Nora to leave her husband, but ends on a note of hope that they could perhaps someday be equals.
Addie in William Faulkner's *As I Lay Dying*	This complex novel centers around the impending and eventual death of a woman whose children react in various ways as they prepare for her death and build her coffin, demonstrating how significant is the death of a

Mother Goddess	Her Story
	mother (at the moment of her death, her two sons are stuck in a ditch trying to free their broken wagon), and yet how insignificant, as her children live on.
Vivi in Rebecca Wells' *The Divine Secrets of the Ya-Ya Sisterhood*	Vivi is at once tragic, beautiful, kind, cruel, sacrificing, abusive, forgiving, and forgivable in this novel that is, essentially, all about mothers, daughters, female friends, and the way they hurt and love each other.
Kate Reddy in Allison Pearson's *I Don't Know How She Does It*	The working mother of two young sons is the protagonist of Pearson's debut novel. Kate Reddy is funny, cynical, irreverent, and lives the reality many of us know: that of ridiculously overextended working mother who, despite all evidence to the contrary, still believes she can do it all. Sometimes we don't quite make it, but that's what makes us human!

Another compelling and fertile source of Mother Goddess archetypes is a deck of Tarot cards. Carl Jung used the Tarot queens in his explication of archetypes, and you can use them, too, even if you have no idea how to read fortunes.

Like a regular deck of cards, the Tarot deck has four Queens. Queens are often read to represent the woman whose fortune is being told, and each of the four Queens symbolizes certain aspects of femaleness.

Every woman is different, and so is every mother. As there are different but equally powerful Queens in the Tarot deck, so are there many different but equally powerful types of mothers. Which Tarot Mother Goddess can you best relate to? Which echoes your personality, your "take" on life, your style of mothering? Take the following quiz to find out.

1. I would most enjoy …
   a) Reclining in front of a roaring fire, preferably getting wined and dined by some admiring suitor.
   b) Flying down the road on my bicycle or rollerblades, alone with my thoughts.
   c) Soaking in a warm bath or a hot tub with candles and New Age music playing in the background.
   d) Taking a long, slow, meditative walk through a beautiful natural area on a cool fall day with deep, rich colors all around me.
2. What I like best about myself is that I am …
   a) Warm, generous, outgoing … okay, maybe even a little bit eccentric.
   b) Intellectual, smart, witty, independent, and a great problem solver.
   c) Creative, gentle, artistic, intuitive, a little mysterious, a dreamer, and in touch with my emotions.
   d) Disciplined, stable, practical, polite, appreciative of nice things, ambitious, and full of grace and style.
3. My best friends are the people who …
   a) Give me lots of attention and admiration.
   b) Can match me in witty banter and verbal gymnastics.
   c) Are sensitive to my emotions and rely on my intuition.
   d) Have made something of themselves, whom I respect, and who have solid values and work hard to get what they need in life.
4. My zodiac sign is …
   a) Aries, Leo, or Sagittarius
   b) Gemini, Libra, or Aquarius
   c) Cancer, Scorpio, or Pisces
   d) Taurus, Virgo, or Capricorn
5. What I most hope for my child is that he or she …
   a) Really learns how to *live* life.
   b) Learns how to be and independent *thinker*.
   c) Is creative and not afraid to *feel*.
   d) Can achieve material and spiritual abundance on his or her own efforts, through hard work and the respect of others.

How did you do? Count up your answers. Here's what your quiz says about the Tarot Queen that most represents *you!* (If your answers were split between two Tarot Queens, you have qualities of both.)

Tarot's Queens of Wands, Cups, Swords, and Pentacles.

If you answered mostly a answers, you are a Queen of Wands. You are a natural leader who enjoys attention. You love to have fun and your natural, gregarious nature coupled with your intrinsic generosity makes you popular with others. You have great empathy. You can deeply understand the problems of others and the fact that an outgoing, beautiful, flashy Goddess like you *understands* can make others feel much better. Your power as a mother is in your ability to make life at home fun, exciting, and stimulating. Your child will be attracted to your natural, vivacious nature and outgoing personality. You also know how to teach your children true generosity, so they learn at an early age to help and empathize with others. Your house is always warm and welcoming, like a crackling hearth fire, and your natural warmth will always make your children feel happy and welcome at home, Mother Goddess of fire!

If you answered mostly b answers, you are a Queen of Swords. You have a flair with words, written and spoken. You are a true intellectual with great analytical powers, and no matter how educated or uneducated you may be, nobody can deny your native intelligence. You love nothing more than verbal banter and while some people might think you can be distant and unapproachable, everyone will agree that you have a natural wit that makes you great fun to have around. You are independent and can be a great help to those who need an objective opinion. You refuse to enable others. Instead, you can help them become independent, too, and therein lies your great strength as a mother.

Your children will learn that it's okay to be smart, and will grow up appreciating the great worth of words, thoughts, and ideas. They will be confident and independent, and are sure to leave the nest when they are ready, as you won't be coddling anybody. You know perfectly well that coddling helps no one, and you're in the business of producing intelligent and confident members of the next generation. You go, Mother Goddess of air!

 It is not the magnitude of our actions but the amount of love that is put into them that matters.

—Mother Teresa (1910–1997)

If you answered mostly c answers, you are the Tarot Queen of Cups. Ultimately feminine, seductively mysterious, and ever intuitive, you are in touch with your emotions and feel emotions strongly. Yet you would never shut off your feelings because your emotional life is such a strong part of who you are. You have a gentle touch and although you may sometimes seem vulnerable to others, you are ultimately a survivor. Like water, you can slide away to somewhere else when the place you are in gets too arid or rocky. You are artistic and creative, and you may find a great attraction in astrology, palmistry, even Tarot! You might even be a little bit psychic, or feel you are in touch with the spirit world. Some call you a dreamer, but your power as a mother is in your deep emotional understanding of your child, even in infancy. You can almost speak to each other because you are so deeply bonded at a spiritual level. You also have the gift of imparting great creativity to your progeny. Your intuition will always help to keep you in close touch with the feelings, both difficult and joyful, of the child or children you love so deeply and with such great waves of emotion, oh sensuous Mother Goddess of water!

If you answered mostly d answers, you are the Tarot Queen of Coins, sometimes called the Queen of Pentacles. You are one classy Mother Goddess who has style, grace, dignity, and a serious work ethic. You would never rely on anybody else to provide for you the things you need. You are self-made and you work long and hard to build the kind of life you think is worth living. You appreciate the finer things in life and chances are, you have plenty of financial resources, or someday you will. You are grounded in reality and you know what it takes to get by. Part of your ability is based in your great people skills. You are polite, genteel, and everybody admires how you can work so hard, can be so steady and stable, and yet look so *good*. You never flaunt your style. You don't have to. It oozes out of you as if you were a natural-born aristocrat. The gift you are so easily able to bestow on your children is the gift of discipline coupled with a healthy dose of ambition. Your steady habits and follow-through set an important example for your children, and even if they don't follow your lead in their youth, they'll eventually come around to your practical and highly effective way of life, turning into effective, ambitious, and graceful adults who know how to make it in the world. You're stylin', Mother Goddess of earth!

> I looked on child-rearing not only as a work of love and duty but as a profession that was fully as interesting and challenging as any honorable profession in the world and one that demanded the best that I could bring it.
>
> —Rose Kennedy (1890–1995), U.S. philanthropist

How to Use This Book

This book is designed to be your companion as you journey through pregnancy and early motherhood. As we've already begun to do, we'll introduce you to many different Mother Goddesses, real and mythical, who can be your partners, your inspiration, and your empowering influences, as you embrace life and nurture the physical and emotional awareness that comes with the healthy experience of pregnancy and motherhood.

That means we'll not only have stories about fantastic, powerful Mother Goddesses but we'll also include all kinds of interactive exercises and explorations to help you find the Mother Goddess you keep inside your own heart and mind. Some of the activities will be familiar and some might not be so familiar, but we hope you'll try them all. Find them at the end of each chapter. They are meant to help you know yourself better and to fully appreciate your own inner power, beauty, strength, fortitude, courage, and compassion.

The last, very important tool we hope you will begin with this chapter and continue throughout your pregnancy and early motherhood ... and even beyond ... is your Motherhood Journal. This record of your pregnancy and early motherhood is far more than a diary, although it can also encompass a diary. In it, you can record your thoughts, feelings, weird pregnancy dreams (oh yes, you'll have them!), stories you've heard, analysis of your emotional overflows, your physical complaints, your joyful epiphanies, your greatest fears. You can map out your ideas for raising your child, the things you don't want to forget to tell her, the dreams you have for him, the hopes and fears. You can even keep a list of baby names, what they mean, and why you like them, to help you choose the name that will finally grace your newborn.

And you don't have to do it all in words, either. You can draw pictures, use markers or crayons, or even cut out meaningful pictures from magazines or that you print from the internet. Draw a portrait. Make a collage. Draw your changing body, or paste in photos you take of how your belly—and the rest of you—change from week to week, month to month.

Let this be your official record of the way pregnancy and motherhood is shaping and actualizing who you are. Express the good and the bad … and yes, even the ugly! House all of this valuable lore in a book that speaks to you. You're a fan of the basic spiral notebook? Great! Go for it. Or maybe a beautiful leather-bound book with a lock is more your style. Lovely! Whatever inspires you, speaks to you, screams "you!" is what you should use, but try to find something that will last. You'll surely be referring back to your own, very personal Motherhood Journal for years to come.

Throughout this book, in addition to exercises and stories, we'll also give you prompts to help you decide what to record in your Motherhood Journal. Maybe you know exactly what you want to put in there, but if you get stuck, we'll help you along with suggestions, such as, "Picture your baby on his or her first day of Kindergarten. Describe how you think your child will look. How will your child react to the experience? How do you think you will feel?" Or "If you are still pregnant, do you know the sex of your baby? Do you have a feeling that you know, even if you don't have the proof? Why did you decide to find out, or to wait and be surprised?"

Most important, no matter what we say or suggest, remember that this Motherhood Journal is yours, and yours alone, a place to record and chronicle this amazing journey on which you've embarked. Every great voyage should have a recorded history. Let this be yours.

Mother Goddesses in History

"For two and a half billion years on earth, all life-forms floated in the womb-like environment of the planetary ocean ... rocked by the lunar-tidal rhythms." So opens the book *The Great Cosmic Mother* by Monico Sjoo and Barbara Mor. Later, we're told that women, not surprisingly, were the first observers of the lunar cycles, using their discoveries for the optimal time to conceive and give birth, and later using the moon's phases in agricultural planting and reaping. The most powerful, awesome human act on earth was, and still is, creating new life. This act was quite naturally revered by ancient peoples.

For thousands of years in the Middle East and the Mediterranean basin, where the ancient civilizations of Sumeria, Babylonia, Assyria, Egypt, and Phoenicia pre-dated Greece and Rome, the people worshipped a deity who personified the Great Goddess. In Sumeria, her name was Inanna. In Babylonia, she was Ishtar, and in Egypt she was Isis. Her name was Asherah in Canaan, and in Syria she was known as Astarte. In Greece she was Demeter, and in Cyprus, Aphrodite. By whatever name she was called, in each language she was being recognized as the Great Mother Goddess, Creatrix of life, protector of children, and the Source of all milk, vegetables, and grain. Different texts now reveal that writing was first invented by women scribes in the temple of the Goddess Inanna of Erech around 3200 B.C.E. They wrote on tablets to keep an accounting of grain and food stores for communal distribution.

About a thousand years later, patriarchal tribes called Indo-Europeans, Indo-Iranians, Indo-Aryans, or simply Aryans began systematic invasions from the north. They brought with them the concept of sky gods, a god on the mountaintop sending down lightening bolts, sacrificial fires, a supreme ruling class of males, and the duality of light and dark as representing good and evil. And guess who was evil? The Goddess and the women who worshipped her. By the fifth century C.E., the Goddess had been stripped of her power, and women were subjugated politically and economically. It's interesting to note that at the same time that women became the property of their fathers or husbands, slavery also became commonplace.

So the very nature of creation has shifted from the original, logical female model to a curiously male version (a male god creating a male and then a female, who as punishment for disobedience would suffer pain during childbirth). Then, a shift back with the re-emergence of the female model over and over again, from ancient eastern, African, and island fertility Goddess worship to early Virgin Mary cults to more recent resurrections of ancient Goddesses by feminists, neo-Pagans, and contemporary members of traditional religions. Even scholars of Christianity and Judaism are searching for a more broad-based and historical theology to support their traditional beliefs by tracing ancient biblical hints to women who have since been cut out of the text.

Remember Kwan Yin from earlier in this chapter? Some scholars say that she evolved in mythology from the Buddhist god of mercy, Juichimen, and there are some male representations of Kwan Yin depicted with a thin moustache. However, in many ancient cultures, the female Goddesses were the source of absolute power and probably spawned the male gods in the first place. Consider India's Devi, who had the universal power of creation, maintenance, and destruction. Also consider Egypt's Isis, probably one of the original Goddesses known as Queen of Heaven and the Mother Goddess. Isis was the daughter of Nut, Goddess of the Celestial Vault who appears as a uterus-shape vessel and whose body was the firmament according to Egyptian myth.

The more we learn about the world we have made, the more we can put religions into perspective and context. What we know today is that motherhood, contrary to the traditional Judeo-Christian teaching about Adam and Eve, was not a punishment but a power, and that mothers were not meant to be subjugated by men or slaves to their domesticity but were meant to be beautiful, radiant rulers.

Can Becoming a Mother Goddess Change *You?*

Your life is changing, and not just changing a little. Pregnancy changes your body, your hormones, your emotions, and your view of life. Childbirth and motherhood push those changes even further so that what you used to do, feel, believe, and know can change dramatically.

Getting in touch with your inner Mother Goddess can guide you to become more acutely aware of and accepting of these inner changes. Whether you are joyful or fearful or a little of both, getting in touch with your Mother Goddess can give you the strength to get through this time of change and upheaval. As your emotions churn, as your center of gravity shifts, as you reexamine your life from top to bottom, feeling the power of Goddess from within can help you to make decisions and changes you know you need but that might require an extra dose of courage.

Maybe you had always decided to return to work, but suddenly feel like you could not possibly leave your baby after those six short weeks. Perhaps you will call on the Persian Goddess Armaiti, creator of life and fertility, who turned barren deserts and wilderness into fertile crops bearing food and beautiful gardens. You, too, can summon prosperity and plenty from within yourself. You can find a way to make ends meet, some way to work at home and be with your child, if that's what you feel you must do. And if you need help adapting your diet during pregnancy or after, then ask the Goddess to help you enjoy what you eat and to bring you a vision of healthy, glowing beauty.

Or maybe you are facing difficulties adjusting your relationship with your partner to the impending addition to your family. This is such a common problem, yet knowing that it is common can help you to summon your inner Goddess. Let the power and commitment of the Roman Goddess Juno, mother and guardian of family, marriage, and children, hearth and home, help you to remain steadfast in your commitment to and partnership with the one you love.

Having trouble getting started with breastfeeding? The Egyptians believed that the Milky Way flowed from the breasts of the moon Goddess. Call on the power of Artemis, whose statue at Ephesus has a torso covered in breasts to overflow with milk for all creation, or Ishtar, the Mesopotamian "Mother of the fruitful breast." Know that within days, the help you need will be forthcoming.

Deathless are those who have fed at the breast of the Mother of the Universe.

—Tantric aphorism

Exercise #1: Create an Altar

Every Goddess should have an altar, but for a Mother Goddess like you, an altar can be particularly special, sacred, and meaningful. Your altar doesn't have to have anything to do with religion. Consider it a quiet, peaceful, and mystical spot all your own where you can relax, dream, contemplate, meditate, and stay in touch with your Inner Self or your Higher Self as it changes and grows.

Choose a quiet corner of your home with room for a comfortable place to sit and a small table of shelves. This shouldn't be an area designed for anything else but your motherhood altar. Don't keep your folder of bills to pay or your extra baking pans or the work you brought home from the office in this spot. Dedicate this spot to your inner Goddess and keep it undisturbed by anyone else.

First, make sure your spot is comfortable. It should have a soft chair with a supportive back and ideally, someplace to put your feet up, such as a padded ottoman. The further your pregnancy progresses, the more you will need to feel comfortable and supported, and if this sacred space isn't comfortable, we all know you won't spend time there!

Next, add atmosphere. Perhaps a CD player with some of your favorite relaxing music. A wind chime or a hanging crystal adds energy. Fabrics draped over furniture or hung on the wall add a feeling of comfort and coziness.

Finally, be creative. On the tabletop or shelf, design your alter by filling it with things that symbolize your pregnancy, motherhood, babies and children, and anything else that makes you feel strong, loving, brave, and empowered, such as a picture of your own mother or grandmother, pictures of your other children, or pictures you like of mothers and children you don't know. Beautiful baby things like silver rattles or booties add a tender touch to your altar, but you can also include images of strength, sensuality, and/or compassion. Consider a statue of Kwan Yin, or the Virgin Mary, or a model of the *Venus of Willendorf*, an ancient fertility Goddess. You might include triangular images representing the maiden-mother-crone or wise-woman triad. A triangle with a downward point is also known as a yoni yantra, a sacred symbol representing the female genitalia, something we may sometimes forget to honor in all its wonder. Bells can symbolize breasts (you don't have to tell anybody you have breasts on your altar, but you can enjoy knowing it yourself!). Vases and urns traditionally represent the uterus, so a beautiful vase can represent the beauty of your own body cradling your unborn child.

If you'd rather not fill up your altar with anatomical symbolism, decorate it instead with images of female power and compassion and comfort. What makes you feel good? What possessions do you have or what pictures do you love that will fill you with a sense of safety and infuse you with joy when you look at them? A desktop fountain, a seashell collection, a vase of fresh flowers—let your altar reflect who you really are. You might also keep a small stack of books on your altar. This one, perhaps, and maybe some books about pregnancy that you can use to answer the questions that come to your mind as you meditate or relax in this sacred place.

As you work through this book and move through pregnancy and childbirth, let your altar change in the same way your body changes. Every few weeks, re-assess the contents of your altar. You might keep a current picture photocopied from one of the many books or printed from the Internet about how your baby looks at your current stage of pregnancy—or your own sonogram images, to keep you focused on his or her growth and development. Change out flowers, shift possessions, remove things that aren't working the way you thought. And don't forget to keep your Motherhood Journal here. This is the perfect place to sit and write about your feelings, hopes, dreams, ambitions, fears and the ways in which you are overcoming them.

Instant Goddess
Every pregnant or new Mother Goddess is beautiful, but we don't all feel that way all the time. What do you see, and know, to be beautiful about yourself? Your eyes? Your complexion? Your curly hair? Your long neck? Your perfect ears? Your strong arms? Your lovely swelling belly? Look at that one thing and marvel at your beauty, and then say it out loud. "I have a beautiful _____." Say it again. And again. Then smile at yourself. You're looking at one beautiful Mother Goddess.

Exercise #2: Your Motherhood Box
For this exercise, you will need:

- A wooden, metal, or other sturdy, permanent box (not flimsy cardboard or paper) at least six inches tall, wide, and deep.
- Glue stick
- Decorative pens and/or paints: Gel markers, glitter pens, acrylic paints in colors you love
- Decorative items such as shells, feathers, beads, crystals, scraps of leather, or anything that you find beautiful.

> Pandora was a Greek Goddess who married Prometheus's brother, Epimetheus. As a wedding gift, Zeus sent the happy couple a box locked with a golden key with the warning that Pandora must never open the box. Yet the box was so beautiful that Pandora was filled with curiosity. At last, she couldn't resist. She decided to take just a tiny peek inside. But when she turned the key and opened the box just a crack, horrible spirits of Hunger, Plague, War, and Despair flew from the box and out into the world, never to be recaptured. Filled with horror and regret, Pandora fell to the floor weeping, but then she heard a sound and looked back toward the terrible box. One spirit remained in the box: Hope. Heartened once again, Pandora set Hope free upon the world to mitigate the negative influences of the evil spirits, knowing that there would always be hope for the end of suffering.

Becoming a mother can feel a lot like opening Pandora's Box. Bringing a child into the world, a child who will rely completely on you for her basic needs, love, and guidance, can be terrifying and can at times fill even the bravest heart with doubts and dread. Yet intrinsic in the birth of a child is the birth of hope, which is born again and again every time a new life enters the world. A life begins, with all its joys and sorrows, cycles and storms, pain and riches along the way. What an amazing journey your child has ahead!

You can make your own Pandora's Box, but let this be a box you *hope* your child will open someday. Fill it with the mementos and memories of your life in all its richness and variety. Sometimes you have felt pain, and sometimes joy. You've done so much and known so many. Someday your child will want to know more about the nature, personality, and experiences of that loving human known so intimately as "mom."

As you and your child grow together, continue to add things to your box. Let it be a treasure trove of hope for your child, helping to demonstrate that life, although it can be difficult and sometimes almost unbearable, is also full of beauty and love and great meaning. Let it be a testament to your inner Mother Goddess and life-giving spirit.

But first, prepare your Motherhood Box. It should be made of something sturdy and durable that can last for years. A box of wood or metal is sturdy. You might use a wooden cigar box, a small metal chest, or even a makeup case or simple tackle box. Your box should also be beautiful. Before you fill it, plan how you will decorate it. You don't have to do it all right away. Plan how you can add beauty to your box by drawing or painting on it, or gluing treasures to its surface. Maybe you will choose to line the inside with velvet or satin or brightly colored contact paper.

Throughout this book, we'll offer you suggestions for what you can put inside your Motherhood Box to begin filling it with the record of you and your great journey as a mother. You might be amazed at how your creativity flows once you begin your Motherhood Box. But we all know how good you are at creation!

After you finish decorating your Motherhood Box, take a few moments relaxing at your altar to write in your Motherhood Journal about the creation of this box and how you feel about it. Do you sometimes feel like Pandora? What do you envision filling your box with? How do you imagine your child will feel one day, when he or she is grown, and you present this treasure?

After completing these initial exercises, you are well on your way along the path of self-discovery. You are finding your own Mother Goddess within, and whether she seems like an old familiar friend or an exciting new one, you have already begun to uncover your own greatness. Keep reading to explore who you are, how you came to the place you are today, and where you are headed. You have taken your place among the Mother Goddesses of the world.

Chapter 2

Celebrate the Female Cycle

The earth spins. The moon sails in its orbit around the earth, and together we careen around the sun. Our solar system turns gently in the great wash of stars that make up the Milky Way, which in turn drifts, perhaps purposefully, through the mighty frontier of the universe. Life at every level is filled with movement, turning, and cycles, and no one understands this better than the mother.

The Sun card in the Tarot deck depicts the giver of light and of life to the planet. No matter the trials, tribulations, and darkness in life—the sun will always come up again in the morning. Revitalized by the power of this perpetual source of energy and light, all who bask in the sun's light can feel contentment, fruition, and the germinating growth force.

Just as the earth travels around the sun, and just as its changes from winter to spring to summer to fall are engendered by our solar system's small and lovely star, so does the Mother Goddess give life, and so does the female body move through cycles of fertility, barrenness, energy and quiet, growth and stillness. Our very solar system is a model for the female body and for the energy and power represented by the Mother Goddess, something we will explore and celebrate in this chapter.

Yin/Yang/You

As a woman, you are probably familiar with the notion that the cycle of a woman's body is similar to the cycle of the moon. The moon is beautiful, soft, reflective, and appears at its brightest and most beautiful when the sun is out of the sky. We love to be associated with the moon, and many ancient cultures have linked the moon and the woman.

Central to traditional Eastern philosophy is the concept of yin/yang, that the universe is a balance of complementary forces. The patriarchal historical interpretation of yin and yang divided these forces by associating light, sun, and male energy (yang) together, complemented by dark, moon, and female energy (yin).

Yet the sun is the source of the moon's light. The sun is a spectacular furnace, an energy generator, the giver of life on Earth. Without the sun, plants wouldn't grow. Crops wouldn't thrive. Perhaps there would never have been life on our little planet. Can a woman, a mother, a Goddess lay claim to the omnipotent sun, the giver of life, the mother to our very own Mother Earth?

One of the particularly empowering and wonderful discoveries that comes from learning about the ancient Goddesses is that, before the patriarchal culture appropriated religion, Goddesses were directly associated with the sun! Ancient cultures understood—because it was a matter of survival—how crucial the sun was to their continued existence. Every morning, the sun rose, and these cultures believed, of course, that the sun itself was on the move. During the day, the sun brought warmth and light, enabling early humans to hunt, play, travel, and eat. Life flourished, nourished and nurtured by the sun.

So of course, the sun would have been associated with the cycle of birth, life, and death, with fertility and creation!

> The name of [the] night goddess is Samanta-gambhira-shri-vimala-prabha, which means "Universal Profound Radiant Undefiled Light." Her name is emblematic of transcendental insight, a fundamental "identity" of the Goddess in Buddhism.
>
> —Thomas Cleary and Sartaz Aziz, from the book *Twilight Goddess*

Rather than relegating femaleness to the moon and the moon alone, ancient cultures saw the Goddess as governing the entire life cycle on Earth: the waxing and waning moon, the rising and setting sun, the cycle of the seasons. This ancient notion that Mother Goddess initiated the life cycles on our planet is urgently relevant today. Rather than feeling victimized by menstruation or controlled by reproduction, recognizing the power of the Mother Goddess, the source of cycles, change, growth, and regeneration, can help us to see that our lives, our cycles, even the decisions we make and the way we decide to build our lives, are ultimately choices that are in our own hands. Every mother is a potent and perfect representation of the universal life cycle.

The *Venus of Willendorf* is a small figure of a woman carved out of limestone, found in 1908 by archaeologist Josef Szombathy near Willendorf, Austria. Archaeologists believe it is among the earliest of all human representations, probably dating from somewhere between 22,000 and 24,000 B.C.E.! This symbol of fertility and creation is small but with proportionally huge breasts, stomach, thighs, and exaggerated genitalia. Clearly these ancient cultures weren't worried about hiding the female body. Instead, they carved it in a form that was exaggerated, emphasizing how much they knew and possibly that they worshipped the power of the female body. This *Venus* might have represented the female power of creation or indeed, the power of universal creation, as many cultures attributed the original supernatural creative force to a Goddess.

Chapter 2: Celebrate the Female Cycle

The Venus is earthy, full, and ripe, possibly suggesting a Mother Earth image. Perhaps it was a statue of an actual woman in a tribe who obviously would not have had to work or be a hunter-gatherer, but who had the luxury to sit, be waited upon, and perhaps reproduce (the heavy stature would prohibit much activity). Another theory about this little stone statue is that it was a fertility charm, imbued with power and carved by a woman. Traces of a red color on the statue when it was first found suggest that it may have been colored in a way that would suggest menstrual blood, and other evidence suggests that in primitive tribes, women would form clay figures and smear them with menstrual blood to increase fertility fortune.

Whether the *Venus of Willendorf* was worshipped as a Goddess or cherished as a charm, she is certainly fertility incarnate: the full breasts, the wide hips, the broad stomach, and the carefully carved vulva are an open, dramatic, and exaggerated representation of sexuality and the female body.

Seeing the *Venus of Willendorf* is an experience, and should you ever visit Vienna, be sure to stop in at the Naturhistorisches Museum to take a look at the Venus in person. You might be surprised at how small she is—just over four inches—but at the same time, how powerful and imposing a figure she makes. Many archeologists believe that the Venus was meant to be held in the palm, and she is just the right size. Imagine that you are holding her in your palm and feel the ancient link to the present: Just as the Venus may have helped women to feel and rejoice in the cycles of their bodies and the creative power within, so you can join in that great cycle of life that has existed since the beginning. Let the *Venus of Willendorf* inspire you to put your own body's cycles and changes into an historical context. As you change, as your body carries life, as your menstrual cycle flows, stops, and, after the birth of your baby, flows again, you are doing just what women have always done, and will always do. You are a fertility Goddess.

 I created a little goddess, Goddess Menses, to make positive association with the menstrual cycle. She is a high-spirited, energetic goddess who plays tricks with our bodies, arriving early or late, quiet or stormy, tugging or rolling over us, but once her presence is acknowledged she is very happy to quietly settle down and wait—until next time.

—Christiane Northrup, M.D., U.S. physician and women's health writer

The Journey of Separation and Individuation

A woman can feel empowered by relating to women from thousands of years before, but what about the woman who came just before *you* … your own mother? Mothers and daughters have a complex relationship, and yet, in some ways, it is a beautifully simple relationship. Maybe your mother is actively involved in your life, and maybe she isn't. Maybe she has already passed on and you miss her, or maybe she's around all too often and sometimes you wish she'd give you some space.

No matter what your mother-daughter relationship, however, becoming pregnant and giving birth will change your relationship to your mother. For the first time, perhaps, you will understand how she felt when she carried you inside her. You will see how she, too, fits into the great universal cycle of birth, life, creation of life, aging, and death. You will know how she felt when she saw you for the first time, and you may finally understand the power and force of the love she feels for you when you first hold your own new baby in your arms.

The mother-daughter relationship is anything but stagnant. It continually grows and changes. First, you are born to your mother. She nurtures you and you grow. Eventually, you become a woman and when you are at last ready to produce your own children, you must in some ways separate from your mother and move into this next stage of life.

Becoming Your Mother?

In your Motherhood Journal, take a few moments to answer the following question: In what ways has becoming pregnant/being pregnant/having a baby changed your thoughts and feelings about your own mother?

This separation can be painful or it can be easy, depending on the individual mother, the daughter, and the circumstances. In some cases, the separation happens earlier, if a mother or a daughter dies or is otherwise taken away by circumstance.

From your point of view as child-bearing daughter, you may still view the mother-daughter relationship from the position of the child, but that's soon to change. And no less important, your mother, who is already further along in the cycle than you, is certain to feel some degree of pain, probably accompanied by plenty of pride (whether she expresses it or not) at the loss of a child who has become a woman.

> Complicated mother-daughter relationships aren't anything new. One of the classic mother-daughter stories from the ancient Greeks, that of Demeter and Persephone, perfectly captures this relationship and the archetypes it encompasses: the wise mother, the young daughter, the coming-of-age that must happen when the daughter is taken away, and the way the daughter returns to the mother, changed and wiser but still and nevertheless a daughter.
>
> Long ago, as one version of the story goes, the world lived in an endless summer of beauty and growth. In this world lived a mother named Demeter, the Greek Goddess of grain and the harvest, and her beautiful daughter, Persephone. One day Persephone was walking alone and Hades, Lord of the Underworld, spotted her. Immediately taken with her beauty, he snatched her and stole away with her, carrying her down to hell. That evening, Demeter began to worry about her daughter, who hadn't returned. She went out to search, but couldn't find her daughter. She searched everywhere, becoming more and more frantic, until at last she encountered a water nymph, who told her the horrible truth: that the king of hell had stolen her daughter away, traveling across the River Styx and into the land of the dead. Devastated, Demeter appealed to Zeus to force Hades to return her daughter, but Zeus refused. In her fury, Demeter withheld the harvest, withering the vegetables and fruits and shriveling the grain, so that famine spread across the earth.
>
> At last, Zeus relented. He agreed that Persephone could return to her mother as long as she hadn't eaten any food while with Hades. He sent Hermes as his messenger to tell Hades he had to return Persephone to her mother. Heartbroken and fully aware of the terms of the deal, Hades offered Persephone a single pomegranate seed as a token of his love. She ate it, and because she ate it, she was forever required to spend only half the year on the earth with her mother—the spring and summer when the harvest flourishes due to Demeter's joy. The other half of the year, Persephone was to spend in the Underworld with her husband, during which Demeter's sorrow causes the fall and winter.

As you can see from this myth, the fertility of the mother extends to the entire earth and its bounty, and this creative power is stunted by the loss of the daughter. In the same way, our mothers, even when they are past their official "child-bearing years," remain creative and have an overarching power that influences, and is influenced by, the lives of their daughters. Demeter lost Persephone, who "came of age" and became a wife, eating of the bright-red pomegranate seed (symbolic of her entrance into the world of fertility), but yet, always returns to the mother so they can be together again. And then, again, returns to her husband to resume her place as Mother Goddess.

Think about how your own mother must feel about you, and the changes and entrance into the world of childbearing you are experiencing. Your initiation into Motherhood also propels your mother into a new stage, as grandmother and mother, as the matriarch over two generations, whose love for you only multiplies as you create the next life.

 We need in love to practice only this: letting each other go. For holding on comes easily; we do not need to learn it.

—Rainer Maria Rilke (1875–1926), German poet

In the Hands of Fate?

Who determines what happens to us as our existence runs its course from birth to life to death? The great cycle of existence determines the basic pattern, but who determines who we are, what we become, how we live, the way we die?

To the ancients, fate was something humans couldn't decide for themselves. It was already set in stone, and no matter what you did, you couldn't avoid your fate. Plenty of Greek tragedies illustrate this notion, but where does the mother fit in? In a very real sense, our mothers do partially determine our fates. They contribute to our genetic destiny. They are the whole sum of our environment as we grow inside them during pregnancy. Once we are born, they are our primary nurturers and caretakers for the first years of our lives, dramatically shaping our personalities according to the way they interact, teach, and love us. Most of us look at least a little like our mothers, and who among us hasn't, at one time or another, said or at least thought: "I'm becoming my mother!"

In this sense, fate—or, in the case of the ancients, who love to divide things into threes, as three is so representative of the cycle of birth, life, and death—the Three Fates are Mother Goddesses of all humanity. Many ancients believed that destiny—that which happens to a person in life—was specifically pre-determined by the Three Fates, who are variously represented in different traditions but are usually in the form of three women.

The Three Fates have different names in different cultures but are probably best known today in their ancient Greek incarnation as Clotho (the spinner), Lachesis (Apprortioner), and Atropos (the cutter).

These three sisters spun, measured, and cut the thread of each human's life. They created each life according to their whims, and as Clotho spun each thread, Lachesis measured out its length, and Atropos made the final cut, the three fates were, in essence, crafting the birth, life span, and death of each human. In some accounts, the Three Fates were in opposition to Zeus and even more powerful than he. Gods can do what they want to do, but no one can change Fate!

In one story, the Three Fates assigned Aphrodite the job of Love Goddess, suggesting that love may indeed be a product of Fate! One story also suggests that the Fates helped Hermes invent the alphabet, the use of weights and measures, and the cultivation of the olive tree. Maybe the Fates helped men extend knowledge of these things, but what we now know is that Divine Guidance led women to create the first writing, plant crops, and domesticate animals at least a thousand years before Hermes and the Greek and Roman civilizations. Perhaps the birth of all cultures came from the hands of these three Goddesses, mothers of civilization itself!

How do the Fates affect your life? You were born. You are living, and will live a certain number of years in this body. Then, you will die, passing on to the next stage. But what happens along the way?

Think about the ways in which your mother, your father, your siblings, your friends, your environment, and your own personality have influenced who you are, what you have become, and what happens to you. How will you, as a mother, influence who your child becomes? Every human on Earth has such an influence on so many others that humanity has become a lovely and intricate web over the face of Mother Earth. Consider how the Three Fates have determined your destiny, and how much of it you take into your own hands as you step into your new role as Mother Goddess.

Moon Power = Your Power

The moon has long been the "planet" of the woman because its cycles are so obvious and so in keeping with the menstrual cycles of women. But the moon reflects more than our menstrual cycles. Many people report mood changes and heightened emotion during the full moon.

For centuries, almanacs have reported when to plant which flowers and vegetables according to the phase of the moon. Some people even place bets and buy and sell stocks according to the moon!

The moon moves the waters of the earth, and many nurses report a noticeable increase in births during a full moon, as if the moon was shifting the very amniotic fluid within the pregnant body. The link has never been definitively proven, but the anecdotal evidence is compelling. The moon—that nighttime source of light so important for women whose work was with herbs, medicine, and healing, often practiced under cover of darkness—orbits the earth like a Goddess, waxing and waning, tugging and releasing, and beaming down upon us with her pale face.

> Lucina, Diana, and Hecate are another triad—a lunar triad of Goddesses who represent birth (Lucina), growth (Diana), and death (Hecate). Lucina means "bringer of light" and this Greco-Roman Goddess is often pictured holding a flower and an infant. She is sometimes associated with Juno, the Roman queen Goddess and protector of women, and she rules the birth of children.
>
> Diana (Artemis in ancient Greece) is the Goddess of the moon, the night, and the forest, and according to some, the Goddess of childbirth and the birth of animals. Diana's presence encouraged the fertility, the life, and the death of the forest, as Diana was also a huntress. Diana is sometimes represented with three heads—a horse, a dog, and a boar—representing heaven, earth, and the dark underworld of death.
>
> Hecate, sometimes her own Goddess and sometimes an aspect of Diana, was seen as the Goddess of the mysterious underworld, of night and darkness, and queen of ghosts and spirits. Hecate controlled the hidden things in nature, including the moon, and presided over birth, life, death, and streets and gates, symbolizing journeys and arrivals. Hecate is often shown holding a torch to light the way for your important decisions and directions. She also is pictured with three heads: a dog, a horse, and a lion, and is sometimes associated with Persephone and Pluto and represents the link between the visible and invisible worlds.

As you prepare for childbirth, you may feel nervous, anxious, even a little scared. Tap the power of these three moon Goddesses to give you courage and strength. Consider Lucina, Goddess of light, presiding over your birth to help guide your baby into the light. Let Diana inspire you to get in touch with your primal side. Think of Diana, who lived in the forest among the animals, inspiring you to venture courageously into this unexplored territory.

Last of all, as the great day approaches and you begin labor, keep Hecate in mind, who governs that mysterious space between visible and invisible, as your infant moves from the world that is a part of your body into the visible world, taking a place as a new human being. Hecate will be there with her torch to guide you through the long dark night and into the next stage of your life: motherhood. (And be sure to watch for the full moon closest to your due date. That just might be the night you go into labor!)

> [At the dark of the moon] life cleanses, revitalizes, and transforms itself in its evolutionary development, spiraling toward attunement with its essential nature.
>
> —Demetra George (1992), writer

Triangle of Power

Lucina, Diana, and Hecate are just one example of the triple Goddesses, who embody the life stages of women—the Maiden, the Mother, and the Crone or Grandmother. Each of us moves through these stages and each stage is equally important and a part of the creative cycle.

This very cycle of female energy is as present in women today as it ever was. We are born and grow into young maidens, when our fertility first begins to bloom inside us. As we become more mature, we give birth to and raise our children. As we age, we move into menopause, substituting mental creativity for physical creativity, a time of intellectual and spiritual fulfillment as the wisdom of years is at our disposal. Today, of course, women are fertile much later in their lives than ever before due to new technology and more knowledge about pregnancy and childbirth. At the same time, two 45-year-old women might be at completely different stages in the cycle, one giving birth to her first child, another enjoying the birth of a first grandchild.

As the boundaries between the stages blur and change, the triple Goddess remains constant because there are no age limitations for the Maiden, the Mother, and the Wise Crone. Every woman moves through these cycles at her own pace, and every one of these cycles is valuable, beautiful, and full of life lessons. In youth, we Maidens grow, change, and first become fertile. As Mothers, we create and produce life, nurture life, and nourish life. As Crones—a word with negative connotations in our culture, but one that in ancient times referenced a woman who had come to be respected for her wisdom and wise counsel—we are leaders with knowledge and experience.

Instant Goddess

Check a calendar, or the night sky, to determine where the moon is in its cycle tonight. Mark the next full moon and the next new moon on your calendar, and then every day for one lunar cycle make a brief note in your journal, at the end of each day, of your overriding emotion that day. After one month, look back and see if you can determine any pattern that matches the cycle of the moon.

> The Triple Goddess involves the three stages of women: the Maiden, the Mother, and the Crone. (And every woman at every age contains all three aspects of this feminine nature. Gail remembers how nurturing and wise her daughters were as they cared for their baby dolls.) Every major culture throughout history has some version of the triple Goddess. The downward-pointing triangle or yoni is, for many cultures, a sign of the Mother Goddess, both in its three-pointed aspect and in its shape representative of female genitalia. From the early Christian Gnostic Female Protennoia to the Indian Goddess Parashakti to the Australian aboriginal Goddess Kunapip, the triangle represented the Triple Goddess. Archetypically, the triple Goddess represents birth, growth, and death; heaven, earth, and hell; the waxing, full, and waning moon; and the overarching cycle of female energy as manifested in the young maiden, the fertile mother, and the wise crone.

As a mother-to-be, you are directly in the middle of the female life cycle, the center of the Mother Goddess Triad. It's easy to forget where we've been and where we're going, but take a moment to remember back to the Maiden you were, and to the Crone you will become ... but wait! If you are regretting that you are no longer a Maiden, consider how beautiful you are in the full manifestation of female creative power! And if you are dreading the idea of becoming a Crone, consider the wisdom, the serenity, and knowledge you will have stored, and the place of reverence and leadership you can take in your family and community. Seeing your life in terms of a spectacular arching spectrum of creativity can make you feel pretty important ... like a Goddess!

Doris revels in Grandmother Goddess joy with granddaughter Becky. When Mother Goddess Nancy told her mother, a retired English teacher, and her daughter, a teenager at the time this book is published, that their favorite picture from Becky's girlhood would be in this book, they both replied, "Cool!"

> I love old moons. There is something humanized about them; they are dulled a little, and rich in color. One can stare all night at an old moon.
>
> —Anne Bosworth Green (1877–?), U.S. writer

Exercise #1: Create Your Personal Triad

Every woman is a triad, encompassing birth, growth, and death, Maiden, Mother, and Crone. And using the concept metaphorically, you can be aware of giving birth to new ideas and personal growth, nurturing this creativity, and letting death take away patterns and past beliefs that are limiting and no longer serve you. Every woman has different wishes, dreams, hopes, and goals. Triangles have symbolized female energy for millennia, and you are no less entitled to your own personal triad than any Mother Goddess!

To do this exercise you will need the following:

- A large sheet of paper
- A ruler
- Colored pens, pencils, or markers
- Scissors
- Glue stick
- Photographs of yourself as a child and as an adult, and any other images that appeal to you, from magazines, postcards, or pictures you find online (If you don't have many photos of yourself from childhood, this is a good time to ask your mother, grandmother, sister, aunts, or other family members if they have pictures or mementos of you from infancy or childhood.)
- Other decorative materials, such as glitter, ribbon, sand, tiny shells, beads, imitation jewels, etc.

Using a ruler and markers or pens, draw a large triangle with the apex pointed downward. Make the lines thick and color them a vibrant, strong color that you love.

Now, at the right corner, glue pictures of you as a child, a grade-schooler, a teenager … in other words, you, the Maiden. The right corner represents the East and sunrise. Also add any images that represent your maidenhood to you … pictures from your favorite childhood places, of your favorite toys or friends. Decorate the area around this corner in a way that reflects your youthful self.

At the bottom corner of the triangle, glue current pictures of you, the Mother. Include pictures of your pregnancy, ultrasound photos, and any images that represent this time of life for you: friends, family, life partner, other children, even pets, places you love, your home. Decorate this area around the bottom of the triangle in a way that reflects your current feelings about your life. Be as creative as you can!

Finally, at the left corner of the triangle, glue pictures that represent what you hope your life will be like as you age; you, the Crone. The left corner corresponds to the West, or the place of sunset. You can include pictures of older women in your life now: your mother, grandmother, aunts, friends. Include images of the things you hope you will find important at that stage in life, and decorate the area accordingly.

Finally, inside the triangle, at each corner, write the following, and fill it in according to your own personal feelings, wishes, dreams, and preferences:

As a Maiden, I was _____.

As a Mother, I am _____.

As a Wise Crone or Grandmother, I will be _____.

After the glue has dried on your triad, hang it up somewhere if it inspires you—perhaps at the altar you created in Chapter 1—or roll it up and store it in your Motherhood Box.

> How to paint your lovely hands, fluttering over the silks like two dark birds?
>
> —Elizabeth Borton de Treviño (1904–), U.S. writer/journalist

Exercise #2: Hands Across the Generations

For this exercise, you'll create a treasured keepsake that you can keep in your Motherhood Box and pass on through the generations. You'll need a long piece of parchment paper, velum, or other acid-free, high-quality paper, about 14 to 17 inches long; an ink pad; and a pen. You'll also need your mother, if possible (or a mother-figure in your life), and your grandmother, if possible (or a grandmother-figure) … even your great grandmother, if possible.

Position the parchment paper vertically. Rub the ink pad over your hand and press your hand in the middle of the paper. Under the print of your hand, carefully and neatly write your full name in pen. Then, have each female in your line ink her hand, press her hand on the parchment above your name, and write her full name below the handprint. Your mother's print should be just above yours, your grandmother's above hers, and so on. Save the paper, then when your baby is born, ink his or her hand and put the print just below yours, carefully writing your baby's full name. Leave just enough space for your baby to add his or her handprint as an adult or, if you want to keep it going through the generations, leave more space below for your future grandchildren.

Chapter 3

Fertility and Conception

Did you know it, the moment you conceived? Did you have a "feeling," even before you took that drugstore pregnancy test, that something profound had happened to your body? Or perhaps you were completely surprised by that little blue line or by the doctor's assertion that yes, you are pregnant. Whether you knew, or thought you knew, or didn't even suspect, the moment of conception, that internal miracle, has taken place within you, like a seed germinating in the womb of the earth.

It doesn't matter how many times it has happened to you, or to a billion other women before you: The joining of the fertile female body and the fertile male body, and the conception that takes place within a woman's body are miraculous, each and every time. Cultures have thought so for centuries, but even in America today, filled with its marvels of technology and "miracles" of intellectual, scientific, athletic, artistic, and philosophical achievement, nothing is more awe-inspiring than the miracle of conception, the ultimate creative act.

But what does fertility and conception mean for a woman? How does it transform a human being into a Mother Goddess? How does it help to spread creativity not only throughout a woman's life but all over the world and into everything she touches? Let's look at the way that fertility and conception have transformed Mother Goddesses all over the world with creative power, now and throughout the course of human history and mythology.

The Celestial Vault Within

Consider your fertile body and the moment of the conception of your child. Whether you know when your child was conceived or not, there is your body. Look at it in the mirror and see it in all its fertile beauty. You have conceived! And while conception is, of course, a highly personal event, in many ways, your body is also a metaphor for the entire universe. You conceived life, and out of the universe the earth was conceived, and out of earth, humans were conceived. You are part of the web that began somewhere in the great vast reaches of space that surround us.

In ancient Egypt, the Mother and Guardian of the Celestial Vault, also called the Great Deep and the Starry One, was a Goddess called Nut pictured as a woman bearing a pear-shape vessel resembling a uterus. This vessel was a representation of the celestial vault, demonstrating that the ancient Egyptians pictured the heavens themselves as a magnificent, starry womb. In some versions, Nut's own great body and belly made up the firmament.

> Unless I am part of everything, I am nothing.
>
> —Penelope Lively (1933–), U.S. writer

This connection between female body and the firmament that cradles our solar system may not be new, but perhaps you've never considered it before. The universe, akin to your own body? It's an ancient idea, one that many still treasure today—the universe as fertile woman.

The more we learn about the nature of the universe, the richer and more fruitful this metaphor becomes. The initial explosion that scientists believe probably caused the universe and all its heavenly bodies is not unlike the explosion of conception that resulted and continues to result in the population of our world. The life cycle is about creation, life, destruction, and rebirth on every level, from the molecular to the planetary.

Spirit artist Rita Berkowitz painted At the Well *to capture an image that came to her during a past life regression. Rita had lived as a slave woman in the Middle East with her two children.*

Isis is the Goddess of Earth and the daughter of Nut, bearer of the Celestial Vault. Many ancient Egyptian myths center around Isis, patroness of wives and mothers. Isis is directly linked to the moon and the cycles of Earth, and is known for her power and her quest for power, tricking the great god Ra into revealing his secret name and transferring more power to her by sending a poisonous snake to bite him. Metaphorically, we could suggest, as the snake represented feminine wisdom in ancient times (remember Cleopatra's gold headdress with the cobra coming out of the third eye?) that Isis cleverly subsumes Ra's knowledge. One of Isis's nicknames is "the cunning one." She is Mother Goddess but never subject to or powerless beneath any God.

> While Isis was always a more popular and more widely worshipped deity than her husband, Osiris, together they represent the female and male sides of civilization as it evolved in the early ages out of a primitive culture into one of higher knowledge and understanding. In many stories, Isis is the savior of Osiris, who is killed and cut into pieces by his jealous brother Set, the God of Evil and Darkness. Isis searched all over the world for the pieces of her husband and found everything but his penis and scrotum. She re-assembled him and brought him back to life by flapping her great wings over him to fill him with breath. Yet Osiris is still missing something! Isis replaced his genitalia with a phallus made of gold. With this golden phallus, they conceived a child named Horus, and Isis, Osiris, and Horus together formed a powerful spiritual trinity for ancient Egyptians.

Consider the relationship between the great Isis and her husband, Osiris. One story reveals that Isis discovered edible grains like wild wheat and barley, while Osiris helped humankind to learn how to cultivate them, and together they brought culture and civilization to the earth. This great partnership was said to have formed and created the whole concept of civilized society!

Consider how the joining of you and your partner has added another aspect to civilization. You needed his fertile seed to give your creative force an anchor, but just as Isis brought Osiris back to life, enabling his fertility, consider the power, love, support, and even salvation that you provide for your partner. In what ways do you save each other? In what ways does your love make something bigger than the sum of the two of you?

If we pay too much attention to stereotypical images of male/female partnership, it's easy to feel that the wife is subject to and a dependent of, even a possession of, her husband. Yet all a modern Mother Goddess need do is look back further into the distant, ancient past to remember what Isis did for Osiris and look at what so many powerful and vibrant Mother Goddesses do: create, nurture, and rule over their charges, even rescue and, in the case of Isis, reassemble and reanimate their men.

> It's not the men in my life that counts, it's the life in my men.
>
> —Mae West (1892–1980), U.S. actor, playwright, screenwriter, and comedian

An old fairytale from ancient Egypt tells the story of a little boy born to a king whose father was told he would fall prey to one of three fates: either death by crocodile, serpent, or dog. As is typical for fairytales, the King did everything he could to protect his son from these horrible but inevitable ends, and in many fairytales, the boy would indeed have fallen to one of his fates. Yet in this story, the prince falls deeply in love with a princess, and she with him. He tells her of his fate, and throughout the long course of their life together, she saves him, through her cleverness, foresight, and quick reactions, from each of his three supposed "destinies." At the end of the story, the prince proclaims, "My wife … has been stronger than my fate."

Sure, fertile women and fertile men need each other to create a child. Consider your partner's contribution in all its magical essence. Even in the case of Nut, the Starry One, four gods (the four directions: North, South, East, and West) held her body aloft in the sky, and it was the god Re, who had tired of Earth and hitched a ride into the heavens on Nut's belly, who filled that celestial vault with the stars that were her children.

Yet also remember how powerful, how cunning, how loving and strong a figure you can be as you create your own life story. While Isis had a husband and a son to complete her holy trinity, all her strength, all her glory and beauty and magic came from within her. She had it all to begin with, just as you do, and she was the most powerful of Goddesses. Find her power within and you can recognize just how clever and strong and benevolent and essential you truly are to the lives of the men, children, and the other Mother Goddesses who love you and who make up the cast of characters in your life.

 Creation is a better means of self-expression than possession; it is through creating, not possessing, that life is revealed.

—Vida D. Scudder (1861–1954), U.S. social reformer and writer

The Many Faces of You

You are, or are soon to be, a mother. But does "mother" encompass all of you? Of course not! Each of us is many different people combined into one multifaceted personality that makes us uniquely who we are. Like any other Mother Goddess, you are a creator, a protector, a nurturer, an adventurer, a reveler, a lover, a destroyer, and a re-creator.

When you are pregnant and when you first give birth to your baby, you will be more focused on your role of creator and nurturer, but the other parts of you remain present and an important part of your whole self. Keeping them in mind may be easier and more fulfilling when you consider how many great and powerful Mother Goddesses had multiple aspects, often represented by many arms, many heads, or many different incarnations.

> The Hindu Goddess Devi is one of the most important Hindu deities. She is seen as the over-riding principle behind the Hindu trinity of Brahman (the creator), Vishnu (the sustainer and preserver of life), and Shiva (the destroyer). Devi provides the energy for all of these eternal functions. Devi is traditionally represented in many different aspects and incarnations, varying in importance, intensity, and power. The word *devi* means "goddess" in Sanskrit but Devi is *the* Goddess among Goddesses. She is the cosmic force that creates, destroys, and re-creates the world. She holds weapons in her many arms to destroy any evil that threatens the world's equilibrium, and is terrifying and violent in her Warrior Goddess aspect, defending and protecting the good, bringing out her "dark side" when necessary (her aspect as the Goddess Kali, often depicted wearing a necklace of skulls).
>
> But other aspects of Devi are much different: Gentle and nurturing, adored by those she protects, Devi is a heroine for women and a lover who will ignore all social convention in favor of true love and devotion. Devi protects local villages and families. She is both fertile and celestial, natural and supernatural, accessible and auspicious. As late as the 1980s, Devi was transformed into the aspect of Mother India and many local temples stand in India today to honor the Mother Goddess. Devi is many Goddesses, and she is one Goddess—the quintessential Mother!

We don't think it's any coincidence that India's most beloved and powerful Goddess was known as a Mother Goddess and has many different "selves." In India, one of the most auspicious times of year is a nine-day celebration called Navaratri during which Hindus celebrate different aspects of Devi on each day. But just because you don't have an official holiday celebrating your own many aspects doesn't mean you can't declare one!

Consider all the many aspects of you that mirror the aspects of Devi: the creator of life, the defender against evil, the keeper of time and schedules, the giver of food, the provider of love, the wrathful defender of right, and the giver of existence. Every mother encompasses these many faces and, just like Devi, every mother probably feels like she has multiple arms (or wishes she did!). During the festival celebrating Devi, many Hindus choose to fast on nothing but fruit and milk, but today, symbolically celebrate yourself with a snack or a light meal of fruit and milk, cream, or yogurt. Take a moment to yourself to enjoy this food and contemplate the many aspects of your own Mother Goddess nature.

Many Arms of the Mother Goddess

Today in your Motherhood Journal, consider how many different Devi manifestations you have. Write about each of your different "selves" and when they emerge. Are you a gentle nurturer around children? A passionate lover around your partner? An assertive problem-solver at work? A clever and witty hostess at parties? Devote half a page to each of your many "selves"; then end by giving each self a name, just like any of the hundreds of ancient Goddesses with multiple aspects. While you're at it, you might also draw a picture of yourself with one arm for each Goddess aspect. If the Hindu Mother Goddess Devi can have all those arms, you can, too!

The Immortal Nature of Creation

Having just conceived life, or shortly to do so, you may be thinking more often about the life cycle and the nature of life and death. While each individual human is mortal, life continues on its cyclical path. While your grandparents, parents, you, your partner, even your children are mortal, your family line and your genetic material persevere through the generations. And you might wish to consider that your soul and the souls of all others are indeed immortal. From *The Devi Gita: The Song of the Goddess*, translated by C. Mackenzie Brown: "I am the Lord and the Cosmic Soul; I am myself the Cosmic Body ... I am certainly female and male, and asexual as well ... I, as Maya, create the whole world and then enter within it, accompanied by ignorance, actions and the life ... How else could souls be reborn into future lives? They take on various births in accord with modifications of Maya."

What if you, your parents, and your children were immortal? Would life have the same sweetness, the same beauty if we knew we would always have it, that we would remain in these same bodies with unenlightened behaviors and the same mindsets forever? Sometimes we may wish that individuals could live forever, but if we really think about it, we see that on the earth plane our energy does live forever ... through each other, and through the love that lives through generations and spreads out across communities and countries and the world through networks of family, friends, even strangers. And on the spiritual plane, we can know even greater, more profound growth with the souls that we love, in the warm embrace of the Goddess.

Our book producer at Amaranth, Lee Ann, gave us this picture of her grandfather, Stephen, as a young boy. He's there in the middle. As a man, Stephen, a Baltimore firefighter, died in a fire when Lee Ann was only four years old. Stephen was the oldest of 11 children born to her great-grandmother, Julia, and great-grandfather, also named Stephen. Pictured here are the first four children born to Julia: Margaret, Stephen, Paul, and Sophia. Lee Ann is told that the eleventh child died in infancy along with Julia and that mother and child were laid to rest together. Lee Ann, now 44, only just given this picture, considers it a timeless gift from her Pop-Pop, a precious glimpse of his boyhood and, miraculously, of his mother, Julia.

Yet as granddaughters, daughters, mothers, and eventually as grandmothers, we all encounter death ... and then, life again. At some point in our lives, each of us comes to see that the whole cycle is all a part of being human ... and being a Mother Goddess, too, as each of us takes our part and plays our role in perpetuating the human life cycle.

> Blackfoot First Woman was the first woman on Earth according to the Native American mythology of the Blackfoot tribe. As other humans began to populate the earth, First Woman asked the creator, "Are we all going to live forever, or is our lifespan limited?" The creator had not considered the question, so First Woman took matters into her own hands. "I will throw this rock into the water," said First Woman. "If the stone floats on the surface, humans will be immortal. If the stone falls beneath the surface, humans will die and remain lifeless." First Woman threw the stone, and of course, it sank. Because each person's life now had an end, Blackfoot First Woman's actions increased sympathy between people for the "human condition," the urgency of love among mortal beings, and engendered the first stirrings of empathy.

More than a pawn or servant of her creator, Blackfoot First Woman cleverly moved forward to take control of a tenuous situation. Just like the biblical Eve, First Woman wanted knowledge, but instead of eating from the tree of knowledge, she set the rules, cast the stone, and became the first cause for the mortal nature of humankind.

And yet, while that may seem a tragedy in some ways—would we all live forever had First Woman just left well enough alone?—the very mortal nature of humans is, according to the myth, exactly what helps us to love, care for, and sympathize with each other. It sparks the great empathy for one another because all that lives must also die. Mortality makes us human. Mortality necessitates the need for the propagation of the species, and so, mortality creates mothers.

 Death was but the unfolding of a long bud-bound flower; the bursting forth of a rock-hampered fountain.

—Mourning Dove (1899–1936), Okanogan writer

Consider your own place in the great cycle of birth, life, death, and re-birth. Have you lost people? Been present at other births? Seen families extend and expand and contract again as the generations are born

Chapter 3: Fertility and Conception

and live and die? Take a moment today to celebrate your unique place in this intricate picture that will never be in the same place along the life cycle as it is today, right now. Let this moment surround you and feel it, for right now; you are no different than First Woman, wanting to know where she stood in the great scheme of things, demanding the knowledge, and seeing all the greatness in the answers.

Mother Earth and You

We all talk about "Mother Earth," but how often do you consider what that really means? The earth was here long before we were, and we would not have evolved without it. In a sense, Earth is our great Creatrix. One theory, called the Gaia Theory developed by James Lovelock, theorizes that Earth itself is a great and complex organism that he calls Gaia, and that humans, as well as every other thing on earth, are all part of this intricate and gigantic being, from the tiniest microbe to the largest of lumbering mammals.

But as we move through our busy lives, taking care of business, cleaning our houses, paying our bills, driving our kids to school, watching television, cooking dinner, and all the other many responsibilities and pleasures and chores we do every day, how often do we step outside and actually notice the earth? Sure, for some of us, communing with nature isn't exactly easy. We live in cities with a nearby park if we are lucky. Even those of us who live near or in the country, in the mountains, in the desert, in the woods, or in the plains might forget to notice the great and magnificent world around us.

Nature can be one of our greatest resources as we work to understand the power of birth, of life, and of motherhood. Conceiving your child links you with all the other creatures on the earth that conceive and give birth to perpetuate their species, each in their own way. The animals, the birds, the insects, even the wildflowers in the field are all a part of this great cycle and process, and now you are a part of it, too. Of course, from the moment you were conceived, you were part of the cycle.

The next time you step outside, notice the color of the sky, put your hand on a stone or pick up a handful of dirt, find a patch of green and really see it. If the earth is your mother, you can learn a lot from her about how to do the job right. You've got the ultimate Mother Goddess mentor right there under your feet.

> The great Grecian Goddess Gaia (sometimes spelled "Gaea") was said to have emerged as the first power out of the great darkness of Chaos at the beginning of time, and she is the personification of the planet Earth itself. Gaia created everything in existence: gods, humans, animals, birds, the oceans and rivers, and the plant life of the earth.
>
> Gaia gave birth to Uranus who represented the sky, and together they bore many races of giants, like the Titans, the Cyclopes, and the Hecatonchires. She is said to have born the Muses, those beautiful inspirers of poetry and art, and many other figures, both monstrous and beatific, in Greek mythology. She gave birth to many other children after that, populating the earth, and, according to the myth, sometimes she bore children with a partner and sometimes she did it all by herself. (Now that's creative!)
>
> When Uranus was horrified at some of the monsters they had created together, he locked Gaia's children away. Out of revenge, Gaia sent her son Cronus to castrate Uranus, and used the severed genitalia to impregnate herself with many other fantastic Gods and Goddesses, including the Goddess of love and beauty, Aphrodite. Gaia would not be thwarted and would not let anyone threaten or control her power or her children. She was the first consciousness; she was the Creatrix of all. She is our own Earth, and we are all a part of her creation.

How can Gaia help you as you conceive a child and make your way toward motherhood? Gaia is the earth who speaks to you in breezes and rustling leaves as you rush from house to car to office. She is the sound of water and the warmth of the sun. She is also the rumble of thunder and the sting of driving rain, the fury of the tornado or the hurricane, and the beauty of the rainbow or the bright blue sky decorated with clouds. Becoming a steward of Mother Earth can help you to feel in closer touch with Gaia as you honor her creation and respect her miraculous body, our planet.

How do you do it? Be mindful: mindful of the pollution you make, the waste you discard, the chemicals you ingest. Even small changes, like instituting a recycling habit in your home, driving less and walking more, reusing grocery bags, thinking twice before tossing that gum on the ground, or switching to organic produce may not seem like big changes, but while they do indeed help the earth, they also effect a profound inner change within you.

You'll find that the more you tweak your life in little ways to honor and respect Mother Earth, the more you'll develop your inner awareness of nature and a feeling of kinship and connection with the earth you inhabit. So many of us barrel through life unaware of where we are or of the beauty and power around us, but tuning in will help you key in to that awareness. You'll also notice your self-respect and self-love growing.

You might eventually find you begin to make more meaningful changes. You might buy a smaller house next time because your life has become simpler and you don't need as much room. You might choose a more fuel-efficient car instead of that monstrous SUV you used to admire. You might become horrified at the thought of simply tossing away newspapers and cans and plastic into landfills. You may even find that your diet evolves to be more in tune with the earth as you lose your taste for processed, chemically laden food in favor of more organic foods, fruits and vegetables, and whole grains.

If we are indeed a part of a giant consciousness spinning through space in an even more giant family of solar systems and galaxies, wouldn't it make more sense to honor that vast Cosmic Mother with every action we make instead of living oblivious to the great order that Gaia brought out of Chaos? Just think of the beautiful gift of awareness you'll be able to bestow on the next generation *you* created.

Mother Goddess Leah relaxes at home with her two boys, Shane and baby Robbie.

> The Great Mother is now powerfully reemerging and rising again in human consciousness … Isis, Mawu-Lisa, Demeter, Gaia, Shakti, Dakinis, Shekhinah, Astarte, Ishtar, Rhea, Freye, Nerthus, Brigid, Danu … She is the beauty of the green earth, the life-giving waters, the consuming fire, the radiant moon, and the fiery sun. She is Star Goddess and Spiderwoman; she weaves the luminous web that creates the universe. As earth, the great planetary Spirit-Being, She germinates life within Her dark womb.
>
> —Monica Sjoo, from the new introduction to *The Great Cosmic Mother*

Exercise #1: Your Turn as Creatrix

You already know you have the power of creativity, as you have already conceived. If you have power like that, you can stretch your imagination beyond to consider what it would be like to be the first Creatrix. What if you had to make a world?

For this exercise, you will need the following:

- A large poster board (the kind you can buy in any discount store in the art supplies section or in any art store)
- Markers or paints
- Glue stick, regular or three-dimensional drawing glue stick
- As many different materials as you can find: scraps of silk, pieces of burlap, bits of fake fur, glitter, sequins, yarn, any kind of material that gives you pleasure (Raid the bargain bin at the fabric store for inexpensive, fun knickknacks.)
- A pin and a piece of string about 6 to 10 inches long
- Pencil
- Heavy-duty scissors
- Paper punch
- Fishing line

Now it's your turn to create a world. Take a few moments to sit quietly and think about what kind of world you would make if you were indeed the Creatrix, having sprung from Chaos and looking for something to create. What kind of lands and seas would you make? What species of creatures? How would you organize it? Think about this for awhile until you feel the spark of your creativity being ignited. Then you can begin.

Tie one end of the yard around the pin and the other around a pencil. The yarn should be a little less than half the width of the poster board so that you can draw a complete circle using as much of the poster board as you can. Pull the yarn taut and draw a circle with the pencil using the yarn and pin as your compass.

Now, cut out your "world" and punch a whole at the top so that you can hang it up when you're done.

Hold your planet in your hands. There it is: a blank slate. What can you make of it? Taking your time, draw land masses and oceans and mountains on both sides of the planet with the pencil until you know you have it the way you like it. Then, color or paint in the land and water. When the color is dry, decorate your world with people, animals, textures, colors, stars. Glue your creation together one side at a time so that the glue on your world can have a chance to set. When you are finished with your creation, tie fishing line to the punched-out hole and hang your world somewhere you can see it and be inspired at your creative power, such as over your desk, in your bedroom, even in the kitchen where you create your meals. Every time you look at the world you conceived, remember the child you have conceived and the great and magnificent creative power you have within you.

Instant Goddess

Right now, before you can be distracted by anything else in your busy life, step outside for one minute. Don't speak. Simply stand outside and notice colors, textures ... everything! Feel yourself as part of a great natural order, whether it struggles to emerge from your urban environment or blossoms all around you.

Exercise #2: Finding Your Inner Artist

Something about conceiving brings out the creativity in every area of life. Even if you never believed you were creative before, now you know you are because you have conceived life.

But creativity comes in many forms. Maybe you can't draw a picture but you can sculpt an interesting image out of clay. Maybe you can't think of a good plot for a story but when it comes to poetry, you can really turn a phrase. Or maybe you think you can't do anything like that. Yet the knowledge that we are fertile and have conceived can bring out all kinds of things from inside us that we never knew were there.

Take advantage of this magical time to unleash your inner artist ... the one you never knew you had inside you!

The goal of this exercise is to find an artistic outlet you haven't ever really tried before, or one you didn't think you could ever do. If you love to write, your assignment is to paint. Don't just paint on scratch paper; buy a big canvas and an inexpensive set of acrylic paints and really express yourself. Who cares if it doesn't look like the Old Masters? You wouldn't want it to. Instead, let your painting express the Mother Goddess within, the inner *you*. Or maybe you love to use your hands but you can't even imagine how to write a poem. Try it! In that case, your assignment is to write a poem about what is inside you right now. You don't have to make it rhyme or have rhythm; all you have to do is write out the images, the colors, the sounds, the textures, and the feelings from inside you. It doesn't even have to make sense to anyone! Or why not buy a block of clay at the art store and work it into something? It doesn't have to be a masterpiece. It need only be from your heart. Take your time and form the clay into your own fertility Goddess or a statue or other sculpture representing your inner creative power. You can do this!

If you never again pick up this new art form you've discovered, you've at least had this one amazing opportunity to exercise the creativity that your body and mind have so recently cranked up a notch. And who knows ... you may have found a whole new hobby, even a whole new profession. You may become the artist within and add a completely new dimension to your life!

We hope you have recognized what a profound and amazing thing has happened within you. Do you feel relaxed, creative, inspired after reading this chapter? Acknowledging the creative act within your body and your place in the natural order of things can truly change your perspective and the way you live your life.

But what about that tiny being within you? Let's move on to the next chapter where we will explore the miracle of carrying a life and what it means to be two lives all wrapped up into the form of one beautiful body: yours! You'll meet Woyengi, the Nigerian Mother Goddess who from the creation stone stands and breathes life into each person as she asks him or her to choose a lifepath. You'll also meet Abraham's biblical wife, Sarah, who conceived in old age; Buddhist Mother Goddess Lakshmi, who holds Vishnu's creative energy within herself and whose name means "lucky sign"; and Sibera's Khotun, whose breast milk forms the Milky Way.

Chapter 4

Embryonate: Potential Takes Hold

Deep within you, creative potential has become manifest. Ovum and sperm have joined to form an embryo, that tiny potential human waiting inside your uterus, practically microscopic but with everything it needs to grow and develop into a fetus and finally, into the baby you will hold in your arms in a few short months.

Long before your body changes its shape, long before anybody can tell anything has changed about you, the fertilized egg, called a zygote, travels down the fallopian tube—two cells become four, four cells become eight, as every sixteen hours or so the cells divide. By the time the embryo reaches your uterus, about the fifth day after your partner's sperm fertilized your egg, the embryo, called a blastocyst, is ready to implant itself there. Without your knowing or planning or instructing it, your body begins to nourish and nurture the embryo as potential takes hold. The embryo connects to your body. Soon the level of the hormone, human chorionic gonadotropin (hCG), that will nurture the placenta connecting mother and baby, begins to rise. By the time you suspect you might be pregnant, there is enough hCG in your body to give you that positive result on your home pregnancy test. And you and your partner or spouse await together the adventure of your lives!

Even as the embryo takes hold, your body is already changing, from the inside out, as you add another layer of life to the Goddess you already are. As potential life stirs within you, we hope to help you stay open to and aware of the great process that begins. The embryo nestles into the endometrial lining of your uterus (remember Nut from the last chapter, whose uterus represented for ancient Egyptians the very universe itself?) and is slowly, miraculously preparing to unfurl.

The Unfurled Flower

How did you become who you are today? Genetics? Experience? The influences of the people around you? The choices you made? Every human is a complex interaction of all of these factors, but just as your genetics affect you, so do your decisions and choices. To a significant extent, you get to choose who you are and who you will become.

Every human is granted this gift, and just as you have formed who you are according to your choices, the tiny human growing within you gets to decide who he or she will become.

Sure, you and your partner have contributed genetic information. Your child's hair color, eye color, face shape and features, and to some extent, even his or her height and body shape are already pre-programmed. Your child will not only inherit certain qualities but will also learn certain tendencies, mannerisms, and behaviors from you. You will be a profound influence as you guide your child through the early part of life.

 God has always been to me not so much like a father as like a dear and tender mother.

—Harriet Beecher Stowe (1811–1896), U.S. novelist and abolitionist

Yet at the same time, while your child came from the joining of you and another, this third little being will take what it receives from the two of you and transform it into something entirely new: a human being existing for the very first time on the planet earth! Your child will be an individual and will also guide his or her own life, just the way you guide *your* own life. You don't really think you are nothing more than a reflection of your parents, do you? This free will to become who and what we desire is one of the great and amazing things about the gift of life.

> According to the Ijo people of Nigeria, long ago there was earth and sea and sky, animals and birds and fish, but no people. One day, the sky darkened and a glowing stone fell from the sky: the creation stone. Then a table and a great chair descended from the sky. The table fell over the creation stone and the chair beside it. At last, Mother Woyengi, the great Goddess of destiny, danced down to earth and sat in the chair. She placed her feet on the warm, glowing creation stone and scooped up earth into her palms. She shaped it into all the people who will ever be—but she left them incomplete.
>
> Then Mother Woyengi spoke: "I have given you the gift of life, but the rest is up to you. Each of you must choose whether you want to be a man or a woman. Each of you must choose the way in which you want to live your life: rich or poor, famous or ordinary. You will choose your vocation—warrior, mother, sorceress, fisher, dancer, craftsperson, artisan. And you will each choose the manner in which you will die."
>
> And so, all the people chose their lives. Some chose to be women, some chose to be men. Some chose to be mothers, some to be dancers, some to be warriors, some to be craftspeople. Everyone chose when they would be born on Earth, how long they would live, and the way they would die. After that day, Mother Woyengi would entertain no complaints about the choices the people had made, because each of them had chosen their own lives and were responsible for those choices.

The Nigerian myth of Mother Woyengi is rooted in the African notion that fate and free will are intricately intertwined. We are given life and we each have a fate but it is one of our own choosing.

When things happen to us, both good things and unpleasant or even tragic things, it's easy to credit or blame fate or luck or some external divine presence rather than to look within at the choices we have made. Certainly, not everything that happens to us is under our own control or due to our own actions, but our every reaction, the way we handle ourselves, and who we have made ourselves are all matters we can influence and shape according to what we do, say, and decide.

Imagine that you were one of those clay beings shaped by Mother Woyengi's hands. Would you have chosen to be the woman you are today? Consider that perhaps you *did* choose, in some pre-birth spiritual state, to be exactly this woman, born this way, living this way, becoming pregnant this way. Consider that perhaps you are *exactly* who you meant yourself to be. Think about that today, and feel the profound inner satisfaction of knowing that, no matter what happens to you in your life, it is all unfolding just the way you planned it. At the same time, your own child may be forming her or his own plans as it grows inside you right now.

 Everyone has a Destiny who knows what kind of destiny he has.

—Rahel Levin Varnhagen (1771–1833), German letter writer

Mother in Many Guises

What makes a mother? Today, the span of life during which a woman can become pregnant is wider than ever before, from the teen years all the way into the late 40s and in a few cases, even into the early 50s. Adoption, foster parenting, and the parenting of grandchildren have extended the boundaries even further so that virtually anyone can be a mother who chooses to be one.

Many of us grew up with what we envision as the classic, stereotypical 1940s- or 1950s-style mother—a woman in her mid-20s who stayed home with the children, cooked three square meals each day and always looked fresh and cheerful for her husband when he returned home from work. Yet because of the way motherhood has evolved, expanded, and encompassed new ways of thinking and necessary cultural changes, and because international boundaries have dissolved and the world has become multi-cultural and ultimately communicative—that profile is somehow strangely foreign to many of us.

So what *is* the face of motherhood? Even though we may not choose our mother's 1950s lifestyle or approach to motherhood and parenting, when we look at those old photos of our own first Christmases, we can't help but admire the strength of those proud moms. The joy of motherhood is universal.

The beautiful thing about being a Mother Goddess in the twenty-first century is that you need not have any particular face. You might feel a little like a "traditional" mom such as June Cleaver of the classic TV show *Leave It to Beaver*, but maybe you feel more like single mom Diane Keaton, divorced mom Meg Ryan, adoptive mom Rosie O'Donnell, or busy working mom Pearson CEO Marjorie Scardino, or mother of the civil rights movement Rosa Parks. Maybe you are a young mother and most of your friends aren't even thinking about having kids yet, or maybe you feel a lot like actress Susan Sarandon, who gave birth at age 46, or Cherie Booth, wife of British prime minister Tony Blair, who gave birth at age 45, or even supermodel Cheryl Tiegs, who had twins at age 52!

Classic moms Ruth and Ethel proudly display their daughters Debbie and Nancy so lovingly for the camera, carrying in their faces the universal expression of a mom's hopes for her child's happy future.

As the Old Testament tells the story, Sarai and Abram were an aged couple well past their childbearing years. Abram was 99 years old and Sarai 90. Yet because they were good and faithful people, God came to Abram one day, along with two angels, to pay a visit. Abram immediately rushed to prepare them food and give them water and a place to rest. God told Abram he was blessed and that he and his wife Sarai would bear a son. As God often did in the Old Testament, the blessing also included a change of names. Abram and Sarai would henceforth be known as Abraham and Sarah, and their offspring would be great and blessed.

Yet as she prepared bread for God and the angels at the command of her husband, Sarai couldn't help but smile. "Give birth? At 90? I don't think so!" she chuckled to herself as she kneaded the dough. But God heard her laugh and called to her. "You laugh? You don't think I can make it happen? You think this is a task too great for God?" Embarrassed, Sarai denied she had laughed, but God knew. Yet he only smiled. "We'll be back in one year, and at that time, you will have a son."

Sure enough, one year later, when Abraham was 100 years old and Sarah 91, Sarah gave birth to a son, whom she and her husband named Isaac. Genesis 21:6 says, "Sarah said, 'God has brought me laughter, and everyone who hears about this will laugh with me.'"

Sarah didn't fit the perfect mother profile of her day by any stretch of the imagination. While Old Testament characters are notoriously old beyond what seems possible to us today (the ages in the Bible may not be counted the same as we count them now), even by Sarah's own accounting she was far too old to bear a child. Yet she did it, and rather than allowing it to frighten or baffle her, Sarah chose laughter. Abraham and Sarah figure prominently in several of the world's most practiced faiths, including Christianity, Judaism, and Muslim beliefs.

In what ways does your own life as a mother or mother-to-be contradict the classic idea of motherhood you used to imagine? Are you younger or older than you used to think a mother should be? More educated or more engaged in your career? Did you always think you would stay home with your child but find you still want to work? Or did you always think you would keep working but suddenly find you simply must find a way to stay home? Maybe you are without a partner and doing it on your own, or maybe your partner isn't at all the person you used to think would be the father of your children. Maybe your partner is not a man, but a woman!

Life is full of surprises, and evolving as a human being and a Mother Goddess may take you in directions you never expected, but rather than feel thwarted or confused or disappointed, why not take Sarah's approach? Why not laugh at all the wonderful ways life has surprised you and brought you to the beautiful place you inhabit today?

The Ideal Mother Profile

In your Motherhood Journal, consider the picture of motherhood you used to imagine. As a child or young adult, what did you think a mother should be? What kind of mother did you think you would be? Then, write a new profile of the ideal mother: a profile that describes you. Write about this Mother Goddess, you, as if from the perspective of the you from long ago. Your profile should describe you as you are right now, today. Begin your profile with the words, "The ideal mother is …."

Born of a Milky Sea

When you become pregnant, one of the first things you may notice, beyond queasiness that may or may not outlast the morning, is that your breasts become tender and sore. Breasts are among the first things to change, and they remain an important focal point throughout pregnancy and early childhood. It's no surprise that breasts and breastmilk are focal points in the mythology of many ancient cultures, as breastmilk is the giver of life. In Vedic mythology, which is sacred literature composed in Sanskrit in India around 1500 B.C., the primordial sea was made of milk.

A Vedic epic called the Bhagavat Pourana tells the story of the primordial sea of milk, which both gods and demons thought would yield a precious elixir called amrita if the milk churned long enough and hard enough. Amrita would make the gods and demons immortal, indicating how much power and importance Vedic culture attributed to milk.

After much toil and over a thousand years of working together, the gods and demons finally had their elixir from the churning sea of milk—but that's not all. The sea also bore several other treasures, including a three-headed elephant, various and sundry nymphs, and the stunningly beautiful Goddess, Lakshmi, who represents good luck and prosperity.

As your breasts change and prepare to generate their own milk, consider how, for thousands and thousands of years, cultures all over the planet have stood in awe of that milky, primordial substance that no one has ever been able to duplicate: a substance that gives life, health, and even emotional stability to every brand-new human that drinks from mother's breast.

> Lakshmi was probably a pre-Vedic earth Goddess appropriated by Vedic mythology, but in the epic Bhagavat Pourana, Lakshmi arose from the primordial sea of milk after the gods and demons had churned it for a thousand years. As she rose from the milk holding a red lotus flower, she was so astonishingly beautiful that each of the Gods hoped she would choose him as her spouse. Lakshmi chose Lord Vishnu and is known in Hindu mythology as his partner in all of his 10 incarnations, representing creative energy and the feminine principle.
>
> Lakshmi has many incarnations as well, but is almost always pictured holding a lotus flower. The lotus flower is an important symbol in Vedic mythology. With its roots sunk deep into the mud at the bottom of a lake, the lotus flower rises up to bloom, pure and untainted, on the surface of the water, symbolizing spiritual transcendence of the material world. Lakshmi, similarly, symbolizes both material and spiritual prosperity.
>
> Those who worship her hope for good luck and material success—whether for their crops, for their business, or for fertility—but she can also liberate humans from the endless cycle of suffering and rebirth. She is beauty and good fortune born from a sea of milk.

Lakshmi is a Goddess who is beautiful, prosperous, and lucky, traits inherent in every Mother Goddess no matter what her material situation. Because she represents inherent universal creativity, Lakshmi bore herself from a sea of milk in much the same way each of us has an inner creative force that helps shape and create us.

Let's look at each of Lakshmi's key traits one at a time and see how they apply to you:

- **Beauty.** Even if you feel nauseous and are finding it difficult to sleep, even if you don't feel beautiful when you look in the mirror, every pregnant woman, every Mother Goddess, is beautiful. Find one beautiful thing about yourself and really see it. Revel in your own beauty.
- **Prosperity.** Prosperity can mean many things. If you are in a materially prosperous place in life, give thanks to the great Goddess for making your life comfortable. If you aren't materially prosperous at the moment, consider all the other ways your life is prosperous. Count the people you love. Count the friends you can rely on. Tally up the food in your cupboards, the electricity and the heat or cooling in your home, the roof above you. Count the community you live in and add all the knowledge you've gained, the experiences you've had, and the fun life has offered you. See how very prosperous you are?
- **Luck.** Luck may seem like an elusive gift. Sometimes you have it and sometimes you don't. Maybe you feel like you haven't had much lately when a string of things in life go awry, but consider how very fortunate you really are. You are lucky to be beautiful. You are lucky to be prosperous. And most of all, you are so very lucky that you were born a woman and are now able to revel in the experience of being a Mother Goddess. (Maybe that's why everybody wants to touch a pregnant woman's belly … for good luck!)

> How can you say luck and chance are the same thing? Chance is the first step you take, luck is what comes afterwards.
>
> —Amy Tan (1952–), U.S. writer

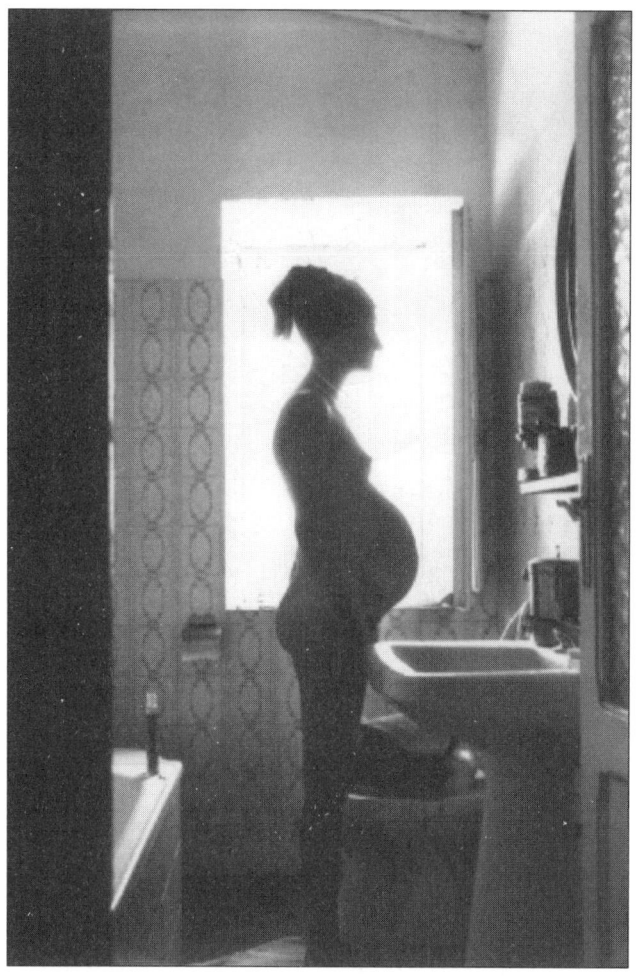

Mother Goddess Wendy, pregnant with son D'arcy, begins her day. We feel this is a beautiful photograph of an expectant mother's blossoming abundance. Soon, your body will blossom, as Wendy's has.

The Universal Embryo

Imagine the embryo nestled inside you, safe and protected by its mother. Now imagine Earth as an embryo, nestled inside the solar system, held tight by the gravitational pull of the sun. And imagine our solar system, nurtured and supported within the vast universe.

Or, consider that each cell within the embryo within you is its own universe, and each atom contained in each cell is its own tiny spinning solar-system-like structure of perfection.

The microcosm and macrocosm of the universe have much in common. We are all built around the same kinds of structures and movements. The embryo within you is a part of the vast space that is your body, just as you are part of the vast space that makes the world, and so it goes on and on. The very universe is a mirror we can hold up to ourselves and say, "Ah-ha! There I am!"

Perhaps this is why the Milky Way, that rotating, spiral-shape galaxy of which our solar system is just a tiny part, is so often and in so many cultures thought to consist of mother's milk. As mythologies form and Goddesses emerge and evolve from culture to culture, passed down through generations, the macrocosm and the microcosm combine, switch places, and mingle like the gasses and clouds of vapor that make up our galaxy and are so faintly visible in the dark night sky like a luminous swath of milk across space.

> The body says what words cannot.
>
> —Martha Graham (1894–1991), U.S. dancer and choreographer

Speaking of astronomy, Jocelyn Bell Burnell, a professor of physics at Open University in England who is credited with discovering the first four pulsars but was denied that credit when the Nobel Prize was awarded in 1974 to Burnell's graduate advisor, also happens to be a mother. In 1995, Burnell said, "Because [physics and astronomy] are predominately male, inevitably, the standards, the norms, are the male. The system doesn't always stop to think, 'Has this person had a career break, perchance, or are there other constraints?' Do we use a quantity of achievement as a measure of ability?"

We think Dr. Burnell is a fantastic example of a space-age Mother Goddess.

> Khotun, also known as Kubai-khotun and equivalent to the Goddess Ajysit or "Milk Lake Mother," was the primordial Mother Goddess for the Yakut people of Siberia. She is the Goddess of milk and the nourisher of all people and animals. Khotun lives in a lake of breastmilk beneath the Tree of Life. Her breasts are huge and overflowing with milk, and it is said that the excess

> milk formed the Milky Way galaxy. Stories surrounding Ajysit say that she determines each individual's fate by writing it in a golden book at the child's birth, and then descends to assist in the delivery and share a meal with the new family. We're guessing she probably advises the new mother on breast-feeding as well!

Your breasts won't begin to produce milk for awhile yet, but if you decide to breastfeed, your breasts will be the primary source of nourishment for your newborn baby. Just as the embryo is growing and developing inside you now, your breasts are slowly changing and preparing for their future role as nourishers.

The Goddess Khotun isn't, of course, supposed to represent anyone's actual lot in life—huge-breasted and wallowing in a pool of milk—but don't be surprised if, in the early days with your newborn, you feel a little bit like that! Remember, however, that Khotun is a metaphor for what our breasts can do and how they represent not only a source of food for your individual child, but also the source of life for the human race. They are, in so many ways, an integral part of your Mother Goddess divinity, so honor them today as they begin their own evolution.

Do you know the anatomy of your breast? Breasts are glands consisting of milk ducts and, especially during the childbearing years, fat. Breasts contain approximately 15 to 25 lobes that branch out into lobules ending in tiny sacs called alveoli. These sacs produce milk when hormones send the message that you have given birth, and muscle cells around the alveoli contract to push the milk through the ducts to a reservoir under the nipple. When a baby sucks on the nipple (this takes some practice for both mother and baby), the milk flows out of tiny openings in the nipple. The "first milk" is called colostrum, a clear substance rich with protective antibodies. After a few days, the colostrum turns into milk.

Exercise #1: The Seed Germinates

As you hold the germinated embryo of your own creation within you, consider how much this life within resembles a bulb. The bulb—of a tulip, a daffodil, an amaryllis, a hyacinth—holds the whole flower within itself. With nurturing, sunlight, and water, that bulb bursts forth into a flower. First, the bulb sets down roots to anchor itself in its new state. Then, it shoots up stalks and at last, a gorgeous bloom.

For this exercise, we will plant a bulb and watch it explode into life from its dormant state, as an external reminder of the life within you bursting from a tiny cluster of cells into a human.

For this exercise, you will need the following:

- An hourglass-shape hyacinth jar, or any narrow-necked jar or vase just wide enough to hold a hyacinth bulb in place
- One hyacinth bulb (Dutch Hyacinth bulbs, or *Hyacinthus orientalis,* work well for this process)

Fill your jar with fresh water and set the bulb, root-side down, in the neck of the jar or vase so that the bottom of the bulb is just touching the water. As you place the bulb over the water, consider how this bulb is like the newly formed embryo within your womb.

Store the bulb in a cool, dark place until the jar fills with roots. Check it every few days to watch its progress; every once in awhile, consider how the life within you is forming and growing and setting down its own "roots" as bones and organs form, buds turn to limbs, and the heart grows stronger and stronger.

When the jar is filled with roots, move the vase to place the hyacinth in the sun. Approximately 14 to 18 weeks after first "planting" your bulb, it should bloom into a beautiful multi-foliate jewel on your windowsill. Admire the beauty and mystery of the blooming bulb as you anticipate the arrival of your own little blossom.

Instant Goddess

To remind you of the flower within your womb and the flowering within your heart as you grow into your new role as Mother Goddess, go outside today and pick a flower or run by the florist and buy a single bloom. Wear it today: in your buttonhole, on your belt, even in your hair! If anyone asks you what the occasion is, say you simply felt like blossoming today.

Exercise #2: Your Milky Way

If you have ever attended a performance of Eve Ensler's controversial play *The Vagina Monologues,* you probably know that this groundbreaking work has become more than just an artistic performance. It has triggered a worldwide movement for openness and honesty about women's bodies and women's lives. Sometimes when this play is performed, exhibitors fill the lobby with educational information for women and even, at one memorable performance we remember, photocopies of a vaginal shape women could decorate with markers, sequins, features, and glitter. "Come decorate your vagina!" the women at the booth proclaimed. "It's fun!"

We think for this chapter, it would be particularly fun to vary this "craft project" just a little. Why not celebrate your breasts, those producers of nourishment for the human race, in a fun and symbolic way?

For this project, you will need the following:

- A large piece of drawing paper
- A black marker
- Colored markers or paints
- Decorative objects you find
- A sheet of gold star stickers (like teachers use to put on student papers)

With a black marker, trace around a cup or a bowl to draw a large circle on the paper. In the center, draw a smaller circle. Now, color and decorate your "breast" in any fanciful way that amuses you. Finally, make a trail of stars from the center of the breast and then populate the area around the breast with stars. Admire your picture for awhile, and then tuck it away in your Motherhood Box.

Now that pregnancy has begun, you have an exciting journey ahead. We hope we have helped to prepare you. In the next few chapters, we'll travel with you through the three trimesters of pregnancy, from the first thrills of walking around conscious of your pregnancy to the birthing process itself. It's going to be a thrilling time, and we want to help you enjoy every minute.

Part 2

Pregnancy: Nurturing the Goddess Expecting

Explore the unique energy of Mother Goddesses for each of the three trimesters of pregnancy: from the sense of wonder that marks your first trimester, through the feel-good power of your second trimester, to the amazing third trimester where your baby precedes you wherever you go. Mother Goddesses help you access your fierce Warrior-Goddess creative instinct and physical prowess during the labor process, as you experience how your body, mind, and spirit collaborate to bring your baby into the world. What happens when that part of you that you've carried for nine months suddenly lies cradled in your arms? Mother Goddesses in your life and in this book will help you and your partner to discover the powerful and sacred nature of birthing another life.

Chapter 5

The First Trimester: Dreaming, Planning, and a Sense of Wonder

The test results are positive. You've seen your doctor. You've told your friends and family. No doubt about it, you are pregnant!

Like most of us, you probably feel awe and wonder every time you think of the new life inside you. Yet you must still continue with daily life: working, paying bills, cleaning the house, seeing friends, and doing everything else you normally do. Despite the way the world spins on as if nothing had changed, you can make conscious choices and dedicate special time to this new and amazing state of being: hosting life within life.

This chapter will help you to make the most of your first trimester so that you don't let it slip away without recognizing and honoring your new status as a pregnant Mother Goddess.

Of course, you probably can't avoid recognizing that some things have changed. You may feel queasy in the morning ... or all day long! Foods you used to love may mysteriously lose their appeal, while things you never would have touched suddenly sound delicious! Your breasts may suddenly become tender and sore, and your aureoles may enlarge and darken. Even your vaginal tissue may change color as your body resets itself to achieve an entirely different state of homeostasis, or balance, than it knew before.

And while you feel pregnant, you don't yet look pregnant. People may wonder what is different about you, but this trimester is marked mainly by internal rather than obvious external changes. You may begin to have unusual, particularly vivid dreams. Your perspective may change, along with your moods. You will feel *different* inside. For that very reason, the first trimester is an excellent time to spend engaging in a little introspection about what lies within you: within your womb; within your busy, happy, worried mind; and within your heart.

 Now I was someone who ate like a wolf, napped like a cat, and dreamed like a madwoman.

—Marni Jackson (1946–), Canadian writer and journalist, from *The Mother Zone*

Moment of Knowing

When you first know, deep inside, that you are pregnant—beyond suspecting, beyond wondering, into truly *knowing*—you may feel totally overwhelmed with the newness of it all. Or perhaps this is your second or third child and you are returning again to a moment of wonder. You recognize that a person will emerge from your body as an individual unique and unknown to you, yet part of you and your partner.

In either case, you are beginning your long wait to meet the person you carry. Who will she or he be? If this is your first pregnancy, you may try to visualize your child, wondering if it is a boy or a girl, what your child will look like as a toddler, a grade-schooler, a teenager, or an adult. If this is the second or third time around, you may be less inclined to visualize the life within and more content to wait and see, knowing that your baby will be born with a personality all his or her own, despite your hopes and fears and vivid imaginings.

As you move through your day, you may find yourself frequently resting your hands on your not-yet-any-bigger belly. As you alternate from ravenous hunger to feeling repelled by food, from joy to panic, from tranquility to excitement, your belly will become a touchstone for you. You will find your hands gravitating there in a deeply rooted instinct to cradle the child within. Feeling your belly now is a great way to monitor the changes, so that as your baby grows, you will be more aware of those changes when they happen. Suddenly your hands will be cupping a barely perceptible swelling. That swelling will grow, and soon it will become like a rise in a hill, and then what may feel like a great mountain. All along, your hands will be there, feeling, waiting, wondering ....

In the Cycladic Islands of the Aegean around 2000 B.C.E., inhabitants created the first life-size female statues, carved in marble. Unlike primitive Paleolithic fertility statues, such as the *Venus of Willendorf*, with their swollen bellies, breasts, and hips, these Aegean Venus figures are tall, thin, almost geometric in character with straight hips, small breasts, sometimes with bent knees, and almost always with hands crossed over the breast or belly.

While art scholars consider this alternative female form a mystery for a fertility Goddess, we Mother Goddesses think we know exactly why these lithe elegant figures represented fertility just as magnificently as the swollen fully pregnant forms of more ancient cultures. These Aegean Venus forms perhaps represented that very moment of knowing, that early internal discovery. The crossed hands over the torso mimic that natural movement every newly pregnant woman feels compelled to make, signifying the internal changes as the thin figure represents the not-yet-changing external form.

During this first trimester, the figure of the Aegean Venus may be something you can relate to more easily than the full-figured Venus of Willendorf. You don't yet *look* pregnant, but you are pregnant and you feel it deeply and with wonderment.

It may seem amazing to you that your belly will grow and expand very soon, but it certainly will. One way to track this process is by beginning a photo record of your pregnancy. Have someone take a picture of you on the first day of each month throughout your pregnancy. Wear something that shows the shape of your belly, such as your exercise gear (perhaps yoga pants and a tank top or leggings and a T-shirt) and keep the series of photos in your Motherhood Box, tied together with a ribbon, or tucked into an envelope. Add a new photo each month, and you'll have documentation of your beautiful transformation.

Another way to further your kinship with the Aegean Venus: Use her pose for meditation. Either standing or kneeling, close your eyes and cross your hands over your solar plexus, just beneath your ribcage, in imitation of the Aegean Venus. Take slow, deep breaths and focus love within your womb, encompassing your unborn child in the glow of your inner light. Stay in the position for a few minutes, or even longer if you desire. Try to spend a short while meditating in this way every day during your first trimester. Consider it your first spiritual communion with the life you have created.

 Though we travel the world over to find the beautiful, we must carry it with us, or we find it not.

—Ralph Waldo Emerson (1803–1882), American philosopher and writer

The Waxing Mother

Is the moon bright, round, and full tonight? Is it a thin silver sliver of new moon? Or is it somewhere in between?

For thousands of years all over the world, people have linked women to the moon. You are closer to the waxing new moon in your first trimester than at any other time in your pregnancy. Pay attention to the gradual changes in the moon over the next three months as you feel and see the gradual changes in your own body.

If you take our previous suggestion to create a photo record of your changing body, you will have an even greater link to the changing moon—your body waxing, right there before you and preserved for you and your children. Just like the waxing moon, your belly will begin to expand into ripeness and fullness. You are at the beginning of a great journey of physical, mental, and spiritual growth, and as your body continues to grow, so will your awareness of the new life ahead.

Yet it's easy to become so engulfed in your physical and emotional changes that you forget what is around you. Your partner, in union with whom you make this child, may feel on the fringes of your experience because you are the only one who can feel what is happening to you right now. Your baby is too small to kick or even to show, and the only change in you, apparent to those who only see what is happening on the *outside* of your body, may be your fluctuating moods and appetites.

What will you choose to share with your partner, who is also a part of the life within you?

> Selene is the Goddess of the Moon, also known as Luna, Diana, or Artemis in ancient Greco-Roman culture. Every evening, after her brother Helios tugged the sun across the sky with his chariot, Selene began her journey pulling the moon across the night sky with her chariot pulled by two white horses. As the ancient Greeks watched the moon set into the Mediterranean, they envisioned Selene ending her journey with a rejuvenating bath in the sea.
>
> Selene, known for her many lovers, loved most of all the shepherd, Endymion, a beautiful mortal whose charm so entranced Selene that she began to neglect her moon-toting duties to lie beside him each evening as he slept. Finally, to secure her lover, Selene, with the help of Zeus, cast a spell over the shepherd so that Endymion would remain in perpetual youth and perpetual sleep. Over the course of their long (if only half-awake) relationship, they produced 50 daughters. Yet because their father remained constantly asleep, Selene and her daughters were never able to interact with him by light of day, or by moonlight. Selene represents the moon at its peak of fullness.

As a newly pregnant Mother Goddess, you can envision how Selene and the ripe full moon represent your pregnant state, full of all the potential of the union with your partner growing in love inside your body. You are the moon, and all the hopes and dreams and plans are there waiting to be born, each one like one of the 50 daughters of Selene and Endymion, circled with love.

 Marriage, to women as to men, must be a luxury, not a necessity; an incident of life, not all of it.

—Susan Brownell Anthony (1820–1906), U.S. suffragist and editor

Yet don't forget your "shepherd," your Endymion, who is far from living a somnolent life and needs to share in your experience. Selene and her daughters never knew the joy of interacting with an awake and alert Endymion. Don't get so caught up in your musing, dreaming, planning, and joy at producing a child through the union with your beloved that you forget to share your dreams and hopes and plans *with* him. Both you and the child that will result from your union can embrace your partner as an integral part of your new family. Let your partner share in your growing sense of wonder at what you discover each day about yourself as a pregnant woman. You carry the power of love and life within you, as well as the magnificent opportunity to communicate your experience with the father of your child.

Instant Goddess
Just as Selene bathed in the deep ocean after her journey across the night sky, you can feel like an instant Goddess with a sea salt bath! Add a sea salt bath product or one cup of plain sea salt (find it at your health food store or enlightened supermarket) to a hot bath and soak for 20 minutes. Close your eyes and imagine you are the moon, dipping into the warm tropical Mediterranean Sea after her long journey across the sky. Relax …

Granter of Wishes

What do you wish right now? Do you wish for a healthy baby? A comfortable pregnancy? A labor surrounded by people you love and trust? Maybe you wish for a bigger house or a more reliable car, or simply more money to support your growing family. Maybe you wish you had a fairy godmother.

The Fairy Godmother is a Mother Goddess archetype who appears in stories all around the world as the guiding light, conscience, and bringer of hope for good souls, from Cinderella to Pinocchio, but real fairy godmothers are everywhere. Think of celebrities like Melinda Gates and Oprah Winfrey, who donate so much of their money and resources to help those in need. Think of the volunteers at hospitals and nursing homes who give consolation and friendship to people who are scared, alone, and sick. Think of the teacher in your child's school who always helps with every school event, giving constantly of her time both in and out of the classroom. Think of the women who sit on crisis lines, the woman doctor who volunteers at the free clinic or the woman lawyer who does pro bono work at the women's shelter. Remember the neighbors who wave and smile at you to brighten your day, the women in your family who help, support, and nurture you. Think of the many Fairy Godmothers who have helped you along the way. We bet you can make quite a list.

Mexico is the home of much sacred belief, and the manifestations of that belief often take the form of various advocations of the Virgin Mary. These Goddesses, centuries-old fusions of pre-Columbian beliefs and Catholicism, have their own festivals, prayers, shrines, and specialties or important qualities.

In the tiny town of Juquila in Oaxaca, Mexico, stands a shrine to the Virgin of Juquila. For centuries, Mexicans have made sacred pilgrimages to visit this Virgin and to make requests for things they need or want—from money to a wife or husband to a child recovering from illness. Myths abound about the Virgin of Juquila: how she has miraculously restored infants to life, healed sicknesses, and rewarded her most devoted supplicants with love, money, and the possessions they need.

The Virgin of Juquila did more than grant wishes, however. She required devotion and purity of those who asked her favors. Many people still travel for miles to visit this Virgin, and some crawl the final two kilometers on their knees across hard stone to display their devotion. While on a quest to ask favors of the Virgin of Juquila, devotees are required to practice chastity, and one story that still circulates today tells of a couple who couldn't contain their lust and veered off the road to make love on the way to Juquila. The Virgin of Juquila turned them to stone, and their belly-to-belly figures are said to remain there today.

The Virgin of Juquila represents hope, purity, and both material and spiritual reward for goodness and devotion. In this way she is both Virgin Mary and a much more ancient manifestation of the Mother Goddess, who rewards, punishes, loves, and gives. She is a moral compass transcending any particular religion, and she has the power to dole out what each person deserves.

This tiny Virgin of Juquila is the work of renowned Oaxacan folk-artist Guillermina Aguilar, who herself has made pilgrimages to ask for special favors. Guillermina is the daughter of a folk artist, with daughters of her own as well. She says of the creative process: "The happiness comes from the moment you pour your heart into what you are creating. The sadness comes from then having to part with what you have just put so much love into." Spoken like a folk-art Mother Goddess!

As a Mother Goddess, we are sure you must have wishes, but as a mother-to-be and the giver of the most pure of loves—the love of a mother for her child—consider how you can transform yourself from receiver of the many gifts of the women in your life to a Fairy Godmother in your own right!

As a mother, you will automatically be the one who grants promises, listens to dreams, and even doles out just consequences for your child as he or she grows and learns about the world. Just like the Virgin of Juquila, you will listen to many requests. Some requests you will grant. Some you will reject. Some you will offer conditionally, and if your child keeps her or his promises, you will be the one who has the power to grant the wishes.

You can also be a Fairy Godmother to other women (and to your partner, brother, father—the men, too!) in your life, returning the favor and perpetuating the cycle of love. Tell your mother how much she means to you. Write your sister a letter describing the positive effects she has had on your life. (Or if the opposite seems true, that she actually made life difficult for you, let her know how much you have learned about yourself from the relationship.) Read a book to your niece or the little girl down the street. Talk to other women who need to talk, and let them ask for what they need from you.

And today, consider how you can even be a Fairy Godmother to yourself. What wishes do you have? What dreams, what desires? Think of one that you can make happen today—something small, like flowers on the table or a big hug from your partner—and grant your own wish. You've been very good, and you have earned it!

 When there is a woman, there is magic.

—Ntozake Shange (1948–), U.S. writer, poet, and playwright

Releasing Your Fears

Even as it is joyful, exciting, and blissful, pregnancy can also be frightening, especially the first time. You might feel that you are no longer in control of your bodily processes. You might feel too ill to function as you did before, or so tired that you can barely keep your eyes open. Your dreams might haunt you, and you might be filled with anxiety at the thought of going through labor.

Many of us feel frightened by the unknown, and what is more unknown than growing a human inside for the first time, and understanding how it comes out after nine months? Childbirth classes and lots of reading and talking to other mothers can help to allay some of your anxiety, although some people are bound to tell you their birth "horror stories," which might make your anxiety even worse.

Remember that as you embark upon this mysterious new journey, it is natural to feel anxious, even scared. Yet creating life and giving birth are some of the most beautiful, natural things a woman can do. Women have been doing them for thousands and thousands of years, and you can do it, too. Consider it your initiation into womanhood, your passage into the realm of the Mother Goddess.

Without mothers, the world's population would eventually die out. You are part of an essential system of life for our planet, and no matter how many people question why you would have a child when the world is overpopulated (someone is sure to say it, inappropriate as it may be), know and always hold in your heart the knowledge that mothers create life. What we are as humans, questing for knowledge and reaching for love and evolving as we have since the beginning of the human race, is all quite simply due to the process of procreation, pregnancy, birth, and the nurture of children. Mothers are more than important: They are absolutely essential for the perpetuation of humanity.

> The Australian aborigines tell the story of the creator of humans, a giant birth-mother snake Goddess called Mother Eingana. She created the earth, the sea, and all the animals by vomiting, but when she began to gestate humans, she was unable to give birth to them. As more and more humans grew within her, she began to writhe in pain until the god Barraiya took pity on her and speared her, creating an opening from which to give birth. Blood and humans flowed from her womb and the human race was born.
>
> The aborigines also believe that Mother Eingana retains a sinewy string attached to the heel of every living creature, and that when she lets go of a sinew, that creature will die. Mother Eingana therefore holds the thread of each life, much like the three Fates who measure and cut the thread of each life to determine its length. Mother Eingana, although represented as the most phallic of animals, is irrefutably female, and the aborigines say that if she ever died, all life would end. Mother Eingana is, therefore, the very essence of life on earth—the creator, maintainer, and destroyer of the world.

Mother Eingana certainly experienced a dramatic labor. Swollen with life, she had no opening from which to give birth. Some women may find the notion of being speared in order to create a vagina and a birth canal a bit disturbing, but this story illustrates how labor can indeed be dramatic, even traumatic. Yet in the end, when life emerges, everything is fine.

Some women have easy labors, and some have more extended, difficult labors. Some assume that their labors will be easy and are surprised when they have difficulties. Some worry incessantly that labor will be traumatic and are surprised at how quickly and painlessly it happens. But like Mother Eingana, who had the support of a fellow deity to help her, you will be surrounded by qualified professionals and friends and family who love you. Learn as much as you can about the birth process and spend time each day meditating on the process of your pregnancy. The more familiar you are with how it all happens, the more comfortable you will feel when the process begins.

In the meantime, remember that you are not alone as you grow life within and prepare to give birth. Your partner, your family, and/or your friends are there to hold you up, support you, and see you through. Labor can be difficult but it is always worth the challenge of the journey for the magnificent reward at the end.

Planning the Birth

In your Motherhood Journal, spend some time today writing about how you envision your labor. Every Mother Goddess should have an organized "birthing plan," which we'll talk about later in this book. For now, just think, dream, and wonder about what your process of giving birth will be like. What do you anticipate? What do you fear? What do you hope? Describe how you think it will go and how you feel about this great experience to come. The more you think about, consider, and plan your birth, the less anxious you will be when the natural progression of life-giving contractions finally begins.

Exercise #1: Yogi-You

For thousands of years, holy men in India have practiced the ancient art of yoga, a path to enlightenment designed to master control over the body so that the mind can fully manifest and apprehend ultimate truth. Yoga has been popular in the West ever since the 1970s and its popularity continues to grow as more people—particularly women—discover the great strength, flexibility, and tranquility of mind possible through yoga.

While most modern historians relate the history of yoga as patriarchal, many "hints" throughout history suggest that yoga was also the realm of the Goddess. For example, in meditation, the classic yogi position (a yogi is someone who practices yoga) was to sit in the lotus pose, with legs crossed, each foot placed on top of the opposite thigh, and to rest each hand, palm facing up, atop each knee, connecting thumb and index finger in a circle and extending the remaining three fingers straight out.

According to *The Woman's Dictionary of Symbols and Sacred Objects* by Barbara G. Walker, this hand position once symbolized the unity of the child (represented by the thumb) and the mother (represented by the index finger). The three extended fingers represent the Triple Goddess, who protects the mother/child union with blessings and love. Walker theorizes that the security and good fortune of this hand position may have evolved into our "okay" sign, a circle made with the thumb and index finger, with three fingers extended. The message? Mother plus child means everything is okay!

Mother Lauren and daughter Claire practice a seated yoga relaxation pose. Only four days after this photo was taken, Claire welcomed her little brother, Jackson, to the world.

Whether or not you have ever studied yoga, the first trimester is an excellent time to begin. While pregnant women should avoid extreme yoga poses if they aren't used to doing them on a regular basis, any pregnant woman can benefit from a simple version of yoga's Sun Salutation. This sequence of yoga poses reverences the life-giving sun, and is a perfect way for the life-giving Mother Goddess to pay homage to the source of life for the earth, with which you now have so much in common.

You don't need much to do yoga, but here is what you do need:

- Comfortable clothes that don't bind and aren't too tight
- Bare feet
- A carpeted surface or surface covered with a blanket, or optionally, an exercise mat, yoga mat, or "sticky mat" (Designed to keep your hands and feet in place without slipping, these mats are widely available at stores that sell exercise equipment, and are well worth the price for any aspiring yogi.)
- A quiet space with enough room for you to lie down on the floor
- About 15 minutes undisturbed

Now, here are step-by-step instructions for doing the Sun Salutation. Different yoga teachers teach this yoga routine in different ways, but this is our pregnancy-friendly modified version. You should be able to do it throughout your pregnancy. (However, never begin an exercise program without the approval of your doctor.)

First, stand in the middle of your mat or on the floor with feet together. Spread your toes out and imagine them gripping the ground firmly. Let your hands extend straight down at your sides and feel the energy flowing all the way to your fingertips. Let your hands hang loosely at your sides. This is Mountain Pose. Imagine feeling firm and tall and steady like a mountain. Breathe naturally.

Inhale deeply, and slowly raise your arms above your head as far as is comfortable.

Exhale deeply, and bend at the waist, bringing your arms straight down so that they hang loosely and comfortably in front of you. Let your knees bend just a bit so they don't lock. Let your head droop and relax. If you can, touch your toes or hold your ankles, but if you can't, that's fine! Just bend forward. If this feels difficult on your back, bend forward holding onto a chair, always bending the knees lightly, and tightening the buttocks muscles to protect the lower back.

Inhale, bend your knees, and place your palms on the floor under your shoulders, fingers facing forward. Walk your legs back so that you form the position for a push-up with arms and legs straight. Or if this is too challenging, come down into a hands-and-knees position. Take your time, breathe naturally, and look up and out.

Tuck your toes under, exhale, and raise your hips so that your body forms an upside-down V, with palms and feet on the floor, hips up, head down. This is called Downward-Facing Dog. It is a modified inversion that sends blood to your brain and is very relaxing. Spend some time in this position relaxing and breathing.

Inhale and walk your legs forward, keeping knees bent if necessary, so that you return to the forward bend position with arms hanging down, touching toes or ankles if possible, or hanging on to a chair.

Inhale and come back up to standing, lifting your arms above your head as far as is comfortable.

Exhale and bring your palms together in front of your chest into prayer pose, also called Namaste (pronounced *nah-mahst-STAY*).

Repeat as often as is comfortable.

This yoga sequence is relaxing and invigorating at the same time. We think you will enjoy it! If you become more interested in yoga or are already more experienced, you may be able to do more for longer and do advanced versions of the Sun Salutation and other yoga poses, but please do so under the guidance of a qualified yoga teacher experienced with yoga during pregnancy.

You might find you love yoga so much that it becomes an ongoing practice for the rest of your life.

 In the symbolism of the hand, the thumb is the Child, extended together with the index (Mother) and middle (Father) fingers in the "hand of blessing" that Christians copied from paganism.

—Barbara G. Walker, from *The Woman's Dictionary of Symbols and Sacred Objects* (Castle Books, 1988)

Exercise #2: Brew a Pot of First-Trimester Tea

Approximately half of all pregnant women experience some nausea and even vomiting during the first trimester, and contrary to the name, morning sickness isn't always limited to the morning. For many women, it lasts all day long. Morning sickness isn't pleasant but at least you know it won't last much longer! However, many home remedies can help alleviate the queasiness.

Although you may not feel like eating when nauseous, morning sickness can get worse on an empty stomach. Never let your stomach stay empty. Carry fruit, cheese, and whole-grain crackers for frequent snacking. Eat high-protein and complex-carbohydrate-rich foods but keep fat intake low. Low-fat cheese on wholegrain crackers makes a perfect first-trimester snack. Eat a protein-rich snack before bed, such as peanut butter on whole-wheat toast with a glass of skim milk, or a slice of turkey and a slice of Swiss cheese rolled in a whole-wheat tortilla.

Finally, ginger is nature's remedy for nausea. An "old wives tale"? Of course! But who do you think the "old wives" are, anyway? Most of them are mothers.

Begin your morning with a steaming cup of ginger tea and keep snacking. Morning sickness will soon be a fond memory (really!).

Here's what you will need to brew your own pot of anti-queasy ginger tea:

- A tea kettle or pan to boil water that will hold about four cups
- About four cups water, preferably filtered or purified
- A ceramic teapot or four-cup glass measuring cup with pouring spout
- A two- to three-inch piece of fresh ginger root (widely available in grocery stores)
- Honey and a wedge of lemon, if desired

Heat the water in the tea kettle or pan over high heat until boiling vigorously (we like whistling teakettles best because they make it hard to forget you put them on the stove, and we all know how those first-trimester hormones can make you forgetful!).

While the water is boiling, peel the tough skin from the ginger root with a vegetable peeler or paring knife.

On a cutting board, slice the ginger root into slices, about ⅛-inch thick. Place ginger-root slices in the bottom of the teapot or measuring cup.

When the water is boiling vigorously, carefully pour it over the ginger root. Allow the ginger to steep for about five minutes, stirring occasionally.

Pour the tea into a mug and add a spoonful of honey and/or a squeeze of fresh lemon juice, if desired. Sip the tea taking tiny sips, very slowly. Relax and enjoy the experience. Repeat every two to three hours, or as needed for queasiness.

We hope you've enjoyed the beautiful if emotionally tumultuous first trimester. You are heading into second-trimester territory now, and the second trimester is a wonderful time of feeling happy, strong, and empowered. Read on to find more ways to celebrate your inner Mother Goddess as your pregnancy progresses.

Chapter 6

The Second Trimester: Feeling Good ... Powerful, and Showing It

Could it be? One morning you wake up, and instead of rushing to the bathroom or balking at breakfast, you feel ... amazing! Your appetite is back, your energy is back, and the nausea is a distant memory. No doubt about it, you are entering the second trimester, a time of feeling strong, powerful, and proudly pregnant!

As your confidence and strength increase, you may also be delighted to discover that you are finally starting to "show." Your baby is growing larger inside you—at the start of the second trimester, it is just over three inches long and weighs about an ounce, but with your expanding uterus, that's enough to give you a brand new belly.

The second trimester is the perfect time to explore empowering images of Mother Goddess strength, power, and vigor, because that's exactly how you are feeling. Gone are the days when pregnant women hid their bodies and stayed out of public during pregnancy. We have returned to a more ancient sensibility of public pride, respect, and reverence for the woman who carries a child.

Just think of the many powerful women today who remain confidently in the public eye throughout their entire pregnancies. Who could forget that famous Annie Leibowitz photo of naked and pregnant Demi Moore on a 1991 cover of *Vanity Fair?* A member of the Dixie Chicks appears in their "Landslide" music video visibly and joyfully pregnant. Supermodels like Cindy Crawford sport pregnant bellies proudly, and designer Liz Lange began the trend of well-made, high-fashion maternity clothes in 1997, finally giving pregnant women the opportunity to look stylish and pregnant at the same time. (Good-bye pink frilly tent tops and Peter Pan collars!)

> We have laugh'd to see the sails conceive
> And grow big-bellied with the wanton wind;
> Which she, with pretty and with swimming gait,
> Following (her womb then rich with my young squire)
> Would imitate, and sail upon the land.
>
> —William Shakespeare (1564–1616), *A Midsummer Night's Dream*

Knowing that we aren't the first generation of women to show ourselves as proudly pregnant connects women of the twenty-first century with the women of prehistory. We are doing just what they did and we probably feel much the way they felt, so while we may wonder if our ancient ancestors ever imagined what life would be like for women thousands of years down the line, we can certainly look back and confirm our own feelings of power and beauty by remembering them.

Pregnancy ... and Plenty of It!

We love the symbol of the horn of plenty for the second trimester. While, at first glance, a horn may look like a phallic symbol (representing the male sexual organ), in ancient cultures, an animal horn symbolized the female vulva, fertility, and the good fortune that came with having a good harvest. Ancient cultures may have honored the horn because it looked like the crescent moon. An ancient name for the Greek Goddess Hera was "Horned One," and pagan cultures believed that the sound of the horn drove away evil spirits.

A horn in the form of a cornucopia, that vessel filled with the fruits of the harvest, is an easy metaphor for the Mother Goddess. This ancient "horn of the Great Mother" sometimes represented Hera or Io in her incarnation as a cow or a goat, or as the nurse of Zeus in a female goat form. The cornucopia or horn of plenty commonly adorned houses, temples, and food stores in ancient Greece, in the hope that the Great Mother would see her symbol and shower down her blessings of plenty.

When Christianity overtook pagan religions, the early Christian fathers interpreted the horn as a symbol of decadence, excess, and, interestingly, excessive fertility in men. Yet long before Christianity, the horn was a vessel that ancient cultures understood to be symbolic of fertility and lasting abundance. Today, whether we are Christian, Muslim, Jewish, or Buddhist, we can reclaim, embrace, and celebrate the horn of plenty as a terrific representation of the miracle of human life.

On a limestone wall in the Dordogne Valley in France 21,000 years ago, someone carved a woman. This carving, discovered in 1911 by physician J. G. Lalanne, which archaeologists refer to as the *Venus of Laussel*, probably decorated a ceremonial shelter. The *Venus of Laussel* cradles a pregnant belly with one hand and in the other, holds a bison horn aloft. The wide hips, the breasts ready for nursing, the curvaceous shape, and the symbolic bison horn reveal this figure as a probable fertility figure and the curved horn, notched with 13 marks, probably corresponded to the 13 lunar months in the year. Some pre-historians also believe the horn represents the Universal Vulva, that key to the propagation of humanity.

Although we know little about who carved this *Venus of Laussel*, and whether or not she is based on an actual woman or was a good luck symbol, charm, or deity figure, this ancient Venus is compelling in her posture, her attitude, her confidence. As a faceless, footless figure emerging from yet blending seamlessly into a sheltered rock face, the Venus certainly suggests a connection to an ancient culture that honored fertility. But it's easy to imagine that this proud naked figure, looking like she might have borne several children before this one, was revered as an important figure in her tribe. As she holds up that symbol of fertility and of plenty, probably also related to the harvest, she encompasses the second trimester sense of strength, good fortune, and magnitude.

You can see the 18-inch bas-relief of this Venus for yourself if you ever visit the Musée d'Aquitaine in Bordeaux, France.

Imagine your life as a horn of plenty. You carry a child within you, and are yourself a cornucopia of abundance, but consider how many other ways your life is filled with rich abundance: the food and shelter you need, family and friends to love and to love you, and the many other material and spiritual resources available to you. Empower yourself by bringing your own personal cornucopia forward in your consciousness.

Fill Your Mother Goddess Cornucopia

In your Motherhood Journal, take a blank page and draw a big horn of plenty, filling as much of the page as possible. Within the horn, write down everything contained in the cornucopia of your life. What are your resources? Your blessings? Your strengths? What constitutes your abundance? Rejoice in how truly rich you are with a wealth that money just can't buy for you or for your family. That horn of plenty is your *life*—bountiful, powerful, amazing, and precious.

Weighing Your Gold

Ah, your weight. It's changing now, isn't it! The scale is creeping up, up ... and yet, somehow, incredibly, *you don't mind,* even if you once watched that scale needle with an eagle eye. As your belly expands and your weight increases, you may feel rich ... richly fertile, richly blessed, rich with love to give to others. Pregnancy has, throughout the centuries, often been associated with both material and spiritual wealth—abundance of body represented abundance of all resources.

The abundance that allows for healthy procreation flows from one area of life into others, and, in many ways, material abundance enters into a synergy with spiritual abundance through the metaphor of pregnancy. It's easy to see how abundance in one area of your life can indeed help to enrich all the others. Of course, material wealth in the form of many possessions and lots of money is not a prerequisite for successful parenting! Nor do you have to be a saint to be a wonderful mother!

But as you feel new life grow within you, it seems natural for you and your partner to begin to prepare a nurturing physical and emotional environment for the child you are expecting. One of our favorite Grandmother Goddesses remembers giving birth to her son, Joe, in December 1929, only a few months after the stock-market crash, marking the start of the Great Depression. Yet this 94-year-old recalls that time as the happiest, and most abundant, of her life. "We had everything we needed," she says, "We had love!"

 Our family never had any hard luck, because nothing seemed like hard luck to it, nor was it ever disgraced, for there was nothing which it would acknowledge as disgrace.

—Boxcar Bertha (dates unknown), U.S. author, depression-era migrant

During your second trimester of pregnancy, you may feel particularly attuned to the abundance of your life as your own belly becomes more abundantly beautiful. When your life is rich with the things you need and rich with love that you give and receive, it's easy to weigh your blessings and give thanks back to the universe. Remember Lakshmi, that Mother Goddess who rose from the primordial sea of milk and represented both material and spiritual wealth? The link between these two types of riches is a common one in Indian lore, but appears in many other cultures and periods throughout history as well. One beautiful example is the Dutch Baroque painting, *Woman Holding a Balance* by Johannes Vermeer, painted in 1664, and now hanging in the National Gallery of Art in Washington, D.C. The painting is sometimes also called *Woman Weighing Gold*. Visit the painting online at www.nga.gov/feature/vermeer/.

A woman, quite possibly pregnant, holds a balance in a dim room. As is typical for the master Vermeer, the world of this painting is meticulously detailed and rich with symbolism. While the table at which the woman stands is filled with pearls and other valuables of the material world, she ignores them. Her scales are suspended in air. What is she weighing?

The woman stands in front of a painting of the Judgment, during which all humankind is called to account, soul by soul. Symbolically, the woman weighs spiritual virtue, as the golden light from the window shines upon her extended belly. Jewels become worthless when weighed against virtue and the preparation of bringing forth a human life. Although many art historians argue that the woman may not be pregnant but merely wearing the fashion of the time, we believe her to be pregnant. For who better to measure the true worth of humankind than an expectant mother—in the process of bringing forth a new, beautiful human being?

The woman weighing in on virtue in Vermeer's painting reminds us of the statue of Lady Justice, a symbol present in our courtrooms even today. Lady Justice may originally have been the Greek Goddess Themis, the Goddess of law and justice and one of the Titans. In some representations, Themis carries both a cornucopia and a set of scales, and gave birth to the Fates, those three deities that determine the length of each human life.

As we depict her today, Lady Justice wears a blindfold so that she can judge right and wrong impartially and without prejudice, and to us, Vermeer's *Woman Holding a Balance* is the spiritually enlightened, maternal version of the Lady Justice, unswayed by wealth or the material world. Today Mother Goddesses can be lawyers, judges, and even hold high office. Look to the example of former Massachusetts governor Jane Swift who gave birth to twins while still monitoring state affairs.

But Vermeer's expectant *Woman Holding a Balance* is not the only wonderful example in art of the beautiful visual metaphor of pregnancy. Two other Northern masters, van Eyck and Rembrandt, created their own famous depictions, as shown in the following table.

More Mother Goddesses from Art History

Masterpiece	Mother Goddess Symbolism
Jan van Eyck, *Arnolfini Wedding Portrait*, 1434 	In this wedding portrait of bride and groom, art historians once again argue that the bride is not pregnant, but wearing the style of the time. However, her intent is clear as she holds the folds of the dress against her stomach to show that pregnancy is a desired (and possibly immediate) outcome of this couple's union. The world of the painting reflects a room carefully created to illustrate the intent to create a prosperous family, both materially and spiritually—the rich reds and golds; the statue of Saint Margaret, patron saint of childbirth, on the chair post; the shoes cast aside to indicate the sacred ground; the dog to represent fidelity; and the mirror, reflecting the witnesses to the ceremony, set with medallions depicting the passion of Christ. The candle represents

Masterpiece	Mother Goddess Symbolism
	the all-seeing eye of the divine. The couple is clearly wealthy and spiritually as well as physically devoted, joined by their clasped hands and tranquil expressions. Check out this painting on the Internet by visiting the website for the National Gallery in London at www.nationalgallery.org.uk/.
Rembrandt, *The Jewish Bride*, 1665 	While some scholars insist that the pair in this painting is neither a married couple nor 1665 Jewish, others insist that they were an actual well-known Jewish couple in seventeenth-century Amsterdam. No matter! Their intimacy, devotion, and bond are obvious as the man places his hand over his partner's breast and heart and the other around her shoulders. She lightly rests one hand upon his as her other hand reaches down to cradle the swell of her abdomen. The rich dress, the luminescent jewelry, and deep yet vibrant colors indicate that this couple was prosperous, yet some believe these were actually meant to be biblical figures, possibly Isaac and Rebecca. Take a look at this masterpiece by visiting the Rijksmuseum in Amsterdam, the Netherlands, online at www.rijksmuseum.nl/.

Balance is key for mothers. We have so much to handle, to deal with, to accomplish, to manage. As we remember the flowering of civilized culture from the Renaissance and Baroque eras, the metaphor of balance extends to include the many areas and resources of our lives. We join with our partner in a life partnership, we give birth to children, we gain wealth in all the areas of our lives—material wealth to support the propagation of life, spiritual wealth to make that life fulfilling—and we do our best to balance the many sides of our existence so that they come together into a rich and rewarding whole.

What elements do you find yourself attempting to balance in your life? Imagine that you hold a scale. What would you weigh? The quest for wealth against the quest for time with family? The spiritual life against the material? The desire for parenthood against the desire to remain a child? One of the wonderful things about being a Mother Goddess is the power to enjoy it all by balancing the right amounts of each of these aspects of life.

Finding Your Balance

On a new page in your Motherhood Journal, draw a simple scale like the one depicted in Vermeer's painting—basically dividing the page in half. This isn't about pros and cons; this is purely a balance, your own personal life scale. What kind of balancing act are you performing? Do you balance partner and family, parents and siblings, working on your spirit with working on your body, time at home with time at work? Write down each pairing, one on the left scale and one on the right. Keep in mind that neither side of this balance is "bad"; it is all simply a part of your life. The Eastern equivalent would be the perfect harmony of yin and yang, the balance of opposites in union.

Having It All

In our quest for balance, we may sometimes feel that we can't have it all. One of the biggest challenges for women in the twenty-first century is the balance of career and motherhood. Women have made such strides in their professional lives. Many of us enjoy fantastic careers, rich with rewards, both financial and emotional. We pursue our creativity in a host of venues—we are writers, painters, sculptors, poets, designers, architects, chefs, graphic artists, website designers, and CEOs of companies from the smallest in-home operations to multinational corporations.

Had we lived a thousand years ago, or even a hundred years ago, we would probably be resigned to the paths of our mothers. We would need to marry and depend on our husbands for financial support. We may have had to work in one of the very few jobs open to women, and if we strayed from the path expected of us, we risked reputation, even ruin.

But today we have so many more choices and personal power. We can do pretty much anything we want. And then, sometimes as we planned, and sometimes quite unexpectedly, we become pregnant—just like a woman living a hundred, or a thousand, or ten thousand years ago. Suddenly our choices seem limited. Are we consigned to give it all up? Or do we have more choices than ever?

> Ogboinba is the daughter of Woyengi, that African Mother Goddess we met in Chapter 4. When all the people of the world chose what they would be, who they would be, how long they would live, and how they would die, Ogboinba declared that, above all, she wanted to be magic, so Woyengi gave Ogboinba magic. She could heal the sick, talk to animals, and tell the future.
>
> But the longer Ogboinba lived and the more she experienced, the more she regretted not choosing to be a mother, as other women had. Yet Woyengi had made it quite clear that once each person chose a fate, he or she would have to live, and die, with that fate. However, Ogboinba's desire for motherhood grew so strong that she embarked upon a great journey to find her mother, collecting great powers from those she met on her path so that she would be strong in the face of her mother's certain wrath.
>
> When at last Ogboinba returned to Woyengi and made her request, the Goddess indeed stood enraged upon the Creation Stone, and all the power her daughter collected was not enough to save her from her mother's fury. "I didn't force you to accept any fate I chose," Woyengi said, her voice cracking like thunder. "I let you choose your own fate, and this is what you chose!" Afraid of her own mother's great power, but still desiring to know what a mother's life is like, Ogboinba fled into the eyes of a pregnant woman. Nigerian myth has it that Ogboinba still lives in the eyes of every pregnant woman today, peering out at the world.

We like to think that Ogboinba waits in the eyes of every pregnant woman as a symbol of that inner creative potential, not as a negative manifestation of wasted creative energy. Unlike Ogboinba, who chose not to bear children but then was unable to change her mind, we do have the choice to do both, with women extending their child-bearing years into their late 30s and even early 40s. Many of us work much of the same kind of magic as Ogboinba. We may not have magic in the traditional sense, but we may work in the healing arts, "talk" to plants and animals through environmental or scientific work, and even predict the future as visionary artists, writers, speakers, or through our work in any of hundreds of other creative professions.

Even if we begin our adult lives thinking that we don't want to have children, we can change our minds. Women today have more choices, and many younger women consciously design their careers and lives to make space for both career pursuits *and* the pursuit of motherhood. Our creativity need no longer be expressed as an "either/or" proposition. We can give birth to our children, but also to our creative potential. We can manifest both.

> I am sure there is Magic in everything, only we have not sense enough to get hold of it and make it do things for us.
>
> —Frances Hodgson Burnett (1849–1924), U.S. writer

In a way, Ogboinba was also able to change her mind, finding her own ultimately creative solution. By fleeing inside a pregnant woman, she lives on eternally experiencing pregnancy through others. You, on the other hand, are experiencing it yourself. Yet you still have all the creativity and magic of Ogboinba inside you, too. Pregnancy itself is the ultimate creative act, and can only fuel and enhance your natural creativity in other areas. Your future can contain everything you need, and you needn't beg any higher power for a new life or a second chance. You have the power within, and just look at you—you are doing it all!

Empress of Your Realm

Even though it isn't quite time to start "nesting," that impulse to clean and organize that strikes so many pregnant women in the third trimester, this second trimester marks a wonderful opportunity to survey and adjust the home in which you live, to prepare for the changes to come.

You may or may not have decided where your new baby will sleep, but during this second trimester, before you are too rushed and while you are still feeling good and a little more mobile than you'll be feeling in a few months, you can still spend time considering and implementing furniture and room rearrangements in a way that works for you and your new family.

First of all, your baby will need a crib or, at least at first, a cradle or bassinet. Many mothers choose to keep the cradle or bassinet in their own bedroom so that they have easy access to their babies during those first weeks when the baby needs to eat several times during the night. Eventually, you will probably make a room just for your baby, or perhaps your baby will share a room with an older sibling.

The way you design your baby's room is entirely up to you, of course. You will need a place for diapers and wipes, but some mothers might prefer a utilitarian design to house toys and books and baby's bed, while others will enjoy decorating with coordinated wallpaper, window treatments, murals, mobiles, furniture, and other accessories.

A house is built by human hands, but a home is built by human hearts.

—Anonymous Goddess

Whether you are a do-it-yourselfer or like to buy everything premade and have it professionally installed doesn't matter. What matters is taking the time to plan your baby's space.

One of the most important spaces you create may not be in the nursery at all. Every Mother Goddess needs a special place to feed her baby. A comfortable chair, a shelf with space for bottles or breast pump and spit-up rags, and perhaps other accessories to create a tranquil mood— a CD player for playing your favorite music, a desktop fountain, a chime, a handful of crystals, or pictures of your favorite Mother Goddesses all make nice additions to this quiet corner. Perhaps you'll want to incorporate your Mother Goddess altar into the space you create to nourish your baby.

The chair you choose might or might not rock, but it should make you feel very comfortable and pampered. Consider adding an ottoman or other type of footrest, a drink holder or coaster, some pillows for propping head, knees, and back, and some reading material for when the baby falls asleep in your arms.

Explain to the rest of your family that the baby's feeding space should be off-limits for noise, clutter, and chaos. Whenever you and your baby sit there, you should be able to relax and concentrate on the business at hand: nursing, or lullabies, or rocking, or gentle playing, or whatever else you need to do when the two of you need a little downtime together.

Finally, give your entire home a once-over. How do you feel about this space? Is it baby-friendly? You won't have to worry about childproofing until your baby is mobile, but what about the mood your home evokes? Is it loud and full of clutter? Are there ways to get better organized?

Evaluate your home space now and try to get your house running according to a system that works for you and everyone else in your home. Purge all the clutter you don't need, because you'll want (and need) the extra space. Babies necessitate lots of brand-new clutter, and you won't have a lot of time for from-the-ground-up reorganization once the baby is here. Now is the time to get started cleaning up, clearing out, and getting ready. Prepare your castle for its newest member and you may just feel calmer about settling into it after the birth.

The third Major Arcana of the Tarot is the Empress. The Empress is the Earth Mother representing fertility, growth, generosity, and healing. Her presence in a Tarot reading indicates both fertility and prosperity, once again joining these two creative forces into a single wave of impending abundance and future happiness.

Tarot's Empress is often depicted on a luxurious chair, holding a scepter and sitting next to a heart-shaped shield decorated with the astrological symbol for Venus, the planet and the Goddess of love. Often surrounded by symbols of luxury such as golden wheat, the Tarot Empress indicates the richness and creative power of the royal life—and she can be your symbol for the rich abundance of your own life!

The Empress you see in the illustration is a painting by artist and psychic medium (and Mother Goddess), Rita Berkowitz. At a workshop on shaman journeying, Rita was asked to see what animal would appear to her in the four directions. A moose appeared and Rita saw the native woman holding her baby up to the great Spirit and then taking the child to her breast as she moved through the four seasons. Rita chose to paint the woman with the buffalo skin on her back, signifying winter. How does the Empress look to *you*?

Before you know it, your pregnancy is half over! These magical nine months are brief and beautiful, and, for this moment, this powerful and empowering second trimester, you hold within yourself both the proof of fertility and the rich abundance of a body expanding to encompass two lives.

You're feeling like royalty this trimester, so let the Tarot Empress be your symbol. Let her presence and power infuse your home, your body, and your mind as you enjoy every second of this feel-good time and as you look toward the third and final trimester, during which your child will prepare to come forth into the world and take its place beside you. The Tarot Empress is both wealthy noble and nurturer, a source of motherly love, growth, potential, and fecundity. Enjoy this regal force within!

Exercise #1: Create Your Mother Goddess Portrait

Involve your partner, your other children (if you have them), family, and friends in remembering this second trimester time of your pregnancy by immortalizing the moment in your own Mother Goddess portrait. Like the great artists Vermeer, van Eyck, and Rembrandt, set your stage by choosing carefully the dress and setting for the world of your portrait. Include details in the portrait that reveal special meaning for you, your partner, and your new family. As van Eyck did, include witnesses to the occasion by inviting your other children, relatives, or friends to be a part of the portrait. A digital camera makes composing your portrait easy. Consider using a video camera to make your masterpiece into a film classic, complete with the laughter and voices of the people who will be there to welcome your new baby into the world. This is a wonderful group project that includes your partner and all your loved ones in the process of your pregnancy. Place the finished photo or video cassette in your Motherhood Birth Box, as a record of your pregnancy that mother, father, and child will cherish as the years go by.

Instant Goddess

Now that you're enjoying the feel-good energy of your second trimester, what better time for taking a Mother Goddess walk? Choose your favorite Mother Goddess, either one from this book or one you've always admired. Now step outside, take three deep breaths of fresh air, and imagine that you *are* that Mother Goddess, taking a walk on Earth just to see how everything is going down here. What do you find beautiful? What would you change? How might you re-create the world a bit differently, in all your Mother Goddess wisdom?

Exercise #2: Toss a Second Trimester Salad

Now that your appetite is back, revel in the bounty and abundance of the healthy, fresh foods available to you by tossing a salad full of delicious organic produce. Nutritious food will help you to feel better and stronger as it nourishes the life inside you at the same time. Better yet, your salad can be sacred!

Certain fruits, vegetables, and nuts are thought to attract certain qualities or things, according to the folklore of many different cultures, and each item in our second trimester salad is also traditionally associated with a Goddess!

Here's what you will need:

- A large salad bowl
- Salad-tossing implements
- Your favorite salad dressing
- Salad ingredients (see the following table for ideas)

First, fill your salad bowl with fresh organic greens. Organic produce is better for your body and the body of your growing child, plus it tastes better! Use packaged salad greens for convenience, if desired.

Next, add your favorite ingredients from the following list, as much or as little as you like. Before adding each ingredient to the bowl, speak to the Goddess associated with that ingredient, asking her to bless your meal. Just before eating, sprinkle sesame or pumpkin seeds on top. These seeds obviously represent the seeds of life, but they also contain essential oils that support the body's creation of estrogen and androgen, important hormones.

Food	**Will Bring You**	**Goddess(es)**
Almonds	Knowledge, money	Athena
Apples	Love	Aphrodite
Avocado	Sexual love	Venus
Banana	Fertility, strength, money	Ix Chel
Blackberries	Protection, wealth, health	Brigid
Carrot	Fertility, sexual love	Freya/Pele
Celery	Psychic power, mental acuity	Hecate
Cucumber	Virtue, health, fertility	Artemis
Ginger	Strength, vitality	Morrigan
Grapes	Fertility, mental acuity, strength	Oya
Honey	Beauty, love, sensuality	Oshun
Lemon	Purity, mental clarity	Amaterasu
Oranges	Luck, prosperity	Oshun
Pomegranates	Psychic powers	Persephone
Strawberries	Compassion, love, luck	Kwan Yin/Demeter
Watermelon	Nurturance, fertility, sisterhood	Yemaya

Finally, enjoy your salad slowly and with full mindfulness. Taste the ingredients, each on its own and the way they taste together. Feel the power of Goddesses infusing and nourishing you, and let yourself feel very, very good.

And now we're heading into the home stretch of your pregnancy. Your third trimester is almost upon you! Turn to the next chapter for guidance and inspiration during this final pregnant stretch leading up to the birth of your child.

Chapter 7

The Third Trimester: Living Large

This morning, you tried to hop out of bed and suddenly found yourself struggling. Almost overnight, it seems, out there in front of you, leading the way wherever you go, is your great and beautiful belly. You are burgeoning with baby and, although you may still be glowing with the joy of pregnancy, you may also be suffering from the swollen ankles, a sore back, heartburn, and fatigue that come from a shifted center of gravity, retained water, and a whole lot more weight than you are used to carrying around with you.

No wonder! You are in your third trimester and that baby is getting bigger and bigger. It might seem like eons before your due date, but it will be here soon … just a few short months away. Your pregnancy is now, or soon will be, obvious to just about everybody. No need to wear that "Baby on Board" maternity T-shirt anymore!

The third trimester is fun—and sometimes a little uncomfortable. It is empowering—and frightening. It is a time for preparation, both mental and physical, and it is a time to revel in your unique and amazing new shape. You won't look like the quintessential fertility goddess for much longer, so enjoy it while you've got it!

In this chapter, we'll help you adjust to your new and (temporarily) larger size by introducing you to lots of dramatically pregnant goddesses, both new and ancient, so you feel in good company. We'll also help you with some Mother Goddess–inspired home remedies to ease your final pregnant months, and offer you some preparatory help for what is soon to come: the birthing process!

This is a magical time, as each trimester has been, but this third and last is special in a unique and spectacular way. Your baby makes its presence known during your every waking moment—and many of your sleeping moments, too! You probably can't lie on your back comfortably anymore. Your walk has changed, and you may often find yourself assuming "pregnant woman" position, hips jutted forward, one hand on the small of your back, the other absently caressing your belly.

Everything you wear is oversize, and everything you eat is undersize because that baby is pushing in on your stomach space, giving you indigestion if you overdo it. Your bladder is feeling the space crunch, too, and you may find yourself running (can you really call it running at this point?) to the bathroom every 15 minutes.

 Women should try to increase their size rather than decrease it, because I believe the bigger we are, the more space we'll take up, and the more we'll have to be reckoned with.

—Roseanne Barr (1952–), U.S. comedian

You might sometimes feel anxious about your impending labor, but you probably also feel excited and elated as you wait to meet your child. Best of all, you've had an introduction of sorts already, as what was at first a gentle flutter has now transformed into frequent healthy kicking, shifting, and even hiccuping inside you.

Your baby can hear your voice now, and can probably hear the voices of others around and near you ... even the family dog barking! When your baby emerges, all of these sounds will be familiar to her or him, but no sound more so than the sound of *your* voice. It's true ... you're almost a mother (or a mother *again*), and you can already feel the ways in which this very special and entirely unique relationship has already begun to take form.

Carolyn welcomes twins—just hours after they were born. That's Lucas on the left and Emerald on the right. Carolyn gave birth at age 38, after two miscarriages. Just as she scheduled an ultrasound to begin fertility treatments, she discovered she was pregnant with twins. The universe has a sense of humor. And Carolyn's joy is double! She cherished her pregnancy and made plaster casts of her hugely pregnant belly.

But I'm a Hippo!

Women in twenty-first-century Western society are programmed from an early age that they will be judged by their appearance, and for American women, so frequently bombarded with images of skinny, stretch-mark-free supermodels, the weight gain of pregnancy can feel like a mixed blessing. We are ecstatically pregnant, and yet it's hard to look at that number on the scale (and not just because our bellies get in the way!).

We might also feel less attractive to our partners as our bellies expand. Although we might feel more like mothers, we may feel less like desirable women, but most of the men we've asked say that they find their very pregnant partners incredibly beautiful, attractive, and sexually desirable. Nothing is more sensuous than a pregnant woman who is comfortable in her body. You are living proof of your own creative power and of the creative power of your partner. Your body is full and ripe with life. This is what sex is all about!

Still, you might be reluctant to look at your body on these days. A belly, a glimpse of a swollen ankle, a puffy hand, a rounder face. Today, take some time alone and stand in front of a full-length mirror. Take a good long look at yourself. Notice everything about your body, and check any negative thoughts. Think through them and past them. Rings don't fit? They will again; you don't need them now. Wearing a larger shoe size? Again, that's temporary, but look at how your body supports and nourishes and surrounds your new baby. It's an all-new you, and you are beautiful in all your bounty.

Rather than mourning the old you (you will get back down to your normal size after your body is finished with this very important job), concentrate on *right now* and look and look and look until you find your inner joy and pride at how well you are doing at this whole pregnancy business. Finally, look yourself in the eye in the mirror and say to yourself, out loud, with conviction: "Carrying this baby makes me incredibly beautiful!" Say it again, and again. Say it until you feel it inside.

Heidi holds newborn Andy. When you hold your pregnant belly and feel your baby move inside you, cherish this moment, feel beautiful, and embrace with your heart a visualization of welcoming your new baby into the world.

Developing a positive body image is important at this stage of pregnancy. You never looked more like a Mother Goddess than you do now, and for thousands of years, people worshipped the very form your body has assumed. Ask your partner to help you if you need reminders of how beautiful you are, but also remember to help yourself. Take good care of yourself, pamper yourself. Eat well, take walks in the fresh air (unless your doctor advises against it), and spend some time every day relaxing and thinking about how well your body is supporting this new life, how perfectly you are fitting into the natural cycle, how full and round and gorgeous you are.

> The cauldron was the prime female symbol of the pre-Christian world, which is why Christians universally associated it with witchcraft. The Egyptian hieroglyph of the great female Deep (womb) that gave birth to the universe and the gods was a design of three cauldrons.
>
> —Barbara G. Walker, from *The Woman's Dictionary of Symbols and Sacred Objects* (Castle Books, 1988)

Getting frustrated about your weight will only encourage less-than-healthy habits, and good health in the form of eating enough healthy food and getting moderate exercise is important now, both for your baby and for you. The healthier you are during your pregnancy, the more quickly your body will regain its previous form. Many mothers find that the health habits they adopted during pregnancy stuck with them afterward and that they were healthier and in better shape *after* giving birth than they were before.

Most important, remember that the number on the scale isn't important. What matters is how you feel, how you eat, how you move, and how you take care of yourself. You may feel like a hippo, but trust us when we tell you that you are beautiful!

Taueret, sometimes called Taouris, was a Hippopotamus goddess of fertility and birth. "The Great One" helped to birth the sun from the sky, and pregnant women in ancient Egypt called upon her to assist in their births, keeping them safe and healthy, and helping them to care for and nurse their newborns.

Represented as a hippo standing on her thick hind legs with large, pendulous breasts, Taueret sports a very pregnant belly. Taueret was quite a

> popular Goddess in ancient Thebes, so much so that many children were named after her and many families decorated their homes with her image. Far from fearing any comparison between pregnant women and hippo, the women of Thebes doted on Taueret and her image and prayed for her presence in their lives.
>
> In her incarnation as the goddess of vengeance, Taueret was sometimes pictured with the head of a lioness, bearing an open-mouthed crocodile on her shoulders. Like any protective mother guarding her offspring, and like the actual hippo itself, Taueret might look mild, even adorable—but in defense of those she nurtured, beware. The hippo is fierce indeed!

By invoking Taueret, we are *not* calling you a hippo ... that is, unless you think it's a compliment, like we do! Taueret's strength, protective power, and ferocity were one with her very pregnant hippopotamus body, and we think she makes a grand metaphor for the third-trimester Mother Goddess who loves and takes strength from her body.

Sometimes it can be difficult to love your body in any shape, but pregnancy is not a sacrifice of body for the life of another. To the contrary! Pregnancy is a glorification of the creative power of the body in celebration of the life of another! Now that you are a mother, your body has changed, and will continue to change throughout your life, but rather than seeing these changes as some sort of "lost youth," we think of these changes as the full flowering and emergence of the Mother Goddess. Your pregnant body is your ticket into this new, exciting stage of life. Enjoy it for all it is worth!

Taking Care of Business, Yah?

Society has some funny ideas about pregnant women. On one hand, everyone seems to have an impulse to do things for you: open doors, give up their seats, carry groceries, tell you to lie down and put your feet up. Then, on the other hand, some of those same people—colleagues, employees, even spouses and children—can seem resentful that you aren't doing all the same things you always did. Where's dinner? What's the problem with that presentation? You're going to take *how* many weeks off? I need cookies for school tomorrow, Mom; you'll bake four dozen tonight, won't you?

Women often feel pulled in many directions at once as they juggle careers, family, and other private and professional responsibilities, but in our third trimesters, the juggling act may feel even more difficult than usual. People want to help us but they don't always know how, and everyone has his or her own agenda. Your pregnancy may necessarily require that some people change their schedules and workloads around. It might require that your family make certain sacrifices. Those of us who are used to trying to smooth things over for everyone else may even feel guilty that we are inconveniencing anyone! If you recognize that impulse within yourself, this is the time to put things into perspective.

Women give birth. We've been doing it for thousands of years. We do what we need to do, we do what we can do, and all we can control is our own reactions to things. You can't force your employer to like the fact that you are pregnant, and you can't force your partner to stop babying you, either. Your job is to stay healthy and do the work you need to do without pushing yourself beyond your limits.

Writing about the pressures you feel can also help to put things into perspective. Don't forget to use your Motherhood Journal as a resource when you begin to feel stressed, overworked, overtired, or simply frustrated. Write about how you feel at your job, or at home, or with your friends.

> One of our favorite Mother Goddesses is Marge Gunderson, the lead character in the Oscar-winning movie *Fargo* (1996). Marge is the pregnant police chief investigating a grisly murder, although she is clearly in her third trimester. In one scene, when Marge gets an early morning call and must go to the murder scene, her husband rolls out of bed to make her eggs because, "You have to eat breakfast, Marge." On the job, Marge is business as usual. Although she doesn't hesitate to take a seat, as she's "carrying quite a load here, yah?" she does her job without hesitation, paying no attention to what other people think or how they act or respond to her pregnancy. When she's hungry, she eats. When a lonely friend needs sympathy, she's there. When she needs to travel out of town to investigate the case, she does so without hesitation. She is the chief of police and her pregnancy is simply part of her at that time.
>
> Marge is a positive symbol of a woman who is both big with pregnancy and functioning perfectly in her responsibilities. She is emotional but controlled, successful, alive, and vibrant, and even when she is tracking horrifying killers, she remains ever life-affirming. When Marge finally apprehends the last living killer and is driving him away in her police car, she asks him

about all the victims, and her words underline the movie's theme: "And for what? For a little bit of money. There's more to life than a little money, you know. Don't you know that? And here you are, and it's a beautiful day. Well, I just don't understand it." Marge's values and beliefs, in the sanctity of life, are clear in her mind. She can't and wouldn't ever comprehend the point of view of a murderer. She is the giver and preserver of life, like some of the most powerful Mother Goddesses before her.

We also love Marge's husband, Norm. They have been married for many years and their relationship is full of mutual support, respect, and affection. In the final scene of the movie, after all her huge accomplishments as chief of police, she sits in bed with her husband and he tells her that his painting of a duck will be published on the three-cent stamp. Her pride for his accomplishments and their mutual love and future together with the baby-to-be end the movie. While Marge remains genuinely dismayed at the evil of the men she captured, she is still powerfully connected to the man in her private life, a man who is not her subjugator but her equal partner.

While we might expect to see Marge give birth, she never does in the movie. She remains a metaphor of ripeness, living on the edge of a new life while dispatching those who would take life. Like early Mother Goddess cultures that fought to preserve a reverence for life, Marge Gunderson's morality is clearly defined. She is a strong, self-confident, powerful authority figure who is, at the same time, loving, nurturing, and empathetic for those who deserve it. Marge is ready for anything life brings, whether two sociopathic killers on the loose, or labor and childbirth—whichever comes first!

Marge Gunderson is a right-now Mother Goddess role model for any working woman. While she certainly must feel the pressure of pregnancy vs. career, and while she isn't afraid to embrace strong emotions when they come her way, Marge is still who she is. Pregnancy has transformed her, but it hasn't changed her. She is still the highly capable chief of police of Fargo, North Dakota, as well as a loving and beloved wife and a mother-to-be.

If you haven't seen *Fargo* and you don't mind a movie with some pretty graphic violence in it, consider renting it and paying close attention to Marge Gunderson's character, played flawlessly by Frances McDormand, a 40-something character actor and a mother herself. Married to the movie's writer/director, Joel Coen, McDormand is mother to two children, and she won an Academy Award for Best Actress for her role in this film. (The movie itself was nominated for Best Picture.)

If you do choose to watch *Fargo* (or watch it again), notice the many nuances of Marge's character. How does she react to people's spoken and unspoken references to her pregnancy? How does she choose to take care of herself while still getting her job accomplished? How does she interact with her husband? We can learn a lot from Marge when the pressure is on! She is never led astray by defensiveness, ego, or self-doubt. She knows who she is, what she thinks, and exactly what she needs to do; it's just that simple.

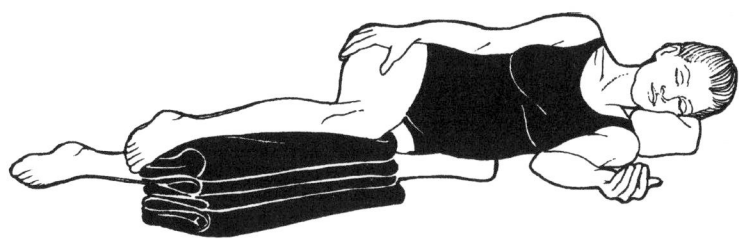

After the twentieth week of pregnancy, get good rest by practicing yoga's Shavasana pose. Lie on your left side and use pillows for your head and between your knees to reduce any strain your big pregnant belly is putting on your neck, back, and hips.

You Can Stop Running Now

Just when you feel like you can hardly move, life seems to speed up. Suddenly, the time of birthing is impending! You may suddenly feel more emotional again, or more nervous, more anxious, and just think of everything you have to get *done!* Wrapping things up before your maternity leave at work, getting that nursery ready once and for all, cooking and freezing meals for when you return home, packing the bag, writing up the birthing plan, making it to those weekly pre-natal visits, and, if you already have children, continuing with all the caretaking they require. If you don't do it all yourself, then who the heck is going to do it?

 True strength is delicate.

—Louise Nevelson (1900–1988), U.S. sculptor

Hold it right there! We know your to-do list is challenging the memory capacity of your PDA these days, but whether or not you get it all done, this baby is coming. The best thing you can possibly do for yourself is to slow down and take it easy. Pushing yourself beyond your capacity in the third trimester can result in stress, damage to already-strained muscles and ligaments, increased swelling and back pain, and difficulty sleeping.

You are better off spending a half-hour meditating before bed each night than painting a nursery wall or cooking a pan of lasagna. Ask for help! Your partner, your parents, siblings, friends, even your other children should be expected to pitch in and help you out right now. Even if "other mothers do it" or family members tell you that you should or must do this or that, listen to your inner voice. It knows what your body needs and how much you can take. Nobody wants you to push yourself too far.

> Macha of the Red Tresses is the Celtic Goddess of war. She may have been an actual Irish monarch who built the Emain Macha, and some historians believe she helped to organize the first hospital in Ireland four centuries before the first hospital was built in Rome. Her legend, however, has evolved to symbolize the way the patriarchal warrior culture and its religion (Christianity) obliterated the peaceful goddess culture in Ireland.
>
> Macha married Crunniuc Mac Agnomain and became pregnant. During a large gathering in Ulster, the new king boasted that none could outrun his horses, but Macha's husband knew his wife was swift enough to outrun them. The king demanded that Macha race the horses, but because she was pregnant, Macha begged that the king wait until she gave birth to make her race. The king refused and forced her to race. She did, and beat the horses—but then fell to the ground and gave birth to twins. After she had given birth, she cursed the king and all the men of Ulster, saying that place would forever be named after her, and that they would experience the pain of childbearing for five days and four nights every time their land fell under oppression, to last for nine-times-nine generations.
>
> Macha's story marks a distinct change in Celtic society. Macha, the goddess of war, fought to preserve a lifestyle that valued birth, the work of women, and life, and respected death. The king represents the male-dominated culture that no longer respected the rights of a pregnant woman, and that subjugated birth and nurturing in favor of competition and, essentially, violence for the sake of violence rather than to preserve a way of life. The king's army, it is said, believed that life was born in the head, not the

> womb, and by cutting off heads, they believed they took the source of all life, undermining the woman's role in the creation of life.

While Macha's story has many levels of meaning, the obvious surface lesson is that other people, who had no business dictating what a pregnant woman should be doing, forced her to overwork herself to such a degree that they induced her labor under extreme conditions. Are you letting others push you too hard?

Don't let outside forces dictate or alter your own priorities, values, and instincts about what you need during pregnancy. Macha's culture was overtaken by forces from the outside, but you needn't let outside forces compromise your experience. Nobody is forcing you to run a race, even if you sometimes feel that way.

As you prepare for labor and birth, remember Macha's story and stay strong in your resolve to take care of yourself and give yourself exactly what you need!

Clarifying Your Values

You are about to become parent to a brand new human who will depend on you for guidance in life. Do you know what you believe? This is a good time to take stock of your own values, morals, and belief system. Take a moment today to begin writing about what you believe is important in life. Good health? Spirituality? Adherence to a certain religion? Commitment to family? Devotion to a calling in life? In your Motherhood Journal, write about what you believe and what you think will be important to teach your new child when the time is right. Writing about your values and beliefs may even help you to clarify exactly what they are.

Go with the Flow

As your third trimester progresses, as your baby grows larger and larger, and as your due date approaches, you will probably become much more focused on that impending event: when your uterus does its final work of miraculously discharging your baby. Of course, you want it to go smoothly! Yet you might feel anxious about embarking upon such a dramatic event, especially if this will be your first birthing experience.

Taoism (pronounced *Daoism*) is a Chinese philosophy and religious system dating back to the fourth century, and we find it a helpful resource, especially in times of worry and striving. Practicing the Tao is about bringing your life into resonance with the universe in all of its natural, articulate inarticulateness. Without speaking or thinking (that is, without using the disciplines of art, science, or other learned knowledge), you act without artifice and in harmony and unity with the mystical power of universal truth. In achieving this, you reach beyond life, beyond death, to an understanding of your essential nature.

While we certainly don't expect you to change your religion, you can use the concept of Taoism to help you as you think about and await the labor process.

In Taoism, the true "way" that brings inner contentment and peace is to follow the flow of life without fighting against it. Imagine that you are being swept away by a great river. Do you panic, cling to the bank, and grasp for tree branches as you fly by them? Do you struggle and slip under the water? Or do you swim with the current, letting it sweep you effortlessly along?

To follow the Tao is to swim with that river. And now that you are nearing the end of your third trimester, that river is sweeping you inexorably toward the birthing process. You can't fight it, so you might as well go with the flow and let it happen. Let your body dictate what you need. Eat when you are hungry. Stop when you are full. Sleep when you are tired (when you can, which may be more often than you think ... do you really need to fold that load of laundry *right now?*). When you need to talk, find someone who will listen. When you need to put your feet up for a moment, do it. If you just can't concentrate another second, take a break. If you need a great big reassuring hug, ask for one.

During this time, you can also call on the many Mother Goddesses of labor and birth to help you. Visualize the way in which your body will open to release new life. Practice breathing, relaxing into the process, embracing it. The more you think about and mentally prepare for labor before it happens, the less anxious you will feel when it finally happens.

During this last trimester, you may also be experiencing Braxton-Hicks contractions. These involuntary muscle contractions across your belly feel like contractions, sort of, except that they aren't usually uncomfortable. Real labor has a regular rhythm and the contractions increase in frequency, duration, and intensity, while Braxton-Hicks contractions are unpredictable, irregular, and nonrhythmic, and feel more like a squeeze than a cramp. When Braxton-Hicks contractions get more intense, they may be mistaken for labor and are called "false labor." One theory is that these contractions help "ripen" the body for delivery, assisting in the effacement and dilation of the cervix. Braxton-Hicks contractions are just one more reminder of the amazing process happening inside you, where your cervix, that cone-shape organ at the opening of your uterus, will thin and open to allow your baby's passage into the world!

As if your belly weren't enough of a reminder, Braxton-Hicks can also help you mentally prepare for the labor ahead of you. We like to use these contractions as little physical reminders to relax, breathe, and just allow your uterus to do its work, visualizing a flowing and easy birth.

> Egeria (sometimes spelled Aegeria) was a Roman water nymph associated with the Goddess of nature and the forest, Diana. This water nymph, it is said, lives in springs deep within the forest. People would come to her and exchange gifts of water and milk for advice. Some legends claim that Egeria was the wife of king Numa Pompilius. He would visit her deep within a cave where her spring erupted, and they would talk, make love, and she would advise him on his work. Egeria is credited with teaching Numa how to lead his people in Earth-worship rituals, and she advised him on political matters, too. After his death, legend holds that Egeria was so saddened that she transformed into a fountain.
>
> Egeria's gift as a mystic and a seer as well as her association with flowing water eventually endeared her to pregnant women, who invoked her presence for easy delivery of their children and for when they wished to know the future of their babies.

As you imagine Egeria, a flowing fountain and Goddess of easy delivery, continue to visualize your own goal for a healthy, easy birth. Any day now, your water could break and flow, signaling the beginning of your labor.

As you near the end of this amazing physical, emotional, and spiritual transformation, don't forget your own king Numa, the partner who waits beside you, also eagerly awaiting the birth of the child you created together. Just as Egeria advised her husband in the matters of his world, you can advise your partner in the matters of your own world because, no matter how he tries, he cannot feel what you feel. He may often try to help you, try to understand you, and he may sometimes fail in his efforts because he cannot possibly fully understand what you need unless you stay open to each other.

Leah and Bob belly bounce in joyous anticipation of the birth of their first child, son Shane.

Let him in on how your body feels, how your thoughts form, and what you expect and imagine and hope for. Let him love you, and let yourself love him back, no matter how focused you both are on the third life that will soon turn your twosome into a trinity. The more you move through these final weeks together, the stronger your bond will be when you meet your child together. Soon you and your partner will hold your baby in your arms, envisioning his or her future and planning it together. Soon you will be a mother and he will be a father, and the love you will both feel for your child—that love already making itself evident in the stirrings of your heart and with every kick and turn of the life inside you—will flow from your hearts like a fountain.

Instant Goddess

Together with your partner, use 3×5 index cards to create affirmations of strength and powerful love for your baby, as well as faith in your body and the birthing process to come. Refer to the affirmations throughout your third trimester and have your partner read them to you during labor if you like, reminding you that you are prepared and that your baby is safe and will be well cared for. The Great Goddess is guiding and loving your new family through the birth experience.

Exercise #1: Creating Your Birthing Plan

A birthing plan is a detailed, written description of your wishes and preferences for childbirth so you have an official record of how you would like things to go, for yourself, your partner, and the hospital staff or midwife. The third trimester is the perfect time to make a birthing plan because, while you may have had set ideas early in your pregnancy about what you think you want, those ideas might have changed and evolved over the course of your pregnancy. You are wiser and more experienced already, so begin your birthing plan today.

You'll need a paper and pen or a computer and printer.

Your birthing plan can be as individual as you are, but it should clearly state your wishes. Write it all out and make copies of it to give to your partner and to any other family and friends who will be present during the birth or who will be responsible for decisions during the birth. Also make copies for your doctor, nurses, and/or midwife. If your birthing plan is long, you may wish to make a shorter bulleted or chart-based version for the medical professionals involved because they may not have time to read pages and pages of text. List only the items relevant to the decisions they will make, such as your feelings on pain medication, epidurals, C-sections, and so on. Reiterate your wishes to the staff so you feel confident that they know and understand them. And don't forget to bring along a copy yourself! Your birthing plan will contain valuable contact information.

As you create your birthing plan, remember that it's a plan, not a law. You never know how your birth will go. For instance, you might think you will want pain medication, but your birth may be so easy that you will find you don't need it after all. You may decide to listen to certain music and practice certain meditations and breathing techniques, but then, you may find the birth happens so quickly that you don't have time! Although it's important to have a plan, it's also important to be flexible.

However, if any medical professional tries to coerce you into changing your plan in a way that makes you uncomfortable and isn't related to the health and safety of you and your baby, don't back down. Have an ally who is also familiar with your plan and will be ready to defend you, because you might be feeling vulnerable once labor begins. Your partner, family member, or close friend are all good choices. They should all have copies of your birthing plan, and should read and understand it.

If you are unsure of how to organize a plan, use the following template.

Birthing Plan for _____

Due date: _____

I plan to give birth at (location name, address, telephone number):

_____
_____
_____

My midwife/physician will be: (name, office address, telephone number):

_____
_____
_____

I will allow the following people to be present during the birth:

_____
_____
_____

I do / do not (circle one) want the birth to be video recorded.

I prefer the room to contain the following amenities (find out which are available in your birthing location, such as adjustable bed, shower, whirlpool bath, television, radio, stereo system, etc.):

_____
_____
_____

Here is my plan for a natural birth/epidural/pain management:

_____
_____
_____

Regarding the induction of labor with drugs (Pitocin), my wishes are as follows:
_____
_____
_____

If my doctor recommends a Cesarean section or feels that one is necessary, my feelings are that this should be performed only under the following conditions:
_____
_____
_____

I would like permission to bring the following items to the hospital (check ahead of time with the nursing staff about bringing nonessential items such as music players; meditation aids like crystals, chimes, or bells; favorite/sentimental items; special kinds of food or drink such as herbal teas; candles; massagers; or anything else that might be against hospital policy):
_____
_____
_____

If for any reason someone other than me must make any decision regarding my care, this person, who will be present with me during the birth, is:

Name	Phone Number	Relationship
_____	_____	_____

Alternate contact person:

Name	Phone Number	Relationship
_____	_____	_____

My partner has the following additional wishes for the labor and birth process:
_____
_____
_____

People to call with the good news and baby statistics after I give birth:

Name	Phone Number
_____	_____
_____	_____
_____	_____
_____	_____
_____	_____
_____	_____
_____	_____
_____	_____
_____	_____
_____	_____
_____	_____
_____	_____
_____	_____
_____	_____
_____	_____
_____	_____
_____	_____
_____	_____
_____	_____
_____	_____
_____	_____
_____	_____

> Creativity can be described as letting go of certainties.
>
> —Gail Sheehy (1937–), U.S. writer

Exercise #2: Playing the Name Game

Some people have a name picked out for their babies even prior to conception, but many couples remain undecided until the birth. Whether or not you know if you have a boy or a girl, you can still play with the idea of names right up until the time when you must fill out that birth certificate. (Some people even wait longer!)

Choosing a name for your baby is fun, especially if you open your mind to the vast possibilities and spend time researching what different names mean. The Internet is full of resources for baby names, and baby-name books grace practically every bookstore.

What will you name your baby?

Some people believe the name you choose for your child will have a profound influence on his or her personality. Some people insist on a common name, while others insist on an unusual name. We love plumbing the names of Goddesses and Gods for names. Your co-author Eve's first child is named after the Celtic cupid, Angus Og, a shape-changing God of love, youth, beauty, and the patron deity of children. Gail named her first child Nicole; while it's not the name of a recognized Goddess, it's a name from ancient Greece meaning "victory for her people."

Choosing a Goddess or God as your child's namesake could imbue your child with some of the qualities of that deity! Ares, the Greek God of storms? Ariadne, the Greek Goddess of dawn? Cassandra, Greek Goddess of prophecy, or Chac, a Mayan rain god and patron of agriculture? Noah, Hebrew survivor of the great flood? Parvati, the Hindu mountain Goddess? The possibilities are practically endless!

Flip through name books, review the names of the Goddesses listed so far in this book, or check out the following list of baby-name websites for some interesting choices, or just to get you thinking. Then make your own list. The more names you think of, the more choices you have. When you hit the right name, you'll know it.

- www.babycenter.com/babyname/
- www.babynames.com
- www.parenthood.com/parent_cfmfiles/babynames.cfm
- www.babynamelocator.com/
- www.babyzone.com/babynames/
- www.indiaexpress.com/specials/babynames/
- www.yourbabysname.com/
- www.kabalarians.com/gkh/yourbaby.htm
- www.zoope.com/about/about_names.html
- www.muslimnames.co.uk/

www.celebnames.8m.com/
french.about.com/cs/babynames/
www.go.to/babynames
www.geocities.com/Tokyo/Ginza/3175/
www.babychatter.com/spanishgirlsnames.html
www.unusual-baby-names.com/

Your top-10 favorite baby names so far:

1. _____
2. _____
3. _____
4. _____
5. _____
6. _____
7. _____
8. _____
9. _____
10 _____

And now it's time ... or almost time ... for that magical moment: the moment labor begins. The moment the water begins to flow or the real contractions first tighten your uterus, and your midwife or doctor or the nurse on duty says, "Yep, this baby's coming!" How exciting! Your great journey into the intense but amazing experience of labor and birth is about to begin. We're here for you! Bring this book to the hospital and keep it open to the following chapter for guidance along the way. (And don't forget to breathe!)

Chapter 8

Labor: Empowering the Pain of Creation

When will you know you are in labor? When will you finally *know* that this is *it*? Maybe your water will break in the middle of the day ... or night. Or maybe those contractions will suddenly become regular, persistent, urgent ... and finally, downright painful! (Breathe, breathe ...)

Labor is rightly named. It is hard work and, in most cases, it takes a while. Labor involves three stages, and the first, longest stage involves three phases: the early phase, the active phase, and the transition phase. (We'll discuss the first two labor stages in this chapter, and the third stage, the delivery of the placenta, in Chapter 9.) As labor begins, you probably have many hours ahead of you before the actual birth, but labor takes a while for a reason: Labor is the gateway, the great passage, from pregnant woman to mother, and an event like this *ought* to take a while. You have to get used to the idea!

Of course, you've been mentally and physically preparing for this time for nine months now, but once labor begins, you (and your partner) might suddenly feel totally unprepared. Fear not, Mother Goddess! You are full of courage and love, and the entire history of Mother Goddesses stands behind you, lifting you up and giving you strength.

Creativity Springs Forth

During the early phase of the first stage of labor, you may not even know you are in labor yet. This early phase, sometimes called the latent phase, marks the point when actual, regular contractions—not Braxton-Hicks contractions, but the real thing—begin. If you have a lot of Braxton-Hicks contractions all day long, you may not notice when the real thing starts, although you may notice, in retrospect, that those contractions *did* feel a little bit different.

Your cervix is slowly dilating and your contractions will slowly become stronger, longer lasting, and more frequent. Throughout the early phase of the first stage of labor, you will still feel comfortable and probably be able to take a walk or relax comfortably. You might even be able to take a nap! (Don't worry about waking up in full-blown labor. If you can still sleep through your contractions, you aren't even close!)

> The pains of childbirth were altogether different from the enveloping effects of other kinds of pain. These were pains one could follow with one's mind.
>
> —Margaret Mead (1901–1977), U.S. anthropologist and writer

When labor begins, your contractions may come every 10 minutes or so and last 20 or 30 seconds. At the end of this early phase, contractions may be down to five minutes apart and last up to a minute. Sometime during this phase, your water may break, but in some cases the water (the sac of amniotic fluid) doesn't break at all. The mucus plug or "bloody show" might be released from the cervix, so don't be alarmed by increased discharge with a little blood in it (call your doctor if you have a lot of blood).

If your water breaks and/or when your contractions are about five minutes apart, call the doctor or midwife, or go right to the birthing center or hospital, unless your doctor or midwife has instructed you to call at an earlier stage. But until that time, you have some time, and this is the perfect stage of labor to work on some meditation and visualization to invoke your inner creative power. You are preparing to bring forth life, the ultimate creative act. Make the most of it now!

> Athena is the Greek Goddess of war, crafts, and wisdom, as represented by the owl with which she is so often depicted. When Athena's mother, Metis, became pregnant by Zeus, Zeus feared that she would give birth to a son that would exceed him in strength and power, so he transformed Metis into a fly and swallowed her. Ironically, that child was not a son, but nevertheless sprang out of Zeus's head, fully armed, helmeted, and bearing a spear, ready for battle—a daughter, the fully grown Warrior Goddess Athena.
>
> Rejecting all suitors, Athena remained a virgin but is credited with the birth of many creative endeavors in Athens, the city for which she is patroness. She created the olive tree, the backbone of Greek agriculture. She first tamed horses and invented the chariot. She taught humans craftsmanship, had a hand in many famous woodworking ventures, and invented the loom and spindle, as well as the flute. She is creativity unleashed!

Remember Macha's story in Chapter 7? The men of Ulster who overthrew Macha's Goddess culture believed that the head was the source of all creative power, not the womb. Athena turns this concept on its head, so to speak, as she reclaims female dominance by birthing *herself* from Zeus's head and then patently rejecting birth on her own in favor of alternative modes of creativity. She subjugates the male notion of birth from the head, but refuses to participate in it after giving birth to herself.

Just as Athena took control over her own creation, emerging fully grown and ready to fight, so can you birth your own bravery and wisdom as you prepare to reclaim your rightful place as woman producing life from the body, not from the head.

Imagine that Athena has helped you to re-establish a woman's power to create in any mode she chooses and using her strength, her resolve, and her fighting spirit, you can forge ahead with your labor, using all your physical and mental resources, toward the successful and ultimate conclusion: the birth of your child. The farther into labor you travel, the more you will feel Athena's raw warrior strength as you go to battle to bring forth and honor life, rather than to take it away, as one might expect from a traditional warrior.

This is Mother Goddess war, and it is a just, loving, and fierce war to preserve the creative energy of the feminine, the bestowing of new life by the mother—the baby that will be born, whether or not the great god Zeus swallows her before birth. Creative energy like this cannot be shut down, and you have access to Athena's energy right now, as the power of labor overtakes you.

What Do You Birth?

As you wait for labor to progress, spend some time describing the experience thus far in your Motherhood Journal. How are you feeling? Describe the physical sensations, your thoughts, your emotions. Then, consider all the other things you have given birth to in your life, up to this point. What great ideas have you had? What things have you created? What plans put into action? Imagine you are Athena, that virgin Goddess of war, of craft, of wisdom, who sprang fully formed from her father's head. She gave birth to so many great ideas; she gave birth to such wisdom, such creativity. Consider your lifetime of creative contributions to the life you have made for yourself and your family, and make a list, perhaps entitled *What I Have Birthed Already, Out of My Own Head*.

Bringing Life to Light

The second phase of the first stage of labor is called the active phase. During this phase, labor starts moving along quickly. You'll really start to feel those contractions as they come more quickly and last longer. And wow ... suddenly they are pretty intense!

The pain or discomfort of labor is actually a sign that your body is doing exactly what it needs to do: dilating your cervix to make a passageway for the baby. That small space quickly expanding to 10 centimeters is a lot of movement in a small span of time, and that much change to your insides can feel like really intense menstrual cramps.

During the second phase of labor, as contractions become increasingly uncomfortable, you might find you are unable to speak or move through them. Although you can probably still walk around, you might need to pause, supported, and breathe deeply during contractions.

 Life gives us what we need when we need it. Receiving what it gives us is a whole other thing.

—Pam Houston (1962–), U.S. writer

For those women who have decided to have an epidural or other pain medication, this is the time—contractions hurt, but you are still early enough in the process to give pain relief a chance to work. For those who plan to forego any medical intervention for pain, this is a great time to practice deep breathing and meditative focus exercises, or self-hypnosis. By suffusing the body with oxygen and pouring deep mental concentration into contractions rather than trying to obliterate or ignore them, you actually aid and facilitate your uterus in its work of moving the baby through the birth canal.

As you progress through this more difficult phase of labor, keep your focus on the life within you as it readies itself, with the help of your body, to emerge into the light. Rather than allowing yourself to become consumed by the physical sensations, keep your mind on your child. After all, you are doing this together!

> Eileithyia is the Greek Goddess of childbirth and the daughter of Hera and Zeus. She may have originally been two separate Goddesses, probably sisters, both daughters of Hera. One sister was the Goddess of easy births, and one the Goddess of difficult births. Eventually, the two were merged into a single figure, perhaps because most women don't know which they are going to have until they are in the throes of it! As labor moves along, you may become more aware of which Eileithyia is watching over you, but in either case, this Mother Goddess protects and nurtures you as you move through the process of labor.
>
> Eileithyia had a strong cult following in ancient Crete and she is often associated with Lucina, the "birth" portion of the triple Goddess along with Diana (growth) and Hecate (death). Lucina means "bringer of light" and, in this incarnation, she was associated with helping to bring newborn babies into the light. This Goddess of birth—easy, difficult, or somewhere in between—was the torchbearer of sorts for the newborn baby making its passage into the world. A protector of women in labor and newborns, Lucina was often depicted wearing a veil—perhaps a symbol of the gauzy space between being almost born and living in the light. She carried an infant in one arm and a rose in the opposite hand, symbolizing purity and perfection. She is the Mother Goddess who watches over you right now!

As your labor becomes more intense, you can invoke the Goddess Eileithyia to assist in the successful completion of the birth, or ask Lucina to help bring your child into the light. Lucina's power is acting upon your body during labor, as your involuntary contractions and changes all help urge your child toward daylight and the external world. Imagine Lucina is acting from within you to guide the life within outward, toward the rest of us.

During this portion of your labor, you might want to help yourself relax by practicing the following meditation. Read it and remember it, or have someone read it to you as you lie quietly, listening with your eyes closed:

Close your eyes and breathe deeply. Take a moment to become as relaxed as you can.

Now, visualize Lucina, a beautiful veiled Mother Goddess glowing with light. In her arms she carries a child—your baby. Imagine her gently rocking the baby as she travels down a long, dimly lit corridor. Her movements are flowing, soft, and easy, almost as if she were floating over the ground. The baby is warm, safe, comfortable, and secure in her arms as she moves forward, forward.

Now, imagine the passageway growing gradually lighter and lighter, the walls opening, and the baby becoming more alert. Lucina begins to glow more brightly until she radiates with a beautiful white light that fills the space and dissolves the cavern walls.

Finally, visualize Lucina walking right up to you and, with a knowing smile, placing your newborn baby into your arms where it belongs. You stare in awe and wonder at your baby, but when you look up to thank Lucina, she is gone. Only a ring of light remains. Watch it slowly fade away. Breathe. Open your eyes and feel Lucina's presence.

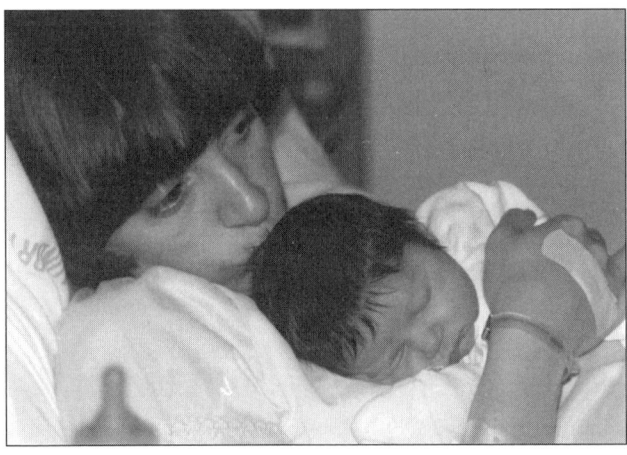

Spirit artist Rita Berkowitz holds her newborn daughter, Erica, in her arms on the day of delivery.

Instant Goddess

Although you probably don't feel like dancing as labor progresses, belly dancing was an ancient labor practice in the Middle East. Pregnant women would practice belly dancing to loosen their hips and help ease the baby into the world. If you have never tried belly dancing before, don't throw out your back, but some gentle hip motions in rhythm with mid-eastern music might help ease your discomfort and even lighten your mood. You might even consider trying to get a copy of the video *Belly Dancing During Pregnancy* by German belly-dancing instructor Gaby Mardshana Oeftering.

The Web of Life

The final phase of the first stage of labor is called the transition phase. During this phase, you will transition into the actual second stage of labor when the baby begins to descend and move through the birth canal and you begin to push.

During the transition phase, if you have already received an epidural or other pain medication, you may begin to feel a more intense pressure and the urge to push. If you are not using any pain medication or an epidural, you may find that your contractions or pulses, as some midwives call them, become incredibly intense during this time. You may be aware of little else during contractions. You might also become very emotional, as this stage of labor can become all-consuming.

During the transition phase, women who are giving birth naturally may sometimes lose confidence in their ability to give birth. Logic doesn't always apply during this extreme phase of labor. Of course the baby will come, but if you suddenly feel like giving up, or if you find yourself grabbing the nurse and screaming, "I can't do this, I changed my *mind!*" nobody will be surprised. They've seen it all before!

 There was no reality to pain when it left one, though while it held one fast, all other realities faded.

—Rachel Field (1894–1942), U.S. writer and poet

This is also the stage when women stereotypically berate their partners for ever putting them into "this situation" (although we've never actually known a woman who really did this). We have known women who scream, cry, curse, or become withdrawn and don't want to speak or hear any noise at all during this stage. How you respond to your transitional phase is highly individual and something you probably can't predict until you experience it. If your partner can be there with you, he (or she) can be your advocate and help to adjust conditions in the room to make you most comfortable.

It's really happening now, and if you do begin to feel weak, or suddenly feel struck with fear, it might help to keep an image of one of your favorite Mother Goddesses forward in your mind, as a point of meditation. Breathe into that Goddess and let her breathe into you, easing the process and facilitating the flow of baby into world.

> Ashke-tanne-mat is a Japanese spider Goddess. Sometimes called "Long-fingered woman," this Mother Goddess helped women with childbirth by pulling the baby from the womb. Impervious to male power, Ashke-tanne-mat protects women from danger and, traditionally, from male marauders.
>
> A magical shaman, Spider Goddess once ignored the advance of Big Demon, who wanted to marry her. Uninterested in his thuggish and unrefined manner, Ashke-tanne-mat ousted him and then continued on with her needlework. She had better things to do!

Ashke-tanne-mat is the ultimate midwife. She protects the vulnerable woman during labor and eases the birth by using her long fingers to guide the baby safely into the world. As labor intensifies, invoke Ashke-tanne-mat's magical powers to ease your baby's passage and to guide the way for both of you.

You may also want to tell your midwife or birthing partner about Ashke-tanne-mat, the Mother Goddess with the long fingers. Your midwife, your partner, your birthing coach, or whoever is standing by your side as your advocate and aid, is playing Ashke-tanne-mat's role in this process. If your partner is your advocate and helper, he may not feel very much like a shaman as he waits and encourages and tries to help, but for this brief moment, that's exactly what he is. He stays by your side as you labor, he helps you in whatever way he can, and he stands over you, instinctively protecting you and the baby you are preparing to bring into the world.

Even if your birthing partner isn't the father of your child, he or she can still play this role. Women who are used to being in charge of their lives all the time may find it difficult to be so vulnerable during the labor process, and they might balk at letting someone else take the reins.

However, having someone there for you, as your protector, coach, and labor partner, will suddenly become much more significant than you may have thought. You will need an advocate, someone to tell you how well you are doing, someone to keep you going and make sure the hospital staff follows your birthing plan, someone to cheer you on and endure your grip when you squeeze that helping hand. You can do this, but when you start to think you can't, your labor partner—with Ashketanne-mat's powers in tow—will help you see that you can indeed do this. You are already doing it. You are in labor, and you are doing a fantastic job.

 Panic is not an effective long-term organizing strategy.

—Starhawk (1951–), U.S. writer and lecturer

No Turning Back!

It's finally time! The transition phase is over and you are entering the second stage of labor. Your cervix is fully dilated and your baby is descending. You knew you couldn't turn back before, but suddenly the actual birth is a reality. It's happening, and it's happening now.

The second stage of labor can be quick, or it can take a while. You might find yourself pushing for an hour, or for a scant 15 minutes. (Typically, the second stage is shorter for each subsequent birth.) After the intensity of the transition period, you might find that your contractions slow down just a little, and you might have a chance to rest a little between them. You are probably exhausted by now, so isn't that good news?

As your contractions help to push the baby out of the uterus and into the birth canal, you might find that you have a very strong desire to push. Even if you had an epidural, which can sometimes dull this urge dramatically, you will probably still feel it, but you may need a little more help in knowing when to push and when to wait.

Your body is telling you that you need to help with the process now. Of course, if your doctor or midwife or the nurse tells you not to push, then you should try to wait. This can be frustrating, but you need to push when the baby is in a position to best benefit from the pushing.

This second stage of labor is tough—it really feels like hard physical *labor*—but it also feels good because after all the waiting, you finally get to do something! You are no longer lying there enduring the contractions. You get to use them and work and help.

As you push your baby into the world, imagine your mind is video-recording the event (whether or not anybody is actually video-recording). As you feel all-consumed by the labor process, let mindfulness enfold your mind and body. Notice everything—the faces of the people around you, the smell of the room, the colors, the sounds—imagine it all in slow motion. Tell yourself: *This is happening, and it's happening right now, and I am here.* Live it. Ground yourself in it. Be your labor, and you will never regret letting it slip away from you.

If you are flexible enough, practicing this squatting pose may help prepare you for delivering your baby. Use pillows to ease any stress on your joints and muscles. Relax and breathe.

While your doctor or midwife may suggest a certain position for pushing, each individual may naturally feel better in one position than another. Some women feel that squatting and pushing is effective. Some women can't imagine pushing in any other position than the traditional one: lying on their backs with their knees up. Some women might even push on all fours or turned slightly to the side. Let your body tell you what you need to do. Of course, if you have an epidural, you won't be able to move your lower body, so you will have to push without assistance from your legs.

When your baby crowns, meaning that the top of his or her head is finally visible, your doctor or midwife may place a mirror so that you can see. You may also want to touch your baby's head as it emerges. Once the head comes through, the doctor or nurses may want to suction out the baby's breathing passages, so if they tell you to stop pushing, do your best. If the umbilical cord is wrapped around your baby's neck, the midwife or doctor can slip it off or cut it. After the head is out, your baby may slip out easily, depending on its position. Follow the advice of your doctor or midwife, and stay closely focused on the way your body feels and what it is telling you to do. You will want to remember this, so pay attention! You are in the midst of one of those rare, defining moments in your life. Once the baby is out, the baby must stay warm, so he or she will be quickly washed up and bundled, but if you ask, you should get to see your baby first in all of its slimy glory. Beautiful!

Harriet Tubman was an African American who escaped from slavery in the mid-nineteenth century, and then worked to lead hundreds of other slaves to their freedom in the north. One of 11 children born to slaves on a Maryland plantation, Harriet Tubman began working at 5 years old, and by age 12 she was a field hand. At 13, a white man hit her on the head with a heavy weight, leaving her brain injured. Tubman suffered from periodic blackouts that lasted her entire life.

In 1849, Tubman moved to Pennsylvania and joined the abolitionists, who worked to put an end to slavery. The Underground Railroad was a network of activists who would help slaves to escape the south, and Tubman became a conductor of slaves. Her first journey in 1850 included her sister and her sister's children. The next year, Tubman helped her brother to escape, and in 1857, she helped her aging parents gain their freedom.

Although Harriet Tubman never actually gave birth to any children, she did play "midwife" for about 300 slaves during 19 journeys from south to north, essentially facilitating a new "birth" for African Americans as free

> citizens. Tubman had to travel in disguise while in southern states, where she was eagerly sought by authorities for her "illegal actions." She was a brilliant manipulator and never lost a single slave. In fact, she carried a gun and threatened to shoot any slave who became scared and tried to turn back. African Americans began to call her Moses because she led her people out of enslavement in the same way Moses led the Hebrews to freedom out of Egypt, and fellow abolitionist John Brown called her General Tubman.
>
> With the underground railroad as the great birth canal, Tubman helped slaves to see that they could not stop on their way toward freedom. They could not give up. They could not turn back, in the same way the laboring pregnant woman cannot give up and her child cannot turn back. Birth, freedom, and new life was, and is, absolutely imminent.

Just as Harriet Tubman led African Americans into a new life, engendering courage and fortitude with her heroism, so can you give yourself to the labor process. You are a wise warrior woman, fierce, free, and devoted to bringing life forward. With the help and wisdom of the thousands of "midwives" before you, all Mother Goddesses, you can perpetuate the process of creation. You won't turn back. You are giving birth. You are a Mother Goddess.

Exercise #1: Mother Goddess Guidance

The beginning of labor can sometimes take hours. As you sit and wait, you may find you are too distracted to read or watch television, too focused on what you know is coming, but yet, you are stuck without anything to *do*. As long as you've got some time, while you wait at home or in the hospital or birthing center, why not plumb the cosmos for some Mother-Goddess guidance by making your own pendulum and asking it some questions?

Whether or not a pendulum actually offers guidance from the great blue yonder or is simply a way to connect with your own subconscious mind, you can decide. You are a Mother Goddess in your own right, and so, with faith and focus, your inner answers bring Goddess wisdom! This fun activity can help pass the time and your partner, labor coach, or friends and family may enjoy doing it with you.

Here's what you will need:

- A 10-inch length of thread
- A small weight, such as a pendant, crystal, fishing weight, or even a heavy nut or washer from the toolbox
- A pen or marker
- A white piece of paper
- A ruler or other straight-edge

Tie the thread to the pendant or other weight. Mark a dot in the center of the paper, and then divide the paper into quadrants with the dot as the center. On two opposite quadrants, write the word *yes*. On the other opposite quadrants, write *no*. You can also designate smaller opposing slivers of your chart to say "Maybe" or "Wait and see" if you prefer the possibility of ambiguity in your answers.

Now, hold one end of the thread over the center of your answer guide so that the weight hangs a couple of inches above the dot in the middle of the paper, and say out loud, "Pendulum, please connect with the Mother Goddesses of the universe to bring me wisdom!" Then, ask your pendulum a simple yes-or-no question, such as, "Am I going to have a girl?" or "Am I going to have a boy?"

At first, the pendulum might not seem to move. Try to keep your hand very still. (You might want to rest your elbow on a hard surface to help steady your hand.) After a few seconds, the pendulum should gradually start to swing back and forth over either the "yes" or "no" areas, and you have your answer.

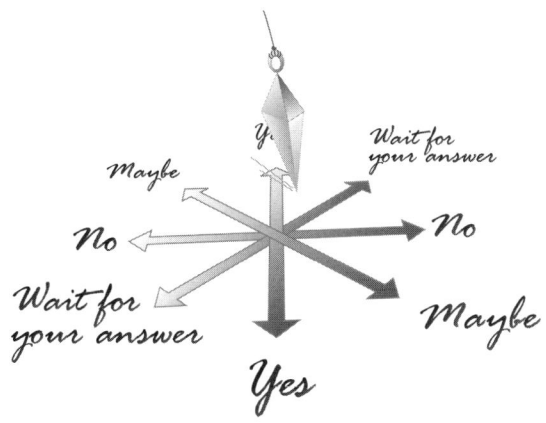

You can ask your pendulum anything you like, but try to stick to questions that are positive and fun. Don't focus on negative things. Let it be a light-hearted game. Here are some questions to get you started:

- Will I have this baby before the stroke of midnight?
- Will my child resemble me?
- Will my partner be loving and supportive throughout the entire labor process, no matter how long it takes? (Make sure to say this while he or she can hear you!)
- Will I really go back to work when I said I would?
- Will I have more children after this one?
- Will my child follow in my footsteps in his or her career?
- Will my baby weigh more than seven pounds? More than eight pounds? More than *nine pounds???*

> Visualization, that seeing of that which is not yet, which is not actually before us, as yet, is essential for the attainment of all the good that man may aspire to.
>
> —Tehilla Lichtenstein (1893–1973), Jerusalem-born U.S. religious writer

Exercise #2: Water Meditation

Flowing water and birth are natural partners, and some women even choose to give birth under water! From the breaking of the amniotic sac to the flowing of the afterbirth, labor and childbirth are visceral and liquid. The notion of flowing fountains, rushing rivers, and pulsing ocean waves can actually help you during labor.

As your contractions intensify, but before you actually start pushing, try the following water meditation to help ease your body into the transition phase as gently as quiet ocean waves washing onto a beach on a calm day. If you have a small desktop fountain you can bring into your room, or alternatively, if you can play a CD or tape with the sounds of ocean waves or a flowing stream during this meditation, so much the better. Have someone read this meditation to you out loud in a soothing voice as you close your eyes:

Imagine you are standing on a wide, solid rock at the edge of a beautiful blue lake. The sun shines and the lake sparkles. A gentle breeze sends quiet ripples over the surface and the air smells fresh and feels clean as you breathe.

You look out over the lake and you notice something in the distance: a little boat made of shiny, solid wood, clean and sturdy. It sails across the surface of the lake and the wind nudges it toward you until it gently bumps against the bank.

Imagine climbing into the little boat. You find it is lined with soft cushions for comfort, and two light oars rest on the floor. You take up the oars and begin to row. You find that rowing is almost effortless as you glide back out onto the lake.

Birds soar high overhead and the sky is almost as blue as the water. The sun is warm on your skin and the breeze guides your boat across the lake. You notice how green the trees and fields are surrounding the lake. In the distance, the green swells into the gentle curve of hills and mountains.

You notice a narrow channel up ahead, so you guide your boat in that direction. The water flow begins to quicken, gently, as your boat heads into the channel, and you find yourself sailing down a gentle river with young green forests on either side, occasionally opening into flower-filled fields or rocky outcrops covered with moss. Deer wander through the trees and come out to drink at the bank, watching you, unafraid. Fish swim at your side, their iridescent scales glinting in the sun. The river moves quickly and joyfully along, carrying you with it, and you find that you no longer need to paddle, so you put the oars down, lean back on the cushions, and watch the sky, the water, the forests, the wildlife.

After awhile, you notice the river quickening. You sit up and look around. Could you be headed for danger? Rapids? A waterfall? No! Instead, you notice that the banks of the river have risen into rocky walls. Tiny waterfalls drop from the cliffs around you but you and the river are safely cradled by a beautiful canyon. Ahead of you, you see a huge rocky arch draped in vines and surrounded by a fine mist from the waterfalls around it. The sun beams in from above, forming thousands of rainbows in the misty spray, and as your boat glides gently through the arch, you enter a grotto that looks to you like everything you ever imagined paradise could be. Your boat has made it through the long passage and here you are, in a land of green and blue with flowers and leaves and the warm spray of tropical mist.

You stand up, peel off your clothes, and dive into the lagoon. The water is warm like a bathtub and you swim, sailing through the water as if you were born just to live here. You are home, you are loved, you have arrived. Breathe in the mist, breathe in the beauty, and then open your eyes.

And now, at last, your labor has culminated in birth. The baby is here, and it's time to celebrate! Your partner may be asked if he would like to cut the umbilical cord. Some people relish this task while others are feeling queasy enough by this point to leave it to the medical professionals. When your baby is clean, dry, and bundled, you should be able to hold him or her. Can you believe it? You did it!

Congratulations, Mother Goddess! In the next chapter, we'll look at the actual birth and consider how it went, and what this means for you, new mama. Yes, we're talking to *you!* Because you are now, officially and forever, a mother.

Part 3

Celebrating Birth and Motherhood

Mother Goddesses act as inspiring, comforting midwives to reveal the nature of birth itself as you experience the profound and transforming moment of new life emerging from your body into the world. Once your baby is born, Mother Goddesses help you to celebrate your postpartum body; to acknowledge, understand, and accept your feelings about new motherhood; to follow your instinct to nourish your child; and to embrace your new life with your baby and with the man (or woman) in your life, your life-partner. Fluctuating hormones can mean fluctuating emotions, but you can use postpartum time of new motherhood to adjust to your new life as a Mother Goddess. We'll talk about the many ways in which you can parent your child with love in an environment suffused with positive spirituality, and the many ways in which you can become the Mother Goddess you want to be. You join the ranks of Mother Goddesses in a line that reaches back to that ancient celestial womb, that first profound creation that birthed the universe. With your baby, you and your partner touch the divine creation. Look to the heavens and celebrate the celestial joy of creation, of life itself!

… *Chapter 9*

Birth: Manifesting Life

Ten billion years ago, scientists postulate, there was an explosion so magnificent and so gigantic that astronomers named it, quite simply, the Big Bang. An ultra-compressed sub-microscopic space containing the potential of the entire universe exploded, giving birth to a universe that has been growing, expanding, and evolving ever since. That fantastic birth engendered not only the earth and everything on it, but also the entire universe.

And here you are, a microcosm of that event but no less miraculous. As you give birth—as baby slips from body and becomes a fully formed, autonomous human being—life has triumphed once again, with you as its vehicle and its progenitor.

Birth marks the beginning of the third and final stage of labor. A few minutes after you've given birth to your baby, your body will begin to experience mild contractions again, and you will deliver the placenta. This process is easy and painless. Your midwife or doctor will check to make sure the entire placenta is delivered and in about 10 to 30 minutes, the third stage of labor will end. You've done it! You've given birth, and you are now a mother.

Birth is such a miracle that tales of it highlight the mythology of every culture, and many great historical and/or religious figures are surrounded with mythological tellings of their births. As a Mother Goddess who has given birth to new life, you can look to other miraculous births to give this celebratory event both a context and a heightened sense of reverence.

Whether your birth was easy or difficult, short or long, with or without great drama, it is no less miraculous than any other birth story, and you will find, as you enter the ranks of mothers, that birth stories are among the favorite topic of conversation. We love to tell our own, and we love to hear the birth stories of other Mother Goddesses. Having a birth story, no matter the plot, no matter the tension or conflict or resolution, makes you a mother, and as you give birth, you are writing that story. It is a story worth repeating.

> And at the end of woe, suddenly our eyes shall be opened, and in clearness of light, our sight shall be full.
>
> —Julian of Norwich (1342–1413), English mystic

The Mystical Divide

For some women, birth is easy and quick, not too painful, an experience they immediately recall with great fondness and joy. One woman we know even called it "fun"! Whether or not you would choose "fun" as your particular descriptor, all births do have an air of the mystical about them. They are transformative experiences that remain etched in our souls and hearts.

Even when birth is difficult, the end result seems almost to obliterate the memory of the pain. In the wake of love we feel for the new life we have brought forth, the birth story may become mythologized—the memories not so harsh as the experience seemed in the moment.

While stories abound about the births of famous figures, scholars often describe the way these stories have adapted details and mystical elements from previous religious traditions. As you remember, tell, and re-tell your own labor and birth story, consider the way birth stories across history have evolved and risen, like cream in a great pitcher, up into the collective unconscious to continue the saga of humanity and the life force that sustains us.

> Maya was a queen in India who had a dream that she was visited by a white elephant. This dream symbolized the spirit of the Buddha entering her body, and when she awoke, she was pregnant, in a way similar to the way that Mary, the mother of Jesus, became pregnant after a dream of being visited by the Holy Spirit. Ten lunar months later, when she was almost ready to give birth, Queen Maya informed the king that she was ready to return to her parents' house, as it was the tradition in India for a woman to give birth in her father's house. The king agreed and arranged a great procession to take his wife back to her childhood home. Queen Maya rode in a magnificent palanquin as the king's soldiers bore her homeward.
>
> During the journey, Queen Maya became weary and asked that the soldiers stop in a beautiful garden at the foot of the Himalayas. The area was filled with trees and flowers. The queen sat beneath a tree to rest, and quite suddenly and with great ease, gave birth to a baby boy: Siddhartha Gautama, the Blessed One who would later in life attain enlightenment and become the Buddha.
>
> The legend tells that Siddhartha emerged from his mother's right side without leaving any opening in her skin and that, just after birth, he took seven steps. With each step, a lotus flower sprung up in his footprint, and he proclaimed, "I am king of the world. I will never be reborn. This is my last incarnation."
>
> Queen Maya quickly returned home with her new son and was filled with bliss and joy, having given birth to the enlightened one. It is said that she died of joy one week later, ascending back into the universal mind, having attained the ultimate life experience.
>
> If you ever happen to travel to Nepal, you can actually visit Lumbini Park, just south of the first foothill of the Churia range, still revered as the birthplace of the Buddha.

Maya, mother of the Buddha, had just about the easiest birth we can imagine. A baby emerging from her side without leaving any opening? Talk about the ultimate C-section. She didn't even have to push!

Yet although Maya and her son, Siddhartha Gautama, are actually historical figures, we can make a pretty educated guess that the story didn't actually happen just the way it is now told. Some scholars believe that Siddhartha's parents weren't even royalty, but wealthy landowners, so that Maya probably wasn't a queen at all. Although she might have given birth on the road to her father's house, we're guessing her baby didn't mystically step out of the side of her body. She may have had an easy delivery and returned home happily, but we imagine her newborn baby probably didn't walk and talk, at least not on that first day!

But like every mother who gives birth to someone exceptional (and all babies are exceptional!), it's easy to change the story. Even as you try to be accurate and remember the experience exactly the way it happened, and because you experience the world from your own perspective, your memory might not be exactly like your partner's, or the midwife's or doctor's, or anyone else's who might have been in attendance.

After you have given birth, write down your own birth story as soon as you can. You will always treasure your immediate perspective on this event, and you might find that as you recall the experience later, details change and don't match what you write down today—all the more reason to do it now! Memories, especially of highly charged emotional and physical events like childbirth, are tricky. If you write your account of the birth of your child right now, you will have a treasured record of one of the most important days of your life.

Dad snaps a photo of Mother Goddess Mary Kay with children Maggie, Pete, and newborn Tess, as the family welcomes the new baby into their lives.

Your Birth Experience

Today if you can, tomorrow if you must, write your birth story in your Motherhood Journal. Include as much description and detail as you can. How did you know you were first in labor? How did it all begin? How did you feel? What did you do? From that first contraction all the way to the final stage of labor (see the next section to read more about this stage), tell your story as well as you can. In this high-tech age, you might want to consider using a digital video camera to film the thoughts of others, if not the birth itself!

"I'll Think About That Tomorrow"

For some women, birth happens unexpectedly. Just as Maya gave birth on the road, before reaching her father's house, just as Mary gave birth in a stable because she couldn't find room in any inn, and just as many other Mother Goddesses have given birth in taxicabs, on subway platforms, in the backseats of cars driven by their anxious husbands, even at home when they had never planned a home birth, sometimes babies come when they are least expected and when it is most dramatically inconvenient.

What do you do when birth surprises you? You become resourceful and make the best of the situation! For thousands of years, women gave birth without any professional medical care, and if you must deliver before you make it to the hospital, well, then you must! Of course, you will seek medical attention for yourself and your baby as soon as you can, but if childbirth comes fast and hard, you won't have much choice but to do what you can. And what a story *that* will make!

> In the 1939 Hollywood film *Gone with the Wind*, Melanie Wilkes, Scarlett's sweet-tempered cousin and rival in love, goes into labor in the midst of the Union Army's invasion of Atlanta. The doctor is gone, tending to the wounded on the battlefield, having left laboring Melanie in the hands of Scarlett and the young servant, Prissy, who claims to know all about birthing babies, but then admits, after the doctor is gone, that she's never even seen a baby being born before.
>
> Scarlett and Prissy must act as midwives to Melanie, whose labor is difficult and painful. Together they must use the resources at hand to help Melanie. With no experience, a pot of boiling water, a roll of twine, and a pair of scissors, Scarlett and Prissy must help Melanie deliver that baby ... and they do it! As Scarlett says throughout the movie when faced with a difficult reality, "I won't think about that today; I'll think about that tomorrow." But today is it for Scarlett, Melanie, and Melanie's baby. And predictably, Scarlett takes action.
>
> While Prissy's character is young and naïve, a frightened child thrown into a desperate situation, she delivers a line in the birth scene that encompasses one of the movie's chief themes. Prissy says her mother told her that during

> birth the midwife should put a knife under the delivering mother's pillow to cut the pain in two. The knife represents that sharp and painful line between birth and life, between life and death. The south was living on the edge of survival during this time in history, and as Scarlett walks out into the bloody battlefield after hearing from Dr. Mead that he cannot assist with Melanie's birth, she sees nothing but pain and death strewn all around her. With Scarlett, we see how close life and death really are. As men die all around them, Scarlett and Prissy help Melanie bring new life into a new world—fragile but successful, they do what they need to do. They improvise, they struggle, and they triumph. Melanie's child is born into a world that is itself being reborn out of the horror of war into a unified country.

During the filming of Melanie Wilkes's birth scene in *Gone with the Wind*, to make her labor seem more convincing, director George Cukor would twist actress Olivia de Havilland's ankle sharply under the blanket whenever she was supposed to be having a contraction. The next time you watch the movie, you might make note of this scene. Is she convincing? Or could you, as an experienced laborer, do an even better job at recreating the scene?

Whether or not you like de Havilland's acting, *Gone with the Wind* is filled with Mother Goddesses of all types. Melanie Wilkes is the long-suffering, pure-hearted mother who understands her own weaknesses and vulnerabilities and must rely on and trust others, no matter what they have done to her in the past. Her open heart and forgiving spirit give her a purity and an abiding sense of love for her fellow humans.

Scarlett O'Hara is another kind of Mother Goddess, but she was also a mother as well as a midwife. Scarlett was strong and enduring, a fiery warrior Goddess in the face of death and destruction. She would not be thwarted and she would not give in. She fought to preserve what she loved. Scarlett did her best to re-create the serene love and ministering care of her own mother, Ellen—but had to do so without the presumed security and calm of her mother's lost time, gone with the wind.

Prissy is the young, naïve Mother Goddess whose almost accidental wisdom smoothes the way for birth in the face of tragedy, and Mammy, played by Oscar-winning Hattie McDaniel, the first African American woman to win an Academy Award for her role in this movie, was the overriding and abiding mother figure to all the women, young and old, whom she managed and nurtured through daily life.

Instant Goddess

As you recover from the birth of your baby, you may be thinking about your mother and how she went through a similar experience, bringing you into the world. Or perhaps you are thinking about a female mentor or other significant female influence who helped shape your life and your ideas about motherhood. Write a thank you note to your mother or mentor to express your new appreciation for what she has given you.

No matter what your home situation, your family profile, or your collection of friends and caretakers, let Melanie Wilkes and the Mother Goddesses who tended and supported her inspire you to look at the other Mother Goddesses in your life who, directly or indirectly, have touched this birth experience.

Our lives are filled with Goddesses, and the ones we envision are no less powerful, mystical, and enduring than the ones who hover around us, either in body or in mind: our mothers, grandmothers, aunts, female cousins, sisters, nieces, daughters, female teachers, mentors, health-care providers, and closest women friends. Your life is blessed with many Mother Goddesses, and together you have brought one more life into the world ... even if you had to wing it!

The Art of Birth

You've thought about your labor and birth experience, and now we hope you have written about it, too. But how would you paint it? Would your painting be a realistic depiction? Or would it be blurred and beautiful like a painting by Impressionists Berthe Morisot or Mary Cassatt? Passionate and ambitious like a painting by Lee Krasner, partner of artist Jackson Pollock? Profound and stained with beauty, such as Helen Frankenthaler's abstract expressionist masterpieces?

> The meaning of a word—to me—is not as exact as the meaning of a color. Colors and shapes make a more definite statement than words.
>
> —Georgia O'Keeffe (1887–1986), U.S. artist

Giving birth is more than a physical process: It is an art. It is creativity incarnate, and every artist who experiences it or even considers it has a depiction that represents it. Not every birth portrait would be all beautiful. Some would be messy; some would be surreal or loaded with expressionistic drama. Art takes real experiences and filters them through the creative mind. What comes out is largely up to you. Consider how you might recreate your birth, not through words, but purely through images.

What comes into your mind? What do you remember? The people? The fetal monitor? Images of the way contractions feel? How would you depict your fear? How would you depict your joy?

Frida Kahlo was a Mexican painter who lived from 1907 to 1954. Her paintings were dramatic, sometimes disturbing, and full of elements of native Mexican art combined with a surrealist sensibility, although she denied being a surrealist, claiming that she only painted the reality that existed within her. Kahlo's paintings were small and personal, while her husband, Diego Rivera, painted huge murals often containing political content. Rivera was himself a huge man, while Kahlo was quite petite, each seeming to be physical manifestations of their art.

While a student, Frida Kahlo was almost killed in a bus accident and began to paint while recovering from her severe injuries. Never able to have children, Kahlo suffered from several miscarriages, but gave birth continually to new paintings that depicted both the intense pain and intense joy in her life.

Much of Kahlo's work is about pain, disintegration, and loss. The injuries from her bus accident shaped her life view from an early age, and her turbulent marriage and continuing health problems helped to sustain this theme. Yet Kahlo's folk-art style, vivid colors, and frank emotion also sometimes reveal moments of pure joy, an open heart, and love. Kahlo's life was full of life and death, pain and beauty, risk and renewal.

Her painting *The Birth* was the first to ever depict birth so graphically: a woman with her head covered, legs spread, surrounded by blood, with a head emerging. Kahlo described the painting as a depiction of her own birth, so that she is both mother and child. The head is covered, said Kahlo, because as she was painting this portrait her own mother died, and this laboring mother is in mourning for her own mother in the moment she becomes a mother. Yet Kahlo is also giving birth to herself because, while she could never

> successfully give birth to another, she continually gave birth: In her journal, Kahlo wrote of this painting, "I gave birth to myself."
>
> The image of Frida Kahlo illustrated here is a sculpture by the family of Guillermina Aguilar, Oaxacan folk artist, where Frida Kahlo is a subject of great interest and exploration—and collectibility.

Frida Kahlo makes us think of the Greek Goddess Athena who gave birth to herself by bursting from her father's head, fully armed and ready for battle. Even though her life was fraught with great pain and loss, Kahlo continued to fight, to create, to live, to give birth to the new, to reinvent herself, and to love stubbornly and defiantly. For more on Frida Kahlo, rent the 2002-released movie of her life, starring Salma Hayek, entitled *Frida*.

In your Motherhood Journal, try sketching images you remember from your birth experience. It doesn't matter if you can't draw very well. All you need to do is to create some visual impressions to complement the written story. Think for a while on what you remember, and don't critique yourself. Just draw what you remember and let it be. After all, you are ultimately creative. You can draw whatever you want to draw. Nobody has to see it, and however it turns out is good and right.

Earth Mother Was with You

Finally, as you look back on your birth experience, consider what Mother-Goddess energies might have watched over you. Did you accomplish a natural birth? Perhaps a Mother Goddess somewhere, in some dimension, stood over you and urged your body to accomplish its task just in time. Did you have a Cesarean section? Perhaps a Mother Goddess somehow invoked medical aid to keep you and your child healthy, strong, and well. Was your baby small or premature? Consider that a Mother Goddess somewhere breathed vitality into your tiny offspring. Were you in crisis during the birth? What Mother Goddess might have eased your mind, fortified your spirit, and coaxed you forward and through the dark night?

Of the many aspects of the Goddess who were Creatrixes, mothers, protectors, and nurturers, imagine which ones might have been at your side, above you, all around you, encircling your labor and birth experience with their positive and protective energies. The Mother Goddess, open to the power and influence of her many sisters, may just get a glimpse of the intricate weaving of influences surrounding every new life, every miraculous birth.

> Haumea is the Hawaiian Earth-Mother Goddess of birth. A shape shifter who could die and rebirth herself at will, Haumea protected mothers in childbirth and gave birth herself to many children who emerged from different parts of her body. Haumea is the Goddess of natural childbirth, and several stories tell of her intervention to invigorate stalled labor or demand that certain potions be administered to prevent Cesarean section—a procedure that used to mean almost certain death for the mother.
>
> Haumea had six rebirths in order to marry her offspring, and was the Goddess of wildflowers and many magical trees. One spectacular fish tree bore fish when submerged into the ocean, and the reason we must now fish for fish rather than having them leap into our hands is because Haumea's son grew greedy and shook the fish tree too violently, scaring the fish away.
>
> Even today, Hawaiian women call upon Haumea to assist in their births. She is said to dwell in human form on the island of Oahu, and to travel back and forth between Earth and the heavenly realm.

When natural birth is possible, it is said, Haumea will see that it happens. When Cesarean section is necessary, Haumea—who herself knows what it is like to bear children from all over her body—keeps the mother and child safe and strong. Some mothers have their hearts set on natural childbirth and feel disappointed and heartbroken when they aren't able to birth naturally, either because they eventually required some kind of pain medication or because a C-section was necessary.

Yet birth is still birth: It is the creation of life. It doesn't really matter how your baby emerged into the world, especially now that medical technology is so advanced as to make C-sections safe. Sure, a vaginal birth is the "natural way," but when a C-section is necessary for your health or the health of your baby (or both!), you can also embrace this miraculous method of birth, a testament to how far we have come in preserving the health of mothers and children.

After your birth, when relaying your own birth story, don't be put down by people who criticize your Cesarean experience. Your own birth happened the way it happened for a reason. It is now a part of your personal history, and anyone who criticizes it is speaking in vain. Everyone has her own story, and whether Haumea helped you to birth naturally or has aided you through a medical procedure, you were in the company of a Mother Goddess. That's all you need to know to believe in your own success.

Exercise #1: Build Your Goddess Web

As you consider the many women who have become a part of your birth experience, you can underline your grateful role in this network of life by designing your own Goddess web. During those early days when your baby is napping and you are resting, collect photos of the women in your life: the family members and friends who are meaningful to you. Use these photos to build your web: a graphic representation of the Goddesses interconnected in your life, which can serve as a permanent reminder of the way we all help, support, nurture, and even give birth to each other.

Here's what you will need:

- A large sheet of heavy white paper
- A fine-line black permanent marker
- Photos of the women in your life
- A glue stick

First, draw a web that extends from every edge of your paper by making lines from one end to the other, and then connecting them with circular shapes extending from the center outward. Your web can look like anything, but envision a spider's web as you draw.

Then, have fun going through photos and cutting out pictures of the women in your life. Find old photos of your female relatives and friends throughout your life. Cut the photos into whatever shapes you like. You can decorate your web with portrait cutouts of head and shoulders, or full-body shapes, or both.

Glue the photos of women all over the web, and then find a photo of yourself and glue that in the center. Your baby will be the center of attention for weeks … even years! … to come, so let yourself be the center of *this* web of life. (Well, all right, if you want to put a picture of yourself *holding* your new baby in the center, that will be lovely as well.)

> Pregnancy doubled her, birth halved her, and motherhood turned her into Everywoman.
>
> —Erica Jong (1942–), U.S. writer and poet

Exercise #2: Designing the Birth Announcement

Sooner or later, everybody—including those beyond your list of must-calls right after the birth—will want to know all about the new member of your family. It's time to send out birth announcements!

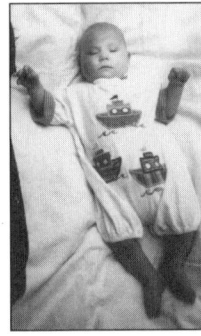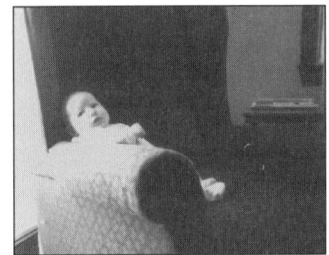

Mary Kay, pictured with her children earlier in this chapter, took these newborn pictures and sent elegant sepia-tinted birth announcements to celebrate the new life of each child. Now, she has a lovely record of the first days of Maggie, Pete, and Tess, seen left to right. Years ago, women typically sent out traditional printed birth announcements, but today, creativity reigns! Many women now design their own birth announcements, hand making them as miniature art projects or designing every imaginable kind of announcement on the computer. We've seen modern, graphic birth announcements, medieval-themed announcements, announcements bedecked with classical cupids, and fantastic photo collages of new baby and happy family. Your birth announcement can be as original as your baby is, but because most people will want to know, it should probably include the following information:

- The baby's time and date of birth
- The baby's weight and length
- The baby's gender

- The baby's full name
- Some mention of proud older siblings, when relevant

Pictures of the new baby are always welcome but not necessary. Other than that, the sky's the limit. You can send postcards, tri-folded letters, traditional cards, and even e-mail messages with attached photo files. Designing a birth announcement is fun, and people really do appreciate knowing that everything—and everyone—came out okay!

To enhance your own home, create a welcoming announcement of your baby's arrival with inkblots of the baby's feet and hands. Frame this important document and hang it on the wall in the baby's room.

Like any major event, after it's over, life is different. Sometimes we feel a post-traumatic letdown. Now what? The new mother, subject to the plummet of hormones, may feel super-emotional and struggle to adjust to a whole new way of existence.

Your own Big Bang has happened, and wow ... it certainly was a *big* bang, wasn't it! Now your universe is expanding, and your Mother-Goddess powers were never so necessary as they are right now, as you begin your brand-new life as caretaker, nurturer, and brand-new Mistress of Your Universe.

Life as a mother is fun, challenging, exciting, baffling, interesting, and rewarding every single day. It may take a little getting used to, or it might come as naturally as sleep. Don't worry: We're still here, and we're with you all the way. Read on through the next chapter to find strategies and inspiration for establishing yourself firmly and confidently in your new way of life.

Chapter 10

Postpartum: One Becomes Two

And now it's over. Pregnancy. Labor. Birth. Those things you've been waiting for, worrying about, anxious over … it's all happened, and now, here you are, you and a tiny little human, totally dependent on you for his or her every need.

Yikes!

The postpartum period is full of confusing emotions: elation, depression, anxiety, bliss. One moment, you may feel flooded with worry that you have no earthly idea how to take care of a baby. Who put *you* in charge, anyway? You're no Mother Goddess! And what were they *thinking?!* The next moment, you may find yourself rocking your baby and gazing into the biggest eyes you've ever seen, struck dumb with wonder at your baby's beauty and perfection and thinking, "I was *born* for this job!"

You might find it hard to believe that you actually created this tiny little human, so small and foreign. At the same time, how familiar your baby seems to you, and how familiar you sound and feel to your baby. For nine months, the two of you moved and breathed as a single being. How peculiar it seems that, suddenly, the one has become two. You are now two separate humans, each autonomous, and yet, you will remain intimately connected for years to come.

> A blossom must break the sheath it has been sheltered by.
>
> —Phyllis Bottome (1884–1963), U.S. writer

The first few weeks after birth mark your chance to bond with and get to know your baby, now that he or she is finally on the outside of your body. You and your partner will also make adjustments to your relationship at this time, and it's important to stay connected and supportive, as you are still recovering from a dramatic physical and emotional event, and he is still your advocate, partner, and protector. He may feel on the outside of your little mother-baby circle, and, in many ways, he is. Yet your conscious efforts to draw him in will pay off tenfold in the coming weeks as he takes on a very essential role in your and your baby's life: father.

During the postpartum period, you will experience many conflicting emotions, but some of the most interesting Mother Goddesses are here to help you cope.

Is That Your Body?

We all know what it is like to finally give birth, and to look down at your belly and think, "Hey … wait a minute … it looks like there's still a baby in there! Did they miss one?"

Your uterus has stretched quite a bit over the last nine months, and so have your muscles. It takes awhile for your body to get back to normal. You are carrying extra weight in the form of both fat and fluid. As your hormones gradually stabilize over the next few months, and with good health habits, your body will gradually shift back to nonpregnant form. But chances are, your body won't look exactly the same.

The first thing a lot of women notice about their new mama bodies is that, even when their stomachs shrink back down, they've still got some extra stomach. One woman we know says that when she lies down on her side, her stomach lies down next to her! Some women sport stretch marks over their abdomens, and even those who seem to bounce right back to the body they had before pregnancy say that their shape has changed—hips or waist may have changed proportion. Even skin tone and hair color and texture may seem a little different, for a while, or even permanently.

Some women find it quite an adjustment, when they bear the obvious marks of pregnancy, to accept their changing bodies. Yet the body of a Mother Goddess—*your* body—is not only more mature, but wiser, too. It has weathered the world, and if you embrace your postpregnancy body as a map of beauty and courage and love, you may find a greater happiness and physical satisfaction than you ever did before.

> Baubo the Belly Goddess is the Greek Goddess of belly laughter, known for her lewd jokes and bawdy manner. In some stories, she has no head but is merely a body with nipple eyes and a vulva mouth. In one version of the story of Demeter, the Greek Goddess of grain and the harvest, and her daughter Persephone, Baubo plays a major role. (We told you the story of Demeter and Persephone in Chapter 2.) After Hades stole Persephone and took her to the underworld, as you may recall, Demeter searched the world over for her daughter. Crops died and the world was cast into winter because of Demeter's misery and despair. Finally, according to one version of the story, Demeter gave up her search. She slumped against a tree, defeated. And then someone came waltzing down the path.
>
> It was Baubo, the Belly Goddess. Whether or not she was headless doesn't matter. She came up to Demeter, and began to tell her an off-color joke. We can imagine Demeter probably stared, humorless, at the strange, bawdy Goddess. But Baubo wouldn't give up. She told another lewd joke, and another. Then she lifted her skirt and bared her belly, flashing her vulva. Finally, Demeter laughed ... and laughed and laughed, until the two Goddesses shared great belly laughs. The headless version of the story describes Baubo walking up to Demeter and actually telling the obscene jokes with her vulva mouth, peering with her nipple eyes, smiling, laughing.
>
> Rejuvenated by laughter and the great generative power of female energy, Demeter had the strength to return to her search. Baubo's belly puts things back into perspective for her. Demeter remembered her status as a Goddess; and no mere God was going to get away with stealing her daughter! Recharged by mirth, Demeter finds her daughter, and you know the rest of the story. Persephone returns for half the year and the world is graced with the seasons.
>
> Baubo also appears in Egyptian mythology, lifting her skirt and baring her belly and vulva to Isis, to cheer her up following her horrible grief at the death of Osiris. A similar belly-baring Goddess appears in Japanese mythology. Uzume coaxed the sun goddess Amaterasu back out of a cave with a skirt-lifting, laughter-filled, vulva-bearing burlesque, rescuing the world from a lethal lack of sunshine.

> The vulva is an ancient image in many cultures, and the ancient caves in southern France that contain some of humankind's earliest markings show outlines of vulvas from as far back as 30,000 years! The gateway to the womb, the vulva and belly are profoundly interconnected, and may have been the first significant elements of the body ever recognized by humankind. That these body parts are intertwined with great humor and belly laughter only makes them more sacred, for in laughter we can find joy, and with joy we understand what life is all about.

Many of us also feel a little less shy about our bodies after giving birth. After all, you spent hours in a room full of people naked from the waist down, pushing a baby out of your body. What's the point of modesty after an event like that?

Remembering Baubo can help you to love and feel pride in the body you have right now. So what if your belly is bigger, or looser, or decorated with stretch marks? Maybe your vulva is healing from a tear or an episiotomy. But these body parts are proof of the remarkable miracle you have experienced. You are infused with the power of the feminine, you are a life-giving Mother Goddess, and you have every right to be proud!

Why not be a little bawdy, a little lewd, a little proud of the vulva and the belly, those body parts that can sustain and produce life? Why not lift up that skirt and take a good, proud look? We can all use a little more Baubo in our lives. You know something? You look beautiful! Celebrate your postpregnancy body's beauty. When you've got it, baby, flaunt it!

Instant Goddess

Are you in touch with your inner Baubo? How easily can you belly laugh? Rent your favorite comedy, or one you haven't seen but have heard is a scream, on video or DVD tonight and watch it, either by yourself or with your partner. Let yourself really laugh. Get loud and rowdy. Better yet, watch it naked. What the heck, have some ice cream while you're at it. Have a really good time. You deserve it!

Who *Is* This Little Person?

Another curious challenge many women face during the postpartum period is ambivalence toward their babies. Some people don't like to talk about this, but it happens, and it is quite common. Most of the time, you may feel so overwhelmed with love for this new little life that you can hardly keep from bursting into tears of joy. Then again, after hours without sleep, difficulty nursing, and ceaseless crying, you may suddenly feel like you simply cannot and absolutely do not *want* to do this mothering thing. And sometimes, when postpartum depression becomes severe, you may lose your desire to care for your baby at all.

Postpartum depression is highly treatable, and if you do feel persistent negative feelings toward your baby, please seek help immediately. It's nothing to feel ashamed or embarrassed about, and your doctor can prescribe medication to help you, and help you fast. Many of us who don't require medication, but just need a little more sleep, some time to talk out our feelings, a little weeping time, and the passage of a few weeks. Meanwhile, we may indeed feel ambivalent. We love that we are mothers. We love our babies. And yet ….

So many things have changed. We are tired. We feel heavy. We feel like milk machines. We are *so* tired. We are already growing weary of changing diapers and we are constantly covered in spit-up. Oh, and did we mention how *tired* we are?

These days, celebrity moms are helping to lead the way in both their on-screen and off-screen personas, to explore the challenges and rewards of giving birth. Miranda Hobbes from HBO's *Sex and the City* is a New York City career-woman, a single mom who struggles with logistics, sleep deprivation, and the enormous change in her identity that her new son brings to her. Miranda confronts her own belief that she is "just not the mother type," while every day making a wonderful new discovery of mother love. Meanwhile, actress Cynthia Nixon, who plays Miranda, delivered her second child in "real life" and celebrated her post-pregnant body with fashion- and comic-Goddess Joan Rivers at the 2003 Golden Globes, where Cynthia was nominated for her work on the show. Being a new mom can be enervating and at the same time elegant and exciting—all without the pressure to wake up one morning and discover that you're June Cleaver!

Newborns are utterly exhausting, and sleep deprivation alone can throw anyone into an extreme emotional state (even June Cleaver!). On top of that, the postpartum woman must endure the powerful effect of fluctuating hormone levels that might make you feel angry and irritable, vulnerable and weepy, or just plain listless.

> Life begets life. Energy creates energy. It is by spending oneself that one becomes rich.
>
> —Sarah Bernhardt (1844–1923), French actress and writer

It's all natural, and the good news is that, in most cases, feelings of ambivalence, uncertainty, or depression will disappear after a couple weeks. Sure, parenting is often difficult and frustrating, but you won't feel as if your emotions are out of control once your body readjusts to not being pregnant anymore (and if you do continue to feel that way after the first few weeks, as we said, please tell your doctor so you can be helped).

Also, remember that you have been the center of attention for almost a year now. Selfish as it may sound, it can be tough to share the spotlight with a seven-pound bald human who can't even hold up his or her end in a conversation—especially when you are working so hard and doing so much!

Other mothers have no problem letting their new babies bask in all the glory, but may still feel a letdown once they are no longer pregnant—once that baby is apart from your body, even though your caretaking efforts are still crucial for its survival, it is a sort of loss when the one becomes two. Consider it a grieving period as you move from one stage to the next—grieving that gets to evolve into a joyful state of manifesting a new relationship.

Aditi is a Hindu Goddess said to have formed herself. The "Mother of Worlds" was at one time considered the mother of all Gods and Goddesses. Aditi was called many names, all revealing her great and encompassing power, including "The Boundless Whole," "Eternal Space," "Supporter of the Sky," and "Celestial Virgin" (virgin used to mean "not for any man" but "a woman unto herself").

In one of the most famous stories about Aditi, she bore 12 children from eggs. One of them hatched out as an unformed lump. Aditi looked at him one time and cast him into the sky. This was Vivasvat, sometimes called Martanda. A God found him and molded him into the sun. The leftover pieces fell to Earth and became elephants.

As for Aditi, we can imagine that even as the "Boundless Whole," perhaps for that one moment, she had had just about enough of motherhood. We can all understand this feeling of frustration, those flashes of anger, that lost feeling. Yet Aditi's momentary lapse, luckily, turned out well. Her child's fate was to become the sun, an auspicious fate indeed!

As the mother of all space, Aditi is invoked for disorders of the head: headaches, epilepsy, and mental problems. Ask for her help with postpartum depression to help you reclaim yourself as you endure the roller-coaster ride of postpartum hormones.

Every woman, every Goddess, must journey through this postpartum adjustment period, and nobody said it was easy. You might feel like part of you has been removed, and indeed it has—but it hasn't been taken away from you, either. It waits in your arms for love, guidance, and nurture. Now that your baby is a human being in its own right, you can enter the next stage: establishing a relationship with this new little person who has emerged from your body.

Unlike Aditi, we know you won't cast your child into the heavens, even if sometimes, after enduring six hours of colicky screaming, the thought might cross your mind. You are doing your best, and that is all you need to do. Nobody expects you to know everything and do everything right. You are new at this job! So were we once, and so is every woman who gives birth to her first child. It's a tough job, and you are doing great.

Finally, let Aditi's presence comfort you when you are feeling frustrated and lost. The self-creating mother of all space is there to calm and still your mind.

Instant Goddess

When you feel frustrated and overwhelmed by early motherhood, take a moment to yourself, sit comfortably, and close your eyes. Breathe in the great energy of life. Let it fill you and reassure you. Close your eyes and clear your mind. Imagine the vast reaches of cool dark space, the billions of stars with their layers of light. Imagine the many worlds out there, and then come back to this green and blue, small, beautiful, whirling world where you and your new baby live. Everything is going to be just fine.

Feed the Need

Many women choose to breastfeed their babies, some for only a week or so, others for the first few years of life. Other mothers decide that breastfeeding isn't for them. Whichever path you choose, you are responsible for nourishing your new baby. Your fulfillment of this primary, urgent, frequent need will sustain your baby's life.

Even if you decide to breastfeed for only a short period, studies show that the benefit to your baby is immense. Colostrum, that clear "first milk" you will secrete for the first few days of nursing, is a potent immune-system protector, imbuing your baby with all your antibodies while his or her own immune system matures. Many scientists and doctors have conducted research into the benefits of breastfeeding, revealing that breastfed babies suffer from fewer illnesses, and may even have higher IQs.

Your breasts are bigger, rounder, fuller, and producing milk, and no matter how you've used them in the past, right now you are using them for the very thing they were intended. The power to feed a baby from your own body is incredible, and is one of the most celebrated female traits in the worship of ancient Goddesses. Many Goddess statues reveal, and often offer, their breasts, a symbol not only for the power to feed a human life but also representing the fruitfulness and nourishing quality of all life on Earth, in the form of agriculture and other natural resources. And remember Chapter 4? Even the Milky Way is thought to be the overflow from the milk-producing breasts of the Goddess.

Get to Know the Gals

How do you feel about your breasts? Think back to when you first became aware of them. Was it in your pre-teen years when you realized you were no longer *entirely* flat-chested? Was it your first trip with your mother to buy a bra? Was it the first time you consciously touched them? The first time you let them be touched by someone else? In your Motherhood Journal, describe how you feel about your breasts, and include how you feel now that they have changed, and now that you are using them for this sacred purpose. Don't feel you have to stick to your positive feelings. Not everybody enjoys all aspects of nursing, so tell it like it is. You'll feel wiser after you're done.

But although breastfeeding seems like the most natural of womanly tasks, it isn't easy at first. Many women, and many babies, have a tough time getting the hang of it, especially in the first few weeks. Teach the baby to latch on the wrong way and your nipples will be so sore and chapped that you won't even want to wear a bra. Most midwives and nursing consultants in hospitals will be happy to instruct you in the proper technique until you get the knack of it, but it really is an art. You and your baby will work it out, but be patient. It takes a while.

Breastfeeding also comes with certain inconveniences. Hear your baby cry or even *think* about your baby crying and, like it or not, your breasts will start producing milk, sometimes at the most inopportune times. (Invest in some nursing pads to put inside your bra—problem solved.) If you go for too long without nursing, your breasts can become engorged, which can be painful, although this process is designed to make sure you feed your baby every few hours. (A breast pump and a freezer will alleviate overflow and give you a supply of breast milk for when you can't feed your baby.)

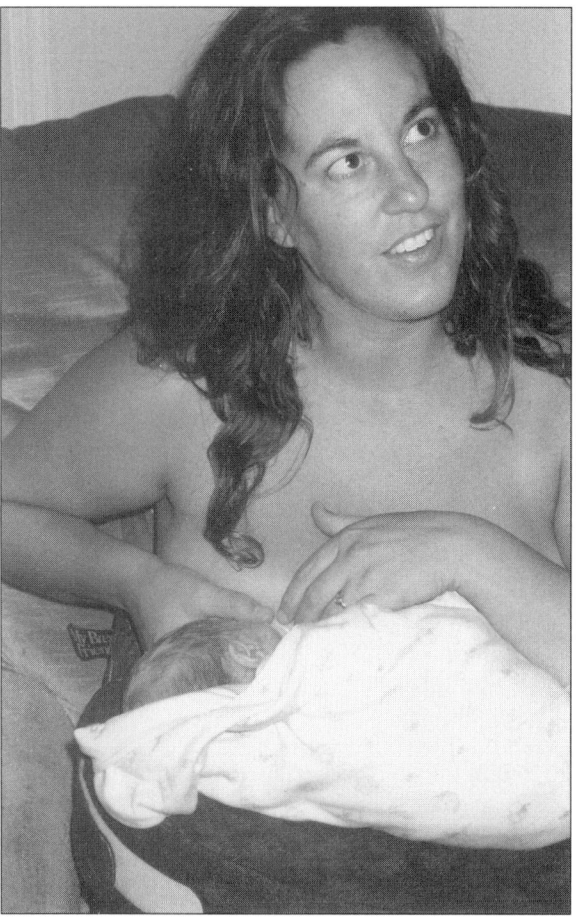

Gail's daughter Niki nurses Gail's newborn grandson Ethan. Turn back to Chapter 1 to see a photo of Gail and Niki when Niki was a toddler. How time flies!

But the benefits of breastfeeding far outweigh the inconveniences. Breastfeeding is a powerful way to bond with your baby, and the process actually releases chemicals into your body that induce maternal feelings, a great way to combat the ambivalence so often associated with postpartum depression. Once you're in the routine of it, nursing feels really good, not only because it alleviates the pressure of the full breast and gives you the satisfaction of seeing your baby happily nursing, but because our bodies are designed to derive pleasure from breastfeeding. It's an evolutionary mechanism that encourages us to do it!

But even if you are unable to breastfeed—some women are too ill or suffer from an infection just after pregnancy and miss the "window" of opportunity, or find that they never produce enough milk (this is uncommon)—or choose not to breastfeed, you will still be the source of your baby's nourishment, and that is a power in itself.

> The Babylonian Goddess Ishtar is called "Mother of the Fruitful Breast." The Mother Goddess of compassion, sex, and war (how's that for a combination?) was intense, aggressive, and passionate about everything she did. Ishtar is often associated with the Mesopotamian Goddess Inanna, the Queen of Heaven.
>
> Known for her sexual exploits, her thousands of lovers whom she took or cast aside at will, and her sometimes violent nature, Ishtar was the deified version of passion in all pursuits. When Ishtar traveled to the underworld in search of her husband, Tammuz, all humans and animals were left without any passion, and Earth was no longer fruitful, producing no food and no life. All despaired in her absence.
>
> Ishtar's ferocity applied primarily to actions related to the whole process of sex, fertility, and feeding. Statues of Ishtar show her offering her breasts, a symbol representing fertility, reproduction, and nourishment of all life. Ishtar had just the kind of power it takes to feed the whole world and sustain the passions required for survival.

In her role as fertility Goddess and nourisher of all, Ishtar was never timid, retiring, sacrificial, or submissive. She was a strong, powerful Goddess who took what she wanted out of life. She reveled in the passion of sex, of birth, of the life-giving capacities of the breast. Some Ishtar cults even engaged in a sacred form of prostitution! Ishtar represents the female power of sexuality in all its stages: the pleasure, the fruitfulness, and the sustaining of the created life.

If you choose to breastfeed your baby, let Ishtar be your guide. Feel her power and her pleasure as you sustain the life of the human you have made. And if you don't breastfeed your baby, let Ishtar also fortify and sustain you. You are also sustaining life, and Ishtar is there to help you nourish your child.

Finally, we hope you will continue to honor your other needs as you care for your baby. In all her glorious fertility, Ishtar was a deeply sexual Goddess. The immediate postpartum period is often a time of low sex drive as hormones readjust, but it's easy to prolong avoidance of sex when you are totally focused on taking care of your baby.

> It's the good girls who keep the diaries; the bad girls never have the time.
>
> —Tallulah Bankhead (1903–1968), American actress

Yet you remain a sexual being. After your doctor has given you the thumbs-up (usually about six weeks after birth), we hope you will draw your partner back into your physical world and seek out your sexuality again. Not only does your body crave the pleasure of touch (even if you've fallen out of synch with that feeling), but you and your partner need to stay in intimate connection as you begin your new journey as parents.

Your partner may not understand how you are readjusting your thinking about your sexuality because his body hasn't undergone the changes yours has. Yet the more you open up to him and tell him how you are feeling, and the more you try to keep that part of your relationship from becoming stagnant, the better you'll understand each other and the closer and more intimate your relationship will be on all levels.

Renaissance You

Sleeping. Eating. Nursing. Cleaning. Changing. Bathing. And suddenly, they want you back at the office … help! As the postpartum period winds down and you finally get into a routine, you may often still feel overwhelmed that you could ever do it all. Everyone seems so needy, and all you really want is eight hours of solid sleep and a nice, hot shower.

But yet, see how well you are learning to do it all? You have transformed, in a few short weeks, from pregnant woman to Renaissance woman. You might not feel very competent yet, but motherhood has a long learning curve, and you are sailing up that curve at just the right speed.

As you master each new skill—nursing, changing, bathing—and as you learn to ask for help and delegate household responsibilities, like laundry, dishes, clutter control, bill paying, etc.—you can continue to add new aspects to the mosaic that has become your life as a mother. If you plan to return to work soon, that will become another piece of the puzzle, and you, like millions of women before you, will find a way to fit that one in, too.

> Labour: to feel with one's whole self the existence of the world.
> Love: to feel with one's whole self the existence of another being.
>
> —Simone Weil (1910–1943), French theologian

Mothers have a great skill for multi-tasking, but this is a learned skill, not an innate one. As you work your way through your long to-do lists each day, don't forget to add yourself to the list. You will only function well and efficiently if you take care of yourself. That means sleeping when you need to sleep, drinking plenty of water, eating healthy foods, and getting some fresh air and moderate exercise. It also means allowing yourself to talk to friends, be with your baby without distractions, and spend time alone with your partner, maintaining your connection.

And about that shower ... strap the baby in the infant carrier, set him or her on the bathroom floor, and enjoy. Believe us, we know. It's been a few days since your last shower, hasn't it?

Finally, keep in mind that life is full of storms, but storms fill the air with life energy, and that life energy sustains us. Staying mindful through these early weeks will carry you through like a miracle cure. Look at this amazing day. This amazing life. This amazing baby. They all belong to you.

Although we know little about the life of the Venetian painter, Giorgione, who lived circa 1478–1510, his painting *The Tempest* was both influential in the world of Renaissance painting and symbolic of the "tempest" of new motherhood.

In the painting, a nude woman nurses a baby on an embankment outside a city. Nearby, a young gentleman watches with a smile on his face. The painting was influential and important because, for the first time, the primary figure or protagonist in the painting is not a person, but the weather. A storm is brewing over the city, and the clouds, lightning, and well-wrought "mood" the storm invokes become the central focus of the painting. This was radical for the Renaissance period, when portraits were about the people and the action of the people, not about the unpopulated sky.

The woman in the painting, though naked, doesn't pose erotically, but rather, wraps her baby in a maternal embrace. The baby, not a newborn but looking more toddler-size, nurses competently while the woman looks out on the world, and perhaps at the viewer of the painting, with a bemused expression. Was she cast out of the city, or simply taking a break from her daily life to enjoy the day? She doesn't seem concerned by the storm. She doesn't seem even to notice the storm or her state of undress, and neither does her happy baby.

The young man in the painting also seems unconcerned by the so-called "tempest," and is more interested in the nursing mother. So why is the painting called *The Tempest?* The storm gathers over the city, and perhaps the painting offers the message that the daily life, from which these two seem to have escaped temporarily, is the tempest of our existence, while a foray into the natural world offers peace and reprieve. Or perhaps the tempest is simply a function of life no matter where one goes, and the three figures in this painting know and accept the fact, waiting unphased for the storm.

Some scholars believe the woman was the mother of some hero from some story we no longer associate with this painting, although the painting does seem secular and not religious. Some speculate the woman's exclusionary status from the city, while others speculate that the storm doesn't look so bad after all, so no wonder no one is worried. Whatever the theme or rationale behind this enigmatic painting, we find it a lovely metaphor for the early days of new motherhood. Oh how we wish to escape from the storm of our busy and sometimes overwhelming lives. But then, oh how we cherish the storm's beauty, too.

Those who see us may or may not understand our lives, our purpose, our comfortable mothering spirit, our round fertile selves, our understanding that we don't need to hide from the world as we do the work of the Mother Goddess. And in the end, no matter what, we are still one with our children.

We love Renaissance art, partially because the women it reveres as beautiful look so much like mothers with their wide hips, rounded bellies, and full breasts; and partly because it reminds us how well we do the job of living lives full of beauty, art, learning, and love. While the Renaissance period of our history—that great revival of art and learning in fourteenth-, fifteenth-, and sixteenth-century Europe—is known primarily for its famously accomplished men, we believe that the twenty-first century is the great age of the Renaissance Goddess.

The more we know and understand about what we can accomplish, the more we will achieve. We will survive despite the tempests life tosses our way, even when we feel frustrated that we can't do it. You *can* do it. Just look into the eyes of the woman in Giorgione's painting and see yourself. You have a child to protect, and you don't fear the storm. You are too strong, too beautiful, too powerful to be lost. You are a Mother Goddess, and you can do whatever you need to do. You are the giver and preserver of life.

Mother Goddess Wendy and baby son D'arcy smile for the camera.

Exercise #1: Your Weather Forecast

How is the weather in your life these days? Sometimes labeling our moods and feelings can help us to more clearly define and master them. Are you having a sunny day? Partly cloudy? Dangerous storms predicted?

Making a weather chart can be a fun way to see your own changing moods in a humorous light while still warning your family members what they can expect, especially in the early postpartum days when your moods, due to hormones and no fault of your own, may change quickly. If your partner or other family members want to get involved, you can each have your own weather forecast on a central household bulletin board. It's a great way to help everyone understand where everyone else is coming from, especially as everybody is working to adjust to a new member of the family.

Here's what you will need:

- Several sheets of lightweight cardboard
- Colored markers
- Scissors
- Package of adhesive Velcro "buttons" or thumbtacks
- Bulletin board

On the cardboard, draw a sun, a sun half hidden by a cloud, a cloud with a bolt of lightning coming out of it, a cloud with rain coming out of it, and a tornado. Each image should be about four to six inches tall. If you can't draw, then look for graphic images on your computer software or on the internet and print them out, and glue them to the cardboard.

Cut out the images and attach one half of a Velcro button to the back of each image (unless you are using thumbtacks instead).

On a centrally located family bulletin board (what, you don't have one? They are invaluable for busy families!), attach the opposite Velcro button. Or, if more than one family member is participating, tack a small slip of paper under each button with the words "Mom's Mood," "Dad's Mood," "Mary's Mood," etc.

Store the weather images in a nearby basket or other easily accessible container, or put them in an envelope tacked to the bulletin board.

Every morning when you get up, make your forecast. How do you think your mood is shaping up today? Post the appropriate weather symbol, and then feel free to change it during the course of the day should your mood turn out to be different than you predicted.

 How we are all more or less creatures of Sun, Shadow, and Imagination, impressed or depressed by weather!

—The Gardener (nineteenth century), English gardener and writer

Exercise #2: Song of Yourself

Have you ever written poetry? Poetry is a wonderful way to express your emotions, especially the strong ones, and we know you've been feeling strong emotions ever since you brought your baby home with you.

Walt Whitman, a famous American poet, first published his famous "Song of Myself" in 1855 (although it wasn't so titled until 1882), in which he expresses his own idea of himself. Look it up and read it for inspiration if you desire, and then write your own song of yourself, but with a special twist. For nine months, you were you with another life inside. Now that life exists outside of you, yet it is still deeply a part of you.

For your Song of Myself, let it be a song of the life that you and your baby share. You might instead call it, "Song of Us." Or call it anything you like. If you don't resonate to poetry, then write a song. Consider Carole King's beautiful song, "Child of Mine," as an inspiring example. Then, create your own.

Whitman's poem doesn't rhyme, and yours needn't either. Let it be a free-flowing expression of your feelings. After you've written it, go back over it and revise it, or leave it as it is if you think it's perfect. You don't have to show it to anyone, but you can certainly share it if you wish. Add more to it later if you feel the inspiration, or write more poems and keep them in your Motherhood Journal. We think every mother is a poet in some capacity. If you can create another life, you can create a poem. Give birth to your inner poet today and write, write, write to your heart's content.

While famous women poets are often notoriously childless, a few notable exceptions, Mother-Goddess poets we love, include Sandra

McPherson, Gwendolyn Brooks, Jorie Graham, and Julianna Baggott. Check them out if you catch the poetry bug and want some more inspiration.

As you gain a greater comfort level with your new status as mother, your journey is just beginning. Motherhood is so complex a job, so complete a persona, and will become such a defining factor in who you are that we could write lots of books about it! For now, though, we'll limit ourselves to two more chapters.

In the next, we'll consider how your role as Mother Goddess will evolve as your child grows into a bigger, more exuberant, more capable baby with a personality all its own. Pretty soon your baby will be crawling, and toddling, and talking, and transforming right before your eyes into an actual human. As one Mother-Goddess friend of ours now says, "Who *is* this person living in our house now?" Are you ready?

Chapter 11

New Mom Fulfilled: Nurturing New Life

Now that your pregnancy is over and your baby is here, slowly but surely you have become a family—a family! Of your own making. After the early weeks of adjustment wind down and you and your partner settle in with your child, life gradually begins to take shape.

Yet the memory of pregnancy is echoed each day by the special closeness you and your baby share. The first several years of a child's life are largely defined by the nurturing presence of the mother. And of course, your partner's presence is also incredibly important, not only for bonding with the baby, but for establishing and maintaining emotional support for you.

At last, life seems to be about more than feeding, sleeping, and changing diapers. As your baby reaches each milestone, you can do more and more together: reading books, singing songs, and playing games like patty-cake and peek-a-boo. The older your baby gets, the more interest he or she will take in everything you say, and watch everything you do with fascination.

One of the most amazing things about being a parent is watching your baby learn. You can almost see the wheels turning in that little head as your baby figures out that applesauce tastes pretty good, that noodles are fun to play with, that Mommy makes silly sounds and funny faces when the food bowl sails onto the floor, that the dog barks but doesn't like his tail pulled, that Daddy is the baby's amusement-park ride, that sleep is nice but waking up is even nicer, that some toys make funny noises and some are soft, that books are interesting, that songs are pleasing, that wet diapers are uncomfortable, and that those tiny hands and feet can actually do some things if you learn how to use them.

What a difference it makes to come home to a child!

—Margaret Fuller (1810–1850), U.S. writer

Now you're getting to the fun part, and that may be quite a relief after the intense neediness of the newborn (lovely as that also is, it is, as you remember, fraught with sleep deprivation). Once babies can sit up and look around, they really begin to reveal their personalities. And the more you stimulate their brains and nurture their bodies, the better they will grow and learn, and the more confidence they will gain in their environment. If they learn to trust you, they will learn to feel safe in their world.

Guardian of Your House

The better you get to know your new baby, the more both you and your partner may feel a fierce sense of guardianship. You might feel less inclined to spend time away from home, preferring instead to make your home more comfortable, livable, and family oriented.

With a baby in the house, safety is crucial. It's time to start childproofing your home, as your baby becomes more mobile: plastic covers on coffee table and fireplace hearth corners, baby gates at the tops and bottoms of stairs, childproof latches on cabinets, screens around decks and open railings.

Cleanliness is also important, and, although you may feel like you don't have much time for cleaning, keeping floors vacuumed, swept, and free of choking hazards should be a priority. Comfort is important, too, not only for your baby but for you. Your furniture should be comfortable, the arrangements of your rooms relaxing. Let your home be a shelter of safety for your family, as homes have been designed to be for thousands of years.

> Uksakka is the Finnish Goddess of Household Affairs, and a Mother and Guardian Goddess to families. She is called "Door Woman," and is said to dwell underground beneath doorways of tents in Finland and Lapland, and to use her magic to change the genders of fetuses, which her sisters place in women's wombs.
>
> Uksakka specifically used her magic to protect newborns and toddlers, and women invoked her to help babies take their first steps. In all matters of the private household, she stood guard. Her sister Juksakka, sometimes called "Bow Old Woman," placed males in the wombs of women and used her magic to make them into good hunters. She is the guardian of children and protects them from accidents.
>
> The third sister, Sarakka, was also a guardian Goddess. She placed females in women's wombs, and was the goddess of spinning and reindeer births. Because reindeer were so crucial for the survival of the people who worshipped these three Mother Guardian Goddesses, this was an important power, and families offered food and drink each day for Sarakka upon their hearths. She was also the protector of parents.
>
> The mother of these three powerful household Guardians was Maddarakka, or "Old Woman." This earth mother cared for the spirits of children before they were born, and then created the fetuses, which she gave to either Sarakka (who would make them female) or to Juksakka (who would make them male). Maddarakka was a healing Goddess whose powers protected women in childbirth, and helped to heal both mothers and babies. Together, this family of four Mother Goddesses, sometimes called the Akkan or creators of life, formed a solid square of protection around northern-European households, exchanging fertility for offerings.

Uksakka and her sisters and mother were powerful guardian protectors of families in ancient Finland, and they can protect your family, too. Call on Uksakka to protect your doorway, keeping the family safe inside. Remember her when your baby takes those first, wobbling steps. You are establishing your new identity as a family unit, so imagine Akkan, that magically protective family unit of women, and let them support and inspire you.

Thank either Juksakka or Sarakka, depending on whether you have a boy or a girl, and let Juksakka's energy protect your baby from accidents while Sarakka helps you to keep your baby, and your entire household, well nourished. When someone in your family is ill, ask Maddarakka to help with healing. Together, families (mainly the women) worshipped these Akkan, who made them fertile and prolific, safe, and well.

 What one loves in childhood stays in the heart forever.

—Mary Jo Putney (twentieth century), U.S. writer

You might relate particularly with the Akkan these days as you explore your own protective feelings toward your child, your worry when he is ill, your delight at her first steps. You are establishing your new identity as a family unit, so imagining the Akkan, that magically protective family unit of women, can inspire you.

Inherent in Uksakka's protective powers is the suggestion that as families nurture each other, they also grow. As your baby gets older and continues to develop, those first steps are inevitable, as are the first words, the first temper tantrum, the first skinned knee. If children never took any risks, they would never grow, and, objectively, you know risks are necessary. Yet you worry. You wish you could keep your baby wrapped up safely in your arms all the time!

Let Uksakka help you. Encourage that growth, those first steps, those measures of growth in your child, while still keeping the environment safe. Your home is fortified and your child is protected by love and diligence, so even when you have a skinned knee to bandage and tears to dry (don't forget the magic kiss that takes away the pain), you'll know you are doing your job.

The spirit of the Uksakka can be found in the care and guardianship of the women of your family, those present now and those who have gone before. Place a family heirloom photo in your child's room to invite the support of the generations to enter, comfort, and guide you and your child.

The woman standing in the center of this photograph looking directly into the camera is the great-grandmother of Becky, the young girl pictured with her grandmother, Doris, in Chapter 2. "Nana" is Doris's mother-in-law, and here, as a young woman, Nana is a lookalike for Becky's Aunt Fran, Doris's youngest daughter. Nana passed before Becky was born, but the vivacious smile, sparkling eyes, and thick dark hair of her Aunt Fran connects Becky to the spirit of this lively young Nana.

Your Baby's Life Path

Parents spend a lot of time just watching their children. Watching them sleep, play, learn ... it's fun to imagine what they will look like later in life, what activities they will most enjoy, what career they will someday choose. It's also tempting to try and shape our kids in a way that pleases us—maybe those "Baby Mozart" tapes will turn him into a musical genius! Maybe baby gymnastics is the springboard to her perpetual physical fitness! Maybe the right kind of environment will be the key to a lifetime of happiness and success!

Yet children are going to be who they are going to be. Stimulating your child's mental and physical growth is undeniably important to making the most of his or her natural abilities, but freedom to explore the world is important, too.

Now, just because your six-month-old would rather chew on those number flashcards than focus on them does *not* mean she will never be a nuclear physicist. Nobody chooses his or her career as a toddler. However, there are certain things about your baby that are the way they are, whether you like it or not. Some mothers who expected a quiet, cuddly baby feel thwarted by a baby who is constantly squirming, struggling, and on the move. Sometimes, highly active, playful parents feel mystified by their introverted, quiet child. Maybe your little girl has no interest in dolls but loves to crash trucks into stacks of blocks, and refuses to wear all those pretty pink dresses you have hanging in the closet. Maybe your little boy has no interest in catching a ball and spends all his time flipping through books and teaching himself to read.

Part of the challenge of parenting is to let go of some of our dreams of how the perfect child "should" be and to take a good look at who our own children *are*. Every child has his or her own unique life path. Each child is an individual with a personality that, while it will be partially shaped by you, is partially shaped simply by your child's own being. Facing the reality of getting to know that person you carried within you for almost a year is an important step down the long road of parenthood. If you understand who your child is rather than clinging to who you *wish* your child were, you can be a more understanding parent and a more useful partner in helping your child become a well-adjusted adult.

> Meshkent, the Egyptian Mother Goddess of childbirth, was a fate Goddess with ties to the upper and underworlds. According to the ancient Egyptians, when someone died, Meshkent would accompany that person to the underworld and testify at the judgment. The wife of Shai, the God of fate, Meshkent was privy to information that enabled her to foretell the future of newborn babies.
>
> In some versions, Meshkent is the Four Meshkents, comprising the four Goddesses who guarded the birth chamber (reminiscent of the four Finnish Akkan Mother Goddesses). In Egypt, the birth chamber contained a birthing stool and two mud birth bricks, approximately one foot long and about seven inches wide. Women would place a foot on each birth brick and squat to deliver their babies, using the birth stool to rest or perhaps for support while squatting. The birth bricks were typically decorated with images of a mother and child and relevant protective childbirth Gods and Goddesses such as the Cow Goddess Hathor.
>
> The Four Meshkents guarded, respectively, the chamber door, the birth stool, and each of the two birth bricks. Sometimes Meshkent is depicted as a birth brick with a woman's head.

In ancient Egypt, infant mortality was much higher than it is today, and the ancient Egyptians tried to protect babies using magic in many forms. Today, we have such advanced health care that most women in developed nations deliver healthy babies without any lasting consequences for mother or baby. Yet those ancient Mother Goddess guardians of the birth chamber and the lives of small children can still support us as we lead our children into the future.

And what future do you see for your child? Take your baby in your arms today and relax at your Motherhood Altar, and then try this Meshkent meditation. Speak or think the following words:

Oh divine Meshkent, Goddess of fate and justice, please reveal my baby's future path to me. Give me a glimpse into the ways my child will grow and develop, the successes and achievements of my child's life, the people my child will love, and the places my child will go.

Now, with your baby still in your arms, or playing nearby if she refuses to comply with your meditative mood, watch your baby and relax. Breathe deeply and let Meshkent show you the future via your imagination. What scenes do you envision? What kind of older child, what kind of teenager, what kind of adult? What profession do you see for your child? What kind of relationships? What learning, what love? And lastly, ask for divine guidance to help your child with all of life's challenges.

Spirit artist Rita Berkowitz painted this portrait, Madonna and Child of Franklin Park, *as part of a series of paintings called* City Folk. *For inspiration, Rita walked around the inner city interviewing and photographing people. When she saw this beautiful mother playing with her child, Rita made this picture to express the sacredness of everyday life.*

We know you worrying types, so we will clarify that, for this meditation, you always focus only on the strengths and positive images that come to your mind. It's easy to imagine things based in worry when you think about your baby, and even to convince yourself that these worries are based in some future reality. However, training your mind to envision positive future scenarios for your baby, and positive resolution for every seeming setback, will open your mind to the many positive possibilities for your child's future and will help draw positive energy into your child's life. This is a productive endeavor, whereas worry only diminishes your energies and takes your mind away from your job as a loving parent.

Baby Stories

As a way to reinforce your positive visions for your baby, spend some time today writing in your Motherhood Journal the fictionalized accounts of your baby's future. Inspired by Meshkent, tell the story of your baby's future life, either in short vignettes or in more detailed and structured accounts. You can use a creative style, a journalistic style, or any other style you choose, but enjoy envisioning scenes from your baby's future life. Have fun with it. Let the exercise fill you with joy and positive expectation.

Your Daily Routine

If you've ever read a parenting book, you've probably read the advice: Children thrive on routine! For the routine-challenged among us, this can be a tough order to follow, but it really is true that children feel calmer, more secure, and are even better behaved when they have a set routine to follow that they can depend on each day.

Sure, sometimes routines must change, on special occasions or when something comes up, as something inevitably does. However, the solid foundation of a routine will help you immensely in your parenting efforts.

Your routine can be as individual as your family, but should consist of eating, napping, and going to bed at the same approximate times each day. You might also add story time, bath time, playtime, and anything else your family does together into your routine. Write it down and post it, and then each morning you will have a visual reminder of your plan. Your routine might look something like this, although, of course, your schedule will consist of your family's individual priorities and activities. This is just an example:

	Monday	Tuesday	Wednesday	Thursday	Friday	Saturday	Sunday
6:00 A.M.	Feed baby/ eat breakfast	Feed baby/ eat breakfast	Feed baby/ eat breakfast	Feed baby/ eat breakfast	Feed baby/ eat breakfast	Feed baby/ eat breakfast	Feed baby/ eat breakfast
7:00 A.M.	Get dressed	Get dressed	Get dressed	Get dressed	Get dressed	Get dressed	Relax in pajamas
8:00 A.M.	Sitter/work	Read books	Sitter/work	Read books	Sitter/work	Family outing	Spirit time
9:00 A.M.	—	Laundry	—	Laundry	—	—	—
10:00 A.M.	—	Feed baby	—	Feed baby	—	—	—
11:00 A.M.	—	Playtime	—	Playtime	—	—	—
Noon	—	—	—	—	—	—	—
1:00 P.M.	Lunch	Lunch	Lunch	Lunch	Lunch	—	Lunch
2:00 P.M.	Read books	Sitter/work	Read books	Sitter/work	Read books	—	Playtime
3:00 P.M.	Clean up house	—	Clean up house	—	Clean up house	Yard work	—
4:00 P.M.	—	—	—	—	—	—	—
5:00 P.M.	—	—	—	—	—	—	—
6:00 P.M.	Dinner	Dinner	Dinner	Dinner	Dinner	Dinner	Dinner
7:00 P.M.	Baby's bath	Baby's bath	Baby's bath	Baby's bath	Baby's bath	Baby's bath	Baby's bath
8:00 P.M.	Books, bed	Books, bed	Books, bed	Books, bed	Books, bed	Books, bed	Books, bed
9:00 P.M.	Grown-up time	Grown-up time	Grown-up time	Grown-up time	Grown-up time	Grown-up time	Grown-up time
10:00 P.M.	—	—	—	—	—	—	—
11:00 P.M.	Bedtime	Bedtime	Bedtime	Bedtime	Bedtime	Bedtime	Bedtime

In addition to simply planning the activities of your day, Mother Goddesses know that the daily rituals of life are sacred. Rather than rushing through meals, dashing through books, and collapsing unconscious into bed at the end of the day, Mother Goddesses know the importance of letting each moment *be*. Mindfulness is the key to this process of honoring the mundane and making daily life more spiritually charged.

> Cuba, Cunina, and Rumina were three sister Goddesses in ancient Greece and Rome who protected the infant in sleep. Specifically, Cuba helped to lull infants into a peaceful sleep, or, according to some sources, protected toddlers no longer sleeping in the cradle. Cunina protected the sleeping infant in the cradle, and Rumina protected and blessed infants while nursing.
>
> As the primary guardian of sleeping children, Cuba worked in concert with the Goddesses Edulica, who blessed the child's food, and Portina, who blessed the child's drink. This triad of protection kept babies healthy and safe as they engaged in the primary activities necessary for survival, working together to protect and honor the infant's daily routine.

As your life rolls on and your child continues to grow, your routine will necessarily require certain adjustments. You will still have those sleepless nights, staying up with your child when he or she is ill, or has a nightmare, or fears a thunderstorm. Eventually, your baby will begin to eat baby food, and you will face the process of weaning your baby, something some babies do easily, and others resist. Finally, you'll find yourself cutting up little chunks of what you are eating, and before you know it, you'll all be eating regular meals together.

Naps will gradually dwindle down to nothing. Cleaning the house will change from washing spit-up rags to grass stains, sanitizing bottles to scrubbing plastic plates and sippy cups. Eventually, you'll give away the infant car seat and buy a booster seat. Playtime will change its quality and books will get longer, with more words and fewer pictures.

If you go back to work, you will need to arrange some kind of childcare—a nanny, an au pair, an in-home daycare provider, or a daycare center. Or perhaps you or your partner will decide to work at home to be with the baby. Soon daycare will turn into preschool, which will turn into kindergarten.

> It is not a bad thing that children should occasionally, and politely, put parents in their place.
>
> —Colette (1873–1954), French writer

Your child will learn how to add, how to read, how to carry on an interesting conversation. He will come up with all kinds of things you never would have considered; she will do things that will amaze you. Every day is a discovery, full of challenges and joy.

Meanwhile, your daily life continues, and mothering gets easier ... and harder. The bond between you and your partner will change and evolve, and through it all, every meal, every nap, every sip of juice, cup of milk, and good night's sleep will be blessed by the Mother Goddesses. Let them help you to recognize the beauty and the sacred nature of every single moment.

Play Time!

Children learn through play, and one of the most amazing things parents get to do is play with their babies. From introducing infants to the basic sounds of language to teaching a grade-schooler how to work a crossword puzzle, playing with children is really communication, bonding, and the expression of love in disguise. As our lives get busy, it's so easy to tell your child "Just a minute, just a minute," until he or she gives up. But if your child gives up asking to play with you altogether, you've lost something.

Instead, let the Mother Goddesses inspire you to creative play with your baby. With your infant, sing, read, and play hand games. Talk to your baby and make lots of expressions and vocal inflections. Toddlers enjoy simple movement games, books with humor and color, and anything musical.

Preschoolers are pre-readers and love to begin practicing letter sounds and memorizing books. They are becoming more athletic and can enjoy more advanced games and simple sports, and their imaginations are fierce and fantastic, so "pretend" games are always an inexhaustible source of play. Kindergarteners are reading and can understand more complicated games. They love to talk, to ask questions, to understand. They might be ready to play an instrument, play a sport on a team, and probably love nothing more than playing anything at all with *you*.

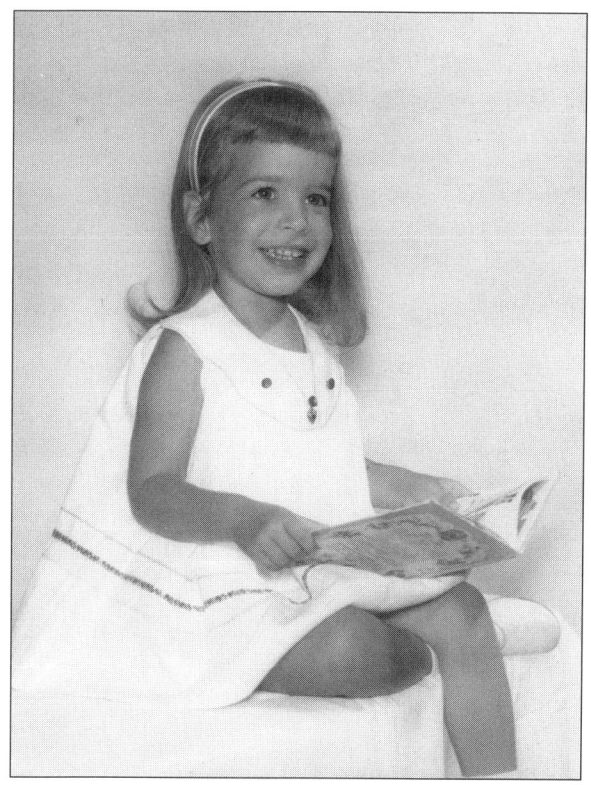

Here's our book producer Lee Ann as a toddler, already well on her way to a literary career with the encouragement of her Mother Goddess mom, Gloria. Lee Ann's grandfather and great-grandmother are pictured in Chapter 3.

> ... children understand what their parents have rejected or forgotten.
>
> —Madeline L'Engle (1918), U.S. writer

No matter how busy you are, no matter how hectic life gets, finding the time to play every day with your child is one of the greatest possible investments of your time. You will never get your children's childhood back again, and if you lose them now because you are too busy to play, you may never get them back.

Play sets a foundation for your future relationship. The more play in your life, the better you will all understand each other, enjoy each other, and laugh your way through your days.

> Nobody knows for sure if Mother Goose was a real person. She might have been Bertrada II of Laon, an eighth-century noblewoman and the mother of Charlemagne. Or she might have been a mythical creation based on a French story of a motherly, magical bird that told stories to children in the seventeenth century. These stories were first collected under the Mother Goose name in 1697 by Charles Perrault.
>
> Most of the nursery rhymes that appear in Mother Goose collections are old folk stories set to rhyme. Their rhythms are captivating and they are full of action, unusual people, and silliness. Although many people have tried to attribute historical meaning to different nursery rhymes, such trivia doesn't matter to kids, who simply love to hear these rhymes. Babies, toddlers, preschoolers, grade-schoolers—something about Mother Goose appeals to children, even when they don't totally understand what the rhymes are about because the references and language are so archaic. We all love them nevertheless:
>
> *Old Mother Goose, when*
> *She wanted to wander,*
> *Would ride through the air*
> *On a very fine gander.*
>
> Or what about this one:
>
> *There was an old woman*
> *Lived under a hill;*
> *And if she's not gone,*
> *She lives there still.*
>
> We like to think that describes Mother Goose ... and many of the other Goddesses who wait on the periphery of our lives.

As you embark on the adventure of learning with your child, we hope that books will play an important part of that process. Sure, it's easier to put a child in front of the television, but reading does so much more for a child's conscious awareness of the world. Plus, reading children's books is great fun for young-at-heart grown-ups, too.

We also hope you will begin to take your child out into the world at an early age: to child-friendly museums, outdoor concerts, children's plays, street fairs, science exhibits, historical landmarks, national forests, parks. The world is an amazing place full of opportunities for learning, and is so much bigger than what's on television. You only have a few short years to help grow this human being of your own making, so we hope you won't waste a single moment.

Exercise #1: Build a Baby Book

Every baby should have a baby book. You probably have one that your parents put together, and although you can buy a huge range of baby books in stores (maybe you already got one for a baby shower gift), you can also make your own with a simple scrapbook and a big imagination.

Here's what you'll need:

- Empty scrapbook or ring binder filled with heavy blank white paper
- Scissors
- Glue stick
- Colored markers
- Colored construction paper
- Decorations like glitter, sequins, ribbons (optional)
- Pictures from magazines for a collage effect

Each page of your baby book can be a work of art. Don't just paste square photos in blocks. Instead, cut the photos out so that the people seem to jump out of the page. Glue collages of photos grouped together by theme, tilted at interesting or humorous angles. Be creative with the way you cut out and arrange your photos, and add your own text and doodles or decorations and designs ... or both! Don't worry if it takes some time. Your baby's book will be a years-long effort, and is the perfect way to relax when you need a few minutes to yourself.

Begin with the cover. Decorate the cover with designs that reflect your baby's personality, and/or photos cut out in interesting shapes and glued to the cover. Put your baby's name on the cover: Anna's Book, or Emmett's Book, for instance. Use calligraphy or print out the name with an interesting font from your computer.

Proceed through the book in rough chronological order. The first page might have pictures of you pregnant, cut out and designed in a way to communicate your excitement. You might include sonogram photos here, if you have them, and some notes, written in marker around the picture, about how you felt when you found out you were pregnant. At the bottom of the page, you could write a short note to your baby about how you imagined her or him while still pregnant, or when you first saw the heartbeat on the sonogram, or found out if it was a boy or a girl.

The next page might show newborn photos of you and your baby in the hospital or birthing center, proud daddy holding baby, and siblings who are now big sisters or brothers. Include the name of the hospital, the doctor, the midwife, nurses that were important to you, and glue in any hospital souvenirs: your or your baby's ID bracelets, that tiny knit cap, the daily menu, your "home care" instructions, etc. Then, write out an abbreviated (and child-friendly) version of your birth story. How did it go?

Finally, in a highlighted box, put your baby's full name, birth weight and length, and, if you saved one, a tiny bit of newborn hair, either taped to the page or tucked in a small envelope and glued there.

In a separate square, you might also list other names you were considering, so that your baby can someday delight—or be horrified—at the names he or she *might have had!*

You can get other ideas for your baby book by looking at published baby books, but the key is to fill it with pictures and information that your baby will someday love to look at. You might spend many hours in the future flipping through your child's baby book together. Children love to hear stories about themselves as they grow.

Don't forget such precious nuggets of information such as these:

- Date of weaning
- Date of the first bite of solid food: What was it? How did your baby like it?
- Date of the first time baby rolled over
- Date of the first time baby crawled, with a description of baby's mobility efforts
- When baby spoke those first words: tell the story
- When baby took those first steps: tell the story
- Date of baby's first and each subsequent tooth eruption
- Story of the first haircut
- Funny sibling interaction stories

- Funny baby-and-family-pet interaction stories
- Clever, amazing, or just plain hilarious things your baby says (these make great quotes to surround family photos)
- Pictures, mementos, and the stories of special events: the first holiday season, the first vacation, the first birthday, the first trip to the park (a pressed flower? a few grains of playground sand glued to the page?)
- Who was your baby's first baby-sitter?
- Who was your baby's first friend?
- Interactions with grandparents
- The first day of school

Your baby book can cover the first two years, or the first five years, or you can expand it indefinitely to become an ongoing scrapbook/photo saga of your child's life. No matter what you do—a little or a lot—your baby's book will be a sacred family treasure and the source of much conversation, laughter, and sharing between you.

Instant Goddess

If you don't have your own baby book, ask your parents to send it to you. Remember the highlights and wonders of your own childhood. If you don't have a baby book, consider making your own. You might not know the dates of your first tooth, your first steps, or what your first words are (though in many families, these stories are passed down orally like legends). But write what you do remember. A late baby book is still a baby book, and still a keepsake.

Exercise #2: Your Evolving Motherhood Altar

The Motherhood Altar that you created in Chapter 1 is probably a well-used area of your home by now, and you may have tweaked it to make it more comfortable for you and your baby, as you relax there to nurse, nap, read, or just spend time together. Continue to adapt this vital center of your home by keeping it stocked with your current favorite relaxing music, a few snacks, the ubiquitous stack of spit-up cloths, books to match your baby's developmental level, and a cozy wrap to keep you both warm. You can also use this center yourself when your baby is asleep, for thinking, daydreaming, meditating, or even just a quick cat-nap. The more you use it, the more you will infuse your Motherhood Altar with potent positive energy.

When your baby is no longer in diapers and no longer nursing, you may think your Motherhood Altar is now without a purpose. Don't dismantle it just yet! Instead, let it remain a fixture in your household, and a center for family togetherness. Maybe it can become a reading center. Replace the changing table with a bookshelf and fill it with books you and your child love to read together. Eventually, you may find your child reading to herself in that very spot. A weekly trip to the library to stock and restock the bookshelf can extend the Motherhood Altar's energies out into the world.

Or maybe your altar could become a game center. The changing table can turn into a game shelf, and a small card table could replace the rocking chair. Spend some time every day or two playing a game with your child in this sacred space and enjoy each other. Have fun. Fill the house with laughter.

Or your Motherhood Altar could become a yoga exercise area. Kids love the way yoga imitates the animals (like downward facing dog, pigeon, rabbit, and cobra) and other aspects of nature like mountains and trees. Find a book on yoga for kids (such as *The Complete Idiot's Guide to Yoga with Kids;* see Appendix B) or register for a mom-and-tot yoga class, and then use this area for practice and yoga play. Depending on the personality of your child (and your own), the Motherhood Altar could also become a meditation center. Keep your relaxing music, crystals, perhaps a fanciful mobile or wind chime, and teach your child how to sit next to you (or on your lap), eyes closed, focused on a sound or a thought, in total relaxation. What a great skill for later in life ... something you can both benefit from!

Whatever you decide to do with your Motherhood Altar, don't forget to let the Mother Goddesses bless it. It is and can continue to be a sacred spot in your home where mother, father, and child can come together peacefully, joyfully, and with reverence for family and for the great chain of life.

Can you believe you've come this far? That mothering seems such a part of who you are? We're almost to the end of this book, and, as a final chapter, we would like to consider motherhood in a broader sense: as a philosophy, a way of life, as a goal and driving purpose, even as a theology. Parenting is the most important job you will ever do, and your child is the most precious thing you will ever make. That little baby has transformed you into a Mother Goddess, and that's no small gift.

Chapter 12

Mother and Child Reunion

Sometimes our friends like to joke, after letting their children watch too much TV, or eat something junky, "What kind of mother *am* I?" We all understand these moments, these temporary lapses of what you think you *should* do as a mother compared to what you actually end up doing. And of course, we believe that good parenting is about doing what is best for the child most of the time. After all, nobody is perfect.

But what interests us more, particularly in the great scheme of things and in the context of Mother Goddesses throughout the history of humankind, is the question: *What kind of mother am I?*

We don't mean the question as a value judgment, but as a character study. Sure, we could cook up some quiz called "What Kind of Mother Are You?" that could neatly pigeonhole each of us into one of five or six "categories," but we know perfectly well that there are far more than five or six kinds of mothers. There are, in this world, billions of kinds of mothers, as many as there are mothers around the globe, as many as have ever existed. There is no quiz to turn that kind of richly hued mosaic into a monochrome, this-or-that summary.

Life began with waking up and loving my mother's face.

—George Eliot (1819–1880), English writer

Yet that doesn't mean we can't ask the question, and that you can't ask it of yourself. What kind of mother are *you*? And further, what is a mother's duty? What is *right action* for a mother? Is there a morality of motherhood that transcends the reality of established philosophical systems? Or ought a mother to be moral according to the standards set up by her religion or by some other pre-set ethical construction?

In a popular philosophy book we enjoy that applies classic philosophy to the television show *The Simpsons*, the fourth essay in the book, called "Marge's Moral Motivation," examines Marge Simpson's behavior as virtuous and moral in the Aristotelian tradition, primarily because she displays classic Aristotelian virtues like courage and temperance and because she avoids the extremes of excess and want in her character (as opposed to other characters on the show, such as the intemperate Homer, her son Bart, who is on a first-name basis with the devil, and even neighbor Ned Flanders, who blindly follows Christian morality without applying logic).

Is Marge Simpson a good mother (even though she is a cartoon)? Is she a Mother Goddess? Sure she is. But that doesn't mean you should act just like she does. Nor must you act like any other mother you've heard about, fictional or real—singer Faith Hill, Carol Brady of *The Brady Bunch*, Senator Dianne Feinstein, former Indian prime minister Indira Ghandi, news reporter Katie Couric, actor Jodie Foster, track star Florence Griffith Joyner, even your own mother, or your siblings or friends who are mothers.

That's not to say you can't and shouldn't have mother mentors. One of the major opportunities of this book is to help you collect mother mentors, fellow Mother Goddesses to help you along your way. But after all is said and done, you are an individual and you will be the kind of mother—the best mother—you can be.

So let's explore the kind of mother you are turning out to be, the kind of mother you plan to be, and your goals and dreams for who you are and what you will become, as well as what you will help your child become.

Taking on the Mantle of Motherhood

Motherhood has become part of your persona, and as you take on this new responsibility, this mantle of motherhood, you may feel a little bit like you have ascended to a new rank in both your personal and private life. Now you can sit comfortably with groups of mothers watching their children play, and the exchange of stories is effortless. Mothers wherever you go will be glad to listen to and address your questions, your concerns, your worries, even listen to your joys and boasts.

Many a mother has had her mind put at ease by talking with other mothers and learning that her baby's loose stools, her toddler's tendency to bang his head on the wall, her preschooler's defiance or immense energy are totally within the great, wide range of "normal."

At home, you may also find you have ascended to a certain new place. You and your partner are now parents, a completely different life stage than "young married couple" or "boyfriend and girlfriend" or whatever you were before. Now you are parents, and that new responsibility carries with it a new sense of self and an evolving identity.

You are now the Queen of your family, and how you govern the household is entirely up to you. It is a learning process and you will make mistakes sometimes, but you will also learn from those mistakes and continue to feel more comfortable in your new role. Hey, even the greatest Mother Goddesses in history sometimes made mistakes. It's all part of parenting.

> The chief Goddess of ancient Greece was Hera, married to the chief God, Zeus. Together they ruled over the world, and Hera was so all-encompassing in her representation of female energy that she transformed from Hera the Virgin in the spring—a ritual bath would restore her virginity—to Hera the Fulfilled One in summer—a ritual wedding took place—to Hera the Widow, an elderly version of Hera surviving death and enduring loss. In and of herself, Hera was the triple Goddess: the maiden, the mother, and the wise woman. Hera's sacred fruits are the apple and the pomegranate. She was always accompanied by her favorite handmaiden, Iris, Goddess of the Rainbow.
>
> Yet Hera's existence was itself stormy. Zeus had many affairs, and Hera was often filled with jealous rages. She sought revenge on many of the Goddesses and mortal women Zeus seduced, and on the resultant children. By some accounts, Hera would sometimes become depressed and wander off

alone in sadness at Zeus's disloyalty. Goddess of the atmosphere, Hera's bad moods were thought to result in violent storms, and she could also grant the gift of prophecy. The most powerful and potent representative of the female principle in ancient Greece, Hera was the supreme Goddess and one of the 12 principle deities on Mount Olympus.

When Rome overtook Greece, Hera became Juno and Zeus became Jupiter. While similar to Hera, Juno incorporated more of the patriarchal society into her persona, taking on the job of Goddess of finance and of war, in addition to her primary functions as Goddess of women, children, marriage, and childbirth. Despite their difficulties, Hera and Zeus, Juno and Jupiter, were central, strong characters whose union symbolized the male/female dynamic and whose worship in both ancient Greece and Rome took on mythic proportions.

Hera/Juno and Zeus/Jupiter produced many children who reigned as Goddesses and Gods over their world. By the very fact that they were daughters and sons of Hera/Juno and Zeus/Jupiter, these deities had a head start in their lives. Yet as celebrated as their children were, none were ever as famous and primary as the parents.

You Rule!

Imagine that you and your partner are Hera and Zeus, rulers over your small but significant world. How can you improve on the stormy relationship of these two primary deities? How can your world be more peaceful and less turbulent? Discuss with your partner how you and he might rewrite the Hera/Zeus relationship in contemporary terms for yourselves and for your growing family, and how you might play these roles as twenty-first-century Mother Goddess and Father God of your universe. How might you resolve conflicts, reach goals, and keep peace?

Harriet Beecher Stowe's brother, orator and Presbyterian minister Henry Ward Beecher (1813–1887), once said, "The most important thing a father can do for his children is to love their mother." Forging a strong, unbreakable bond between you and your partner will create a firm foundation for your family that can extend through generations to come.

No matter the state of the marriages of your own parents, let your partnership be the beginning of a great tradition of strength, resolution, loyalty, and love. Your children will always know they come from love and a solid base of power, and that is one of the best gifts you can give them.

 Remember, Ginger Rogers did everything that Fred Astaire did, but she did it backwards and in high heels.

—Faith Whittlesey (1939–), U.S. lawyer and politician

Out in the World

Sooner or later, you will be sending your child off into the great big world. Whether to daycare or preschool or just next door for a play date, you can't keep your baby under your wing forever. Yet part of your job as a mother is to help prepare your child for dealing with the world beyond the walls of your home.

Living in a society means interacting with that society, a skill we all must learn. The child who is well cared for, well loved, and well taught will have no problem entering into and thriving in the world while keeping what you have taught locked safely within.

Yet understandably, many of us are reluctant to place the care of our children in the hands of the world. We agree with Hillary Clinton that it takes a village to raise a child, but can you trust the other members of the village? Letting go of your children is a gradual process for good reason. When your child is still young, you must carefully monitor the other caretakers in his or her life, as well as the places your child goes, the things he or she does, and what influences he or she may be exposed to.

This isn't easy and sometimes it's downright scary. It's a big world out there with a lot of things we don't want our young children—even our older children—to see. So we do our best to protect our children—with the help of the other Mother Goddesses in our lives—while still imbuing them with the moral strength and fortitude to do the right thing.

Whether you are making decisions about which movies your child may and may not see at this or that age, or whether you are considering more dramatic measures, such as quitting your job to be with your child more often or home schooling instead of public or private school, the next decade and beyond will be filled with opportunities for key decisions about sheltering or exposing your child to the world, as well as shoring up your child with guidance about how to handle what he or she sees and learns about.

Once again, you can only do your best, and that is enough. Call on other mothers for help, read as much as you can, and seek guidance, but finally, listen to your heart, your moral compass, and your partner. Together, you can walk with your child through the first part of life to ensure that he or she stays safe and yet has the opportunity for the broad-based learning experiences so important to becoming a fully realized human being.

> Xi Hou is an ancient Chinese Goddess who gave birth to 10 suns. A Mother Goddess and Guardian Goddess, she is also responsible for the proper workings of daylight. Every morning, Xi Hou bathes her 10 children in a lake at the eastern edge of the world. Then, each day, one of these suns has the important job of traveling across the sky to bring daylight to the world.
>
> Xi Hou takes the child sun that is scheduled for that day and lifts him into a tree. He climbs to the top and Xi Hou puts him into a great chariot pulled by dragons. She sees off her child with a wave and he goes out into the world to journey across the sky. At night, the sun returns home to Xi Hou, and the next morning, each sun again receives its bath and the next sibling prepares for the journey.
>
> Xi Hou's is just a beautiful story of nurturing where each child becomes a sun and goes into the sky one by one when it is his or her turn—a great metaphor for nurturing your child and watching him or her grow and shine.

Xi Hou is a supreme nurturer whose 10 children require daily care. Yet protective and diligent a mother as she is, part of that nurturing means seeing a child travel off into the world without her each morning.

We all know the feeling of letting our children go—that tear-choked moment when they first board the school bus or walk into the preschool classroom with barely a wave, or worse, with clinging and heart-wrenching sobs of "I want to go home!" It can be a difficult job to teach a child how to enter the public world after living in the sheltered and carefully controlled world of the home.

Yet eventually, at some age, our children will go on without us, and even when they return to us after a few hours or even a few minutes, we always feel the loss of ourselves as part of us toddles away gleefully or tentatively chooses a seat next to another child and offers up a greeting.

Eve shares a quiet maternal moment with sons Angus and Emmett.

Nobody ever said mothering was easy, and letting our children go off into the bright sky to do their own work, to grow their own lives, is perhaps the hardest part of all. And yet, it might be the most rewarding part of all, too. Just look at your little sun. Just look at how your child brings more light to the world.

 My mother had a great deal of trouble with me, but I think she enjoyed it.

—Mark Twain (1835–1910), U.S. writer and humorist

Chapter 12: Mother and Child Reunion 199

Investing in Faith

As mothers, we learn all about faith, whether or not we were ever much for the religion-based variety of faith before we became mothers. Sometimes, letting our children make their own way in the world, letting them make their own decisions and suffer their own consequences, is a matter of faith. For a few years, we can dictate to our children what we know is best for them, but after awhile, it's a puzzle they need to work themselves. Sure, we can suggest that this piece go there or that piece go over here, but each child puts together the masterpiece that will become his or her own life, and in the end, we need to stand back and watch.

When our children travel away from us, we must have faith that they will come back to us, either physically or emotionally or even morally. All children rebel several times in their lives—as toddlers, as pre-adolescents, as teenagers. They are likely to battle with us, to defy us, at best to disagree with us, sometimes vehemently. Although our children are a part of us, they are not *wholly* us. They are themselves, and that can be a hard pill to swallow.

At the same time, watching the individual blossom before you can also be the culmination of a glorious personal epiphany that reveals to you who *you* are: not an archaic version of this new life, but an individual, too, with your own life.

You are Mother Goddess, and a Goddess apart from your motherhood as well. You are an individual and so are they, and the relationship you have with your child will be forever burned into the very veins and sinews of your body. It has changed you. It has probably, in some sense, given birth to a new you. And yet, you are *you*. You are your own person. That part of you that emerged from within and took off on its own has changed you forever, and when it is gone, know that you are still you—and within this great understanding of who you are, you also know, deep within, that your child is never really completely gone. You know because you have faith in the love bond, that invisible silver cord that connects the two of you forever.

> Celie is the main character in the Alice Walker novel *The Color Purple*. She had an extremely difficult life as a victim of poverty and assumed incest. She bore two children from the man she thought to be her father, and the babies were quickly taken away from her. Her only friend as a child was her younger sister, Nettie, who was also taken away from her. Celie spent much of her life waiting, in faith, to be reunited with her blood, with those she loved.

> Yet in all the pain and suffering she endured, Celie never lost her faith and her compassion and love for her children. Her love for her children and for her sister endured against all odds and under the most extreme of circumstances. In a pivotal scene (also the most memorable scene of the movie, starring Whoopi Goldberg), Celie is reunited with her children, who are almost grown, and with her sister, after so much time apart. Afterward, Celie offers up an almost involuntary prayer:
>
> > *Dear God. Dear stars, dear trees, dear sky, dear peoples. Dear Everything. Dear God. Thank you for bringing my sister Nettie and our children home.*
>
> Celie's faith, love, and courage have finally rewarded her. After a life that few would survive, Celie returns to a sort of paradise of family now made whole. The book ends with Celie's speculation about love, family, and the nature of youth:
>
> > *I feel a little peculiar round the children. For one thing, they grown. And I see they think me and Nettie and Shug and Albert and Samuel and Harpo and Sofia and Jack and Odessa real old and don't know much what going on. But I don't think us feel old at all. And us so happy. Matter of fact, I think this the youngest us ever felt. Amen.*

It's a funny thing how motherhood can make you feel so much younger and so much older all at the same time. As you endure pain you never imagined, as you find courage you never knew you had, and as you watch your heart walking around on the outside of your body every day, you gain immeasurable wisdom and experience.

And yet, living life in the company of a child and in the constant remembrance of your own childhood can infuse your life with the incredible fervor of youth. You get to see the world through a child's eyes again. What better way to keep one foot in heaven?

As your child grows and changes and moves outward into the world, renew your faith often by continuing to add mementos to your Motherhood Box and by spending time at the altar you built to honor your mother/child bond, from nursing and nursery rhymes to fairytales and board games. Remember always to move forward in your parenting with one eye on the past and keep your household filled with love. You and your partner will always be the most influential people in your child's life, whether they admit it or not, so let that influence glow and shine in every interaction you have with your child. Hold on with your faith, and your parenting efforts will be true and right and good.

Mother Goddess Tamara, with husband Gary and daughter Sydney: a family captured in time.

> Most of the beautiful things in life come by twos and threes, by dozens and hundreds. There are plenty of roses, stars, sunsets, rainbows, brothers and sisters, aunts and uncles, but only one mother in the whole world.
>
> —Kate Douglas Wiggin (1856–1923), U.S. writer

Generations

Meanwhile, history rolls on. Perhaps you will have more children, and perhaps you won't. Perhaps your children will have children, and someday you will be a Grandmother Goddess (and that's a whole book in itself!).

Every generation is not only affected by family but also by the character of the world in which it lives. Perhaps your children will experience long periods of peace and human achievement. Perhaps they will see war and tragedy. Perhaps they will travel across the world to seek knowledge or experience. Perhaps they will stay in their hometowns for most or all of their lives. Where they go and what they do will become a matter of history, perhaps personal, perhaps also on a broader scale.

Just as your life has spanned several decades already, so will your children's lives, eventually, coinciding with history at every level. Stepping back to see the lifespan of your family line can put love and loyalty in greater perspective. You are part of a generation, but your family lasts for generations, and you have perpetuated that tradition. May each generation make the world a little bit better!

> Queen Elizabeth the Queen Mum, mother to Queen Elizabeth of Great Britain and the consort of George VI of Great Britain, died in 2002 at the sagacious age of 101. We chose the Queen Mother as our final Mother Goddess for this book because her life spanned the entire twentieth century, from 1900 to 2002.
>
> The Queen Mother saw and participated in the many changes and challenges for women and motherhood in the twentieth century. From the flood of immigrants from Europe to the United States during the start of the century through two world wars, imagine her perspective on life, family, and what is important to pursue and achieve! Queen Elizabeth became queen quite unexpectedly through George's ascension to the throne following King Edward's famous abdication. Queen Elizabeth proceeded to lead the nation in courage during the First World War, while raising her children with a profound commitment.
>
> Her independence and determination make her a model to the world and to Mother Goddesses everywhere facing a world ever balancing on that narrow ledge separating peacetime from war. Prince Charles once called the Queen Mother "quite simply the most magical grandmother you could possibly have," and her indomitable optimism, sense of humor, and great support of her family were legendary. She is an inspiration to Mother Goddesses everywhere as they aspire to build a memorable and loving family line.

Think of your own family history, your mother, grandmother, great-grandmother. What are their stories, where is their courage? Hunt down old photos of the women in your family's matriarchal line and preserve their photos in your Motherhood Box, as a record of the female history you have built. If you don't have a daughter, your sons and their partners will nevertheless treasure these photos and historical records of your family, and so will their children, and their children's children.

This sacred storehouse may still be around long after you have moved on to the next realm, and your children and grandchildren and great-grandchildren may continue to treasure it and fill it with their own records of your family's history and future. Whenever a child or a grandchild asks you, "Who was your mother?" or "Who was your grandmother?" or "Who was my grandma's grandma?" you'll be ready with an answer—and a few great stories, too.

Here is Nana, from Chapter 11, one more time. Nana holds Doris's husband Frank, Becky's grandfather, in her lap. For a picture of Doris and Becky, see Chapter 2. A mother's expression, as her love, radiates warmth, faith, and confident joy through generations.

> There is a wonderful word, *why?*, that children use. All children. When they stop using it, the reason, too often, is that no one bothered to answer them; no one tried to keep alive one of the most important attributes a person can have: interest in the world around him. No one fostered and cultivated the child's innate sense of the adventure of life. One of the things I believe most intensely is that every child's *why* should be answered with care—and with respect.
>
> —Eleanor Roosevelt (1884–1962), U.S. First Lady

Exercise #1: Your Touch-Base Ritual

The busier our lives get, and the busier our kids' lives get, the harder it can be to stay in touch without a solid and established commitment. We think one recent television commercial, where a parent goes to his son's room and encounters a secretary who will make an appointment for him to get together with his son, is particularly telling. Between school, homework, sports, and other extra-curricular activities, friends, and keeping up with popular culture, kids are overbooked!

Some parents begin by signing up their kids for every new activity that comes along: soccer, T-ball, gymnastics, ballet, piano lessons, violin lessons, horseback-riding lessons, basketball, flag football, volleyball, and all manner of day camps and other clubs and activities. Eventually, though, some of us recognize that our kids need some downtime, and all they really want is to spend some time with us! Are you too busy working? Too busy cleaning up the kitchen? How many times this week have you told your child, "Not now," or "Just a minute," or "I really have to get this done first; I can't listen to this right now!"

Sound familiar?

If you aren't to that stage in parenting yet, it pays to be prepared for it. It's easy to say, "I'll never let housework or my job come before the needs of my child," but it's a lot tougher to follow through on that vow when life gets out of control and children get demanding. And then one day, your child may tell you something along the lines of, "Mommy, you never hear what I say when you are working." Ouch.

As Mother Goddesses, we owe it to our kids to take up arms against this trend. Scale back the activities and, instead, schedule touch-base time. Depending on the age and inclination of your child, this could be a daily time or a weekly time, but don't let more than a week go by without a touch-base session.

Mothers can get pretty creative about the ways they choose to touch base with their kids. Here are some ideas we've heard:

- A weekly "beauty salon" for a daughter. Mother gives daughter a hairstyle, facial, manicure, pedicure, or other special beauty treatment, or they both share a treatment, during which they can be alone and talk.
- A daily "do-nothing" session between a mother and her son after school each day, during which she sits with him on the couch and gives him complete, undivided attention: phone off the hook, e-mail turned off, television and radio off, nothing in the oven, and no fair picking up or dusting anything during this all-for-him 30 minutes.
- A weekly mother/child field trip to the destination of the child's choice. Don't underestimate travel time to and from your destination, a great time to talk in the car. Some kids are more willing to open up to their parents if they know their parents' eyes are on the road, not on them. Some parents also exchange weeks so that every other week, one parent gets alone time with one child. With two kids, trade off every other week.

Moms can play sports, too. Don't think you can toss a ball or shoot some hoops? Think again. This is a great way to hang out with and relate to your athletic child. Ask for pointers. Kids love to teach their parents cool stuff.

Just be there. After a busy day, some kids simply want some undivided attention. Is that so hard? Certainly not. Your children will never forget those times when you were really there ... and they will never forget those times when you weren't there at all. Make some good memories. Start today. Initiate your touch-base ritual and keep your family together. (This is a good ritual to practice with your partner, too.)

Instant Goddess

Nix the knee-jerk "no." One mother friend of ours recently told us that she had seen a call for essays in a parenting magazine on "The one time you surprised your child and said 'yes' when they expected a 'no.'" "I couldn't think of a single time I said 'yes' when they expected a 'no,'" she said, in horror. She has since vowed to say "yes" to something at least once a week, or at least to consider whether the knee-jerk "no" need really be a no.

Exercise #2: Celebrate Your Mother Goddess Nature

Now that you have achieved full and complete Mother Goddess status, we want to end this book in celebration of *you*. Throughout the ages and in every culture, Goddess worship included rituals, rites, and sacred practices. Hera's sacred fruit was the apple. Athena's sacred bird is the owl. Aphrodite's sacred flowers were the red poppy and the rose. Goddesses were sometimes honored with sacred processions, sacrifices, and festivals.

But what about you? You are a Mother Goddess, too. Before you leave this book behind (although we hope you will refer to it often), we would like to help you establish your own Mother Goddess status officially. Decide what your sacred fruit, flower, bird, and animal will be. What are you the Goddess of?

Many Goddesses were patrons of or governed over many things. Consider Isis, the Egyptian Goddess of loving wives, mothers, Earth, the dead, and the protector of seamen. Remember Kwan Yin, from the first chapter of this book? She was the Goddess of mercy, of fecundity, the protector of women, the Goddess of rain, and the protector of sailors. The Hindu Goddess Kali was the Goddess of war, fertility, time, mysteries, death, and the opposing forces of destruction and creation. So don't you feel limited in your choices, either! Maybe you feel like you could be the Goddess of the moon, of poetry, and of affection toward children. Or maybe you feel more like the Goddess of women's professional lives, of passionate kissing, of gardens, or of children's ability to read. Maybe you could be the Goddess who honors curiosity or protects families from a lack of communication. Use your imagination. What do you value? What do you honor? What do you represent?

> For women, there are, undoubtedly, great difficulties in the path, but so much the more to overcome. First, no woman should say, "I am but a woman!" But a woman? What more can you ask to be?
>
> —Maria Mitchell (1818–1889), first woman astronomer in the U.S.

Fill out the following to help you decide your own Mother Goddess qualities. You can even give yourself a different Goddess name. Many Mother Goddesses had multiple names, so why shouldn't you?

Your Mother Goddess Stats

My name is _____

I am sometimes also known as _____

I am the Goddess of _____

_____

_____

_____

My sacred animal is _____

My sacred bird is _____

My sacred flower or plant is _____

I am the protector of _____

_____

_____

These objects are sacred to me: _____

_____

_____

My birthday, which is on _____, is known as the Festival of _____. During this time, I am honored by the following activities:

_____

_____

_____

_____

_____

During my life as a Goddess, many myths surround me. Here are some of the stories of how I have exercised my powers in the world (if you need more space, use your Motherhood Journal for overflow):

_____

_____

_____
_____
_____
_____
_____

Everyone knows I love the God _____.
Together, we produced the following Gods/Goddesses:
_____
_____

Finally, I believe that in centuries to come, I will always be remembered as a Mother Goddess for this:
_____
_____
_____
_____
_____
_____

And now, Mother Goddess, we will leave you to journey out into the world, with all your powers, resources, and great halo of love to sustain you. We have really enjoyed getting to know a Goddess as magnificent as you are, and we are proud and honored that you have chosen us as your guide through the sacred journey of pregnancy, childbirth, and new motherhood.

Now that you have established your Mother Goddess identity, you can continue to work your magic in the world, in the realm of your family, in the life of your child, in the relationship with your partner, and across the generations of your family. Imagine the Goddess Iris's rainbow arcing from the women before you, over your head and far beyond you in a never-ending, vibrant extension of Mother Goddess power. You are part of that rainbow, and it is everlasting.

Appendix A

A Who's Who of Mother Goddesses: Ancient and Contemporary

Addie From Faulkner's complex novel *As I Lay Dying*, Addie is the mother of a family whose children react in various ways as they prepare for her death and build her coffin, demonstrating how significant is the death of a mother (at the moment of her death, her two sons are stuck in a ditch trying to free their broken wagon), and yet how insignificant, as her children live on after she passes on.

Aditi A Hindu Goddess said to have formed herself. The "Mother of Worlds" was at one time considered the mother of all Gods and Goddesses. Aditi was called many names, revealing her great and encompassing power, including "The Boundless Whole," "Eternal Space," "Supporter of the Sky," and "Celestial Virgin" (virgin used to mean "not for any man"). In one of the most famous stories about Aditi, she bore 12 children from eggs. One of them hatched out an unformed lump. Aditi took one look at him and cast him into the sky. This was Vivasvat, sometimes called Martanda.

A God found him and molded him into the sun. The leftover pieces fell to Earth and became elephants.

Aegean Venus Figures carved by inhabitants of the Cycladic Islands of the Aegean around 2000 B.C.E., Aegean Venuses were the first life-size female statues, carved in marble. Unlike primitive Paleolithic fertility statues with their swollen bellies, breasts, and hips, these Aegean Venus figures were tall, thin, almost geometric in character with straight hips, small breasts, sometimes with bent knees, and almost always with hands crossed over the breast or belly.

Aegeria *See* Egeria.

Ajysit Equivalent to Khotun, this Siberian Goddess determines each individual's fate by writing it in a golden book at the child's birth, and then descends to assist in the delivery and share a meal with the new family.

Ashke-tanne-mat A Japanese spider Goddess, sometimes called "Long-fingered woman," this Goddess of women helped with childbirth by pulling the baby from the womb. Impervious to male power, Ashke-tanne-mat protects women from danger and, traditionally, from male marauders. A magical shaman, Spider Goddess once ignored the advances of Big Demon, who wanted to marry her. Uninterested in his thuggish and unrefined manner, Ashke-tanne-mat ousted him and then continued on with her needlework.

Athena Athena is the Greek Goddess of war, crafts, and wisdom, as represented by the owl with which she is so often depicted. When Athena's mother, Metis, became pregnant by Zeus, Zeus feared that she would give birth to a son who would exceed him in strength and power, so he transformed Metis into a fly and swallowed her. Ironically, that child was not a son, but nevertheless sprang from Zeus's head, fully armed, helmeted, and bearing a spear, ready for battle—a daughter, the warrior Goddess Athena.

Atropos One of the Three Fates of ancient Greece, Atropos was the cutter who cut the thread of each human life, determining that life's time of death.

Baubo Baubo the Belly Goddess is the Greek Goddess of belly laughter, known for her lewd jokes and bawdy manner. In some stories, she has no head but is merely a body with nipple eyes and a vulva mouth. In one version of the story of Demeter and Persephone, Baubo tells lewd jokes to Demeter and lifts up her skirt to bear her belly and vulva, cheering up Demeter and coaxing her to keep searching for Persephone. Baubo also appears in Egyptian mythology, lifting her skirt and baring her belly and vulva to Isis, to cheer her up following her horrible grief at the death of Osiris.

Blackfoot First Woman   Blackfoot First Woman was the first woman on Earth, according to the Native American mythology of the Blackfoot tribe. First Woman asked the creator if humans would live forever, and when he didn't know, she proclaimed that she would throw a stone into the water and that if it floated, humans would be immortal. If it sunk, humans would die and stay dead. Blackfoot First Woman's casting of the sinking stone engendered mortality and also mutual sympathy for the human condition and the urgency for love, as humans can now look at each other and know that each of us will eventually die.

Bow Old Woman   *See* Juksakka.

Carol Brady   The famous mother character on the 1970s television show *The Brady Bunch*, played by Florence Henderson.

Celie   The protagonist in the Alice Walker novel *The Color Purple*. A victim of poverty and incest, Celie bore two children as a result of that incest, and they were quickly taken away from her. Her only friend as a child was her younger sister, Nettie, who was also taken away from her. Celie spent much of her life alone. Yet in all the pain and suffering she endured, Celie never lost her faith and her compassion and love for her children, and was finally reunited with them.

Clotho   One of the Three Fates in ancient Greece, Clotho was the spinner who spun out the thread of each human life, creating each human life.

Cuba   Cuba, Cunina, and Rumina were three sister Goddesses in ancient Greece and Rome who protected the infant in sleep. Specifically, Cuba helped to lull infants into a peaceful sleep, or, according to some sources, protected toddlers no longer sleeping in the cradle.

Cunina   Sister of Cuba and Rumina, this ancient Greek/Roman Goddess protected the sleeping infant in the cradle.

Demeter   Demeter, the Greek Goddess of grain and the harvest, had her daughter stolen away by Hades, lord of the underworld. Demeter cut off all fertility from the earth until she was able to find her daughter with the help of a water nymph and inspiration from the Belly Goddess, Baubo. Demeter bargained to bring her daughter back for half of each year, during which the earth experiences spring and summer.

Devi The Hindu Goddess Devi is one of the most important Hindu deities; she is seen as the overriding principle behind the Hindu trinity of Brahman (the creator), Vishnu (the sustainer and preserver of life), and Shiva (the destroyer). Devi provides the energy for all of these eternal functions. She is traditionally represented in many different aspects and incarnations, varying in importance, intensity, and power. The word *devi* means "goddess" in Sanskrit, but Devi is *the* Goddess among Goddesses. She is the cosmic force that creates, destroys, and recreates the world. She holds weapons in her many arms to destroy any evil that threatens the world's equilibrium, and is terrifying and violent in her Warrior Goddess aspect, defending and protecting the good, bringing out her "dark side" when necessary. Many Hindu Goddesses are aspects or incarnations of Devi.

Diana Part of the Roman trifold Goddess with Lucina and Hecate, Diana represented growth and was also the Goddess of the moon, nature, the woods, and hunting. She is the Roman equivalent of Artemis.

Dianne Feinstein California State Senator Dianne Feinstein was the first woman to serve on the Senate Judiciary Committee. In 1994, she won a difficult battle to pass a measure to prohibit the manufacture and sale of 19 types of military-style assault weapons. She has also made great strides in environmental protection and in raising money for breast-cancer research.

Door Woman *See* Uksakka.

Edulica Greek/Roman Goddess who blessed the food of children and worked with Cuba, who blessed their sleep, and Portina, who blessed their drink.

Egeria Egeria (sometimes Aegeria) was a Roman water nymph associated with Diana, the Goddess of nature and the forest. This water nymph lives in springs deep within the forest. People would come to her and exchange gifts of water and milk for advice. Some legends claim that Egeria was the wife of King Numa Pompilius. He would visit her deep within a cave where her spring erupted, and they would talk, make love, and she would advise him on his work. Egeria is credited with teaching Numa how to lead his people in Earth worship rituals, and she advised him on political matters, too. After his death, legend holds that Egeria was so saddened that she transformed into a fountain.

Eileithyia Eileithyia is the Greek Goddess of childbirth and the daughter of Hera and Zeus. She may have originally been two separate Goddesses, probably sisters, both daughters of Hera. One sister was the

Goddess of easy births, and one the Goddess of difficult births. Eventually, the two were merged into a single figure.

Eingana   The Australian aborigines tell the story of the creator of humans, a giant birth-mother snake Goddess called Mother Eingana. She created the earth, the sea, and all the animals by vomiting, but when she began to gestate humans, she was unable to give birth to them. As more and more humans grew within her, she began to writhe in pain until the god Barraiya took pity on her and speared her, creating an opening from which to give birth. Blood and humans flowed from her womb and the human race was born.

Eve   Eve is the biblical mother of all humankind, whose story is related in Genesis, the first book of the Old Testament. The Book of Genesis was written by Hebrew priests to describe the patriarchal history of the Israelites. During the time of its writing (fifth to ninth century B.C.E.), shifting power away from Goddess worship and destroying matrilineal descent was the first order of business. Poor Eve took the hit.

Faith Hill   Country/pop singer and mother to three daughters.

Florence Griffith Joyner   "The World's Fastest Woman," Florence Griffith Joyner, or Flo Jo as she was called, was an Olympian track and field champion as well as a wife and mother.

Four Meshkents   *See* Meshkent.

Frida Kahlo   Frida Kahlo was a Mexican painter who lived from 1907 to 1954. Her paintings were dramatic, sometimes disturbing, and full of elements of native Mexican art combined with a surrealist sensibility, although she denied being a surrealist, claiming that she only painted the reality that existed within her. Never able to have children, Kahlo suffered from several miscarriages, and much of her work is about pain, disintegration, and loss. Her painting *The Birth* was the first to ever depict birth so graphically: a woman, head covered, legs spread, surrounded by blood, with a head emerging. Kahlo described the painting as a depiction of her own birth, so that she is both mother and child. The head is covered, said Kahlo, because as she was painting this portrait, her own mother died and this laboring mother is in mourning for her own mother in the moment she becomes a mother. Yet Kahlo is also giving birth to herself because, while she could never successfully give birth to another, she continually gave birth to her art. In her journal, Kahlo wrote of this painting, "I gave birth to myself."

Gaea   *See* Gaia.

Gaia The great Grecian Goddess Gaia (sometimes spelled "Gaea") was said to have emerged as the first power out of the great darkness of Chaos at the beginning of time, and she is the personification of the planet Earth itself. Gaia created everything in existence: gods, humans, animals, birds, the oceans and rivers, and the plant life of the earth. The contemporary "Gaia theory" suggests that Gaia is the earth herself, and a complex living creature. All of nature, including humans, is part of Gaia's anatomy.

Giorgione Nursing Mother The woman in the painting *The Tempest* by Italian Renaissance painter Giorgione (c. 1478–1510), though naked, doesn't pose erotically, but rather, wraps her baby in a maternal embrace. The baby, not a newborn but more of a toddler, nurses competently while the woman looks out on the world, and perhaps at the viewer of the painting, with a bemused expression, unconcerned by the tempest brewing in the city behind her.

Harriet Tubman Harriet Tubman was an African American who escaped from slavery in the mid-nineteenth century, and then worked to lead hundreds of other slaves to their freedom in the north via a network of activists called the Underground Railroad.

Hathor An Egyptian Mother Guardian Goddess, Goddess of domesticated animals, Goddess of the Underworld, Hathor was sometimes called the Celestial Cow, the Queen of Heaven, the Queen of Earth, the Lady of the Cemetery, and the Goddess of Joy. She created herself and is often pictured with a solar disk on her head between two horns, and the face of a cow.

Haumea Haumea is the Hawaiian Earth-Mother Goddess of birth. A shape shifter who could die and rebirth herself at will, Haumea protected mothers in childbirth and gave birth herself to many children who emerged from different parts of her body. Haumea is the Goddess of natural childbirth, and several stories tell of her intervention to invigorate stalled labor or to demand that certain potions be administered to prevent Cesarean section—a procedure that used to mean almost certain death for the mother.

Hecate Part of the Roman trifold Goddess with Lucina and Diane, Hecate represented the mysterious underworld of night and darkness. She was queen of ghosts and spirits. Hecate controlled the hidden things in nature, including the moon, and presided over birth, life, death, and streets and gates, symbolizing journeys and arrivals. Hecate is often shown holding a torch to light to way for your important decisions and directions, and she represents the link between the visible and invisible worlds.

Hera   The chief Goddess of ancient Greece was Hera, married to the chief God, Zeus. Together they ruled over the world, and Hera was so all-encompassing in her representation of female energy that she transformed from Hera the Virgin in the spring—a ritual bath would restore her virginity—to Hera the Fulfilled One in summer—a ritual wedding took place—to Hera the Widow, an elderly version of Hera surviving death and enduring loss. In and of herself, Hera was the triple Goddess: the maiden, the mother, and the wise woman. Strong storms were thought to be the result of Hera's bad moods, and Hera's sacred fruits are the apple and the pomegranate. She was always accompanied by her favorite handmaiden, Iris, Goddess of the Rainbow.

Hillary Rodham Clinton   Former First Lady and current New York State Senator Hillary Rodham Clinton is both an influential public force and mother to Chelsea. Hillary Clinton is responsible for the widespread use of the quote, "It takes a village to raise a child," from her book *It Takes a Village, and Other Lessons Children Teach Us.*

Inanna   The ancient Sumerian Queen of heaven, Inanna may be the first Great Goddess or Earth Mother. The Sumerians, who established one of history's earliest civilizations in the region that is now Iraq, honored Inanna as the Goddess of date groves, grain, love, and wine. She was also the Queen of Battles. She is associated with the Babylonian Goddess Ishtar.

Indira Ghandi   Former Indian prime minister and mother.

Ishtar   The Babylonian Goddess Ishtar is called "Mother of the Fruitful Breast." The Goddess of compassion, sex, and war was intense, aggressive, and passionate about everything she did. Ishtar is often associated with the Mesopotamian Goddess Inanna, the Queen of Heaven. Known for her sexual exploits, her thousands of lovers whom she took or cast aside at will, and her sometimes violent nature, Ishtar was the deified version of passion in all pursuits.

Isis   Isis is Egyptian Goddess of Earth and the daughter of Nut, bearer of the Celestial Vault. Many ancient Egyptian myths center around Isis, patroness of wives and mothers. Isis is directly linked to the moon and the cycles of Earth, and is known for her power and her quest for power, tricking the great god Ra into revealing his secret name and transferring more power to her by sending a poisonous snake to bite him.

Jocasta   Jocasta, the mother of Oedipus in the famous play *Oedipus Rex* by Sophocles, mistakenly marries her son and bears his children.

Juksakka   Sister of Uksakka and Sarakka, this Finnish Goddess was sometimes called "Bow Old Woman," and placed males in the wombs of women, using her magic to make them into good hunters. She is the guardian of children and protects them from accidents.

Julian of Norwich   A medieval English mystic and possibly Carmelite nun who experienced profound visions in youth while gravely ill, and spent the rest of her life meditating on and writing about her visions, in which God revealed many truths about the nature of reality.

Juno   The Roman incarnation of Hera, married to Jupiter (the Roman incarnation of Zeus). While similar to Hera, Juno incorporated more of the public society into her persona, taking on the job of Goddess of finance and of war, in addition to her primary functions as Goddess of women, children, marriage, and childbirth.

Kali   The Warrior Goddess aspect of the Hindu Goddess Devi, often depicted wearing a necklace of skulls.

Katie Couric   News reporter and mother to two daughters, Katie is a widowed mom whose husband died of colon cancer in 1998. Couric is now a colon-cancer activist in addition to hosting NBC's popular news program *Today*.

Khotun   Khotun, known as Kubai-khotun and equivalent to the Goddess Ajysit or "Milk Lake Mother," Khotun was the primordial Mother Goddess for the Yakut people of Siberia. She is the Goddess of milk and the nourisher of all people and animals. Khotun lives in a lake of breastmilk beneath the Tree of Life. Her breasts are huge and overflowing with milk, and it is said that the excess milk formed the Milky Way galaxy.

Kubai-khotun   *See* Khotun.

Kwan Yin   Sometimes called the Chinese "Virgin Mary" and sometimes pictured with many arms, each with an eye in the palm, Kwan Yin is the subject of many different and sometimes contradictory legends, but everyone agrees that this Goddess was a bodhisattva, or someone who has attained enlightenment but delays entrance into heaven in order to stay on Earth and help others toward finding the truth.

Lakshmi   Lakshmi was probably a pre-Vedic Earth Goddess appropriated by Vedic mythology, but in the Hindu epic *Bhagavat Pourana*, Lakshmi arose from the primordial sea of milk after the Gods and demons had churned it for a thousand years. As she rose from the milk holding a red lotus flower, she was so stunningly beautiful that all the Gods hoped she would choose them as her spouse. Lakshmi chose Lord Vishnu and is known in Hindu mythology as his partner in all of his 10 incarnations, representing creative energy and the feminine principle.

Lechesis One of the Three Fates in ancient Greece, Lachesis was the apportioner who measured out the thread of each human life, determining that life's length.

Lilith Lilith was the true first wife of Adam. She refused to be subservient to Adam and left him in the Garden of Eden, after which God created Eve to be a more suitable "wife." The Goddess Lilith represents courage, wisdom, justice, and freedom.

Long-Fingered Woman *See* Ashke-tanne-mat.

Lucina Part of the Roman trifold Goddess with Diana and Hecate, Lucina represents light and bringing newborns into the light, and is often portrayed as a veiled figure holding a flower in one hand and an infant cradled in her opposite arm.

Macha Macha of the Red Tresses is the Celtic Goddess of war. She may have been an actual Irish monarch who built the Emain Macha, and some historians believe she helped to organize the first hospital in Ireland four centuries before the first hospital was built in Rome. Her legend, of being forced by the king to race against his horses while very pregnant, then falling down, giving birth, and cursing the men of Ulster, has evolved to symbolize the way the patriarchal warrior culture and its religion (Christianity) obliterated the peaceful Goddess culture in Ireland.

Marge Gunderson The lead character in the Oscar-winning movie *Fargo* (1996), Marge Gunderson is the very pregnant police chief investigating a grisly murder. Cleary in her third trimester, Marge nevertheless does her job with a cheerful pragmatism, supported by a loving and nurturing husband and a town that respects her and the work she does. She is the chief of police and her pregnancy is simply a part of her at that time.

Marge Simpson Marge Simpson, mother of the notorious Bart Simpson, might be animated but strives daily to embody right behavior and goodness while maintaining her family. Marge finds the balance between the classic Aristotelian extremes of excess and want, as opposed to the extreme male characters on the show *The Simpsons,* such as the intemperate Homer, the morally barren Mr. Burns, her son Bart, who is on a first name basis with the devil, and even neighbor Ned Flanders, who blindly follows Christian morality without applying logic.

Maya   Maya was the mother of the Buddha. This Indian queen had a dream that she was visited by a white elephant, and awoke pregnant. When Maya gave birth to the Buddha, he stepped effortlessly from her side, leaving no wound, and immediately took seven steps. A lotus flower sprung up in his footprints, and he proclaimed, "I am king of the world. I will never be reborn. This is my last incarnation." Having given birth to the enlightened one, Maya died of joy one week later, ascending back into the universal mind.

Melanie Wilkes   Scarlett O'Hara's sweet-tempered rival in the Margaret Mitchell novel and 1939 Hollywood film *Gone with the Wind*, Melanie Wilkes goes into labor in the midst of the Civil War, and, after a difficult labor, gives birth with the help of Scarlett and the young servant, Prissy.

Meshkent   Egyptian Goddess of childbirth, Meshkent was a fate Goddess with ties to the upper and underworlds. According to the ancient Egyptians, when someone died, Meshkent would accompany that person to the underworld and testify at the judgment. The wife of Shai, the God of fate, Meshkent was privy to information that enabled her to foretell the future of newborn babies. In some versions, Meshkent is the Four Meshkents, comprising the four Goddesses who guarded the birth chamber.

Milk Lake Mother   *See* Khotun.

Morgan le Fay   In direct opposition to the beautiful and ideal (if flawed) Queen Guinevere, Morgan le Fay was both a mother and a powerful enchantress who secretly studied the dark arts. In ancient versions of the Arthurian legend, she was Arthur's foe; in some modern versions of the legend, she was Merlin's adversary. In all cases, she was strong enough to be at odds with the most powerful of men.

Mother Eingana   *See* Eingana.

Mother Goose   The embodiment of playfulness, Mother Goose might or might not have been a real person. She was perhaps Bertrada II of Laon, an eighth-century noblewoman and the mother of Charlemagne. Or she might have been a mythical creation based on a French story of a motherly magic bird that told stories to children in the seventeenth century. These stories were first collected under the Mother Goose name in 1697 by Charles Perrault.

Mother Woyengi *See* Woyengi.

Nora The protagonist of the Henrik Ibsen play *A Doll's House*, Nora is a beautiful, cheerful, happy wife and mother, or so it seems. When her husband realizes she has actually been managing their difficult financial situation on her own, he considers her independence and deceit a betrayal, and this recognition that their love wasn't based on equality forces Nora to leave her husband, but ends on a note of hope that they could perhaps someday learn to see each other as equals.

Nut Ancient Egyptian Guardian of the Celestial Vault, also called The Great Deep and The Starry One, Nut is represented as a woman bearing a pear-shape vessel resembling a uterus. This vessel was a representation of the celestial vault, demonstrating that the ancient Egyptians pictured the heavens themselves as a magnificent, starry womb. In some versions, Nut's own great body and belly make up the firmament.

Ogboinba Ogboinba is the daughter of Woyengi, that Nigerian Goddess who made humans and let them each decide the conditions of their lives and deaths. Woyengi's daughter, Ogboinba, declared that she wanted to be magic, so Woyengi gave her magical powers. However, later Ogboinba regretted her choice and wished to become a mother. When Ogboinba presented her revised request, Woyengi became enraged and Ogboinba ran away, hiding in the eyes of a pregnant woman.

Patty Murray This Washington State Senator is known as the Mom in Tennis Shoes because, when she first attempted to confront a legislative office about a problem, she was told she could do nothing because she was just "a mom in tennis shoes." This comment prompted her to run for, and win, a senate seat.

Persephone Demeter's daughter, Persephone, the Greek Queen of the Underworld, was stolen away by the Lord of the Underworld, Hades, when he encountered her innocent beauty. Persephone's mother searched for her as the world was cast into barrenness. Because Persephone ate one pomegranate seed, she was required to stay in the underworld and serve as its queen for half the year, during which the world is cast into fall and winter. When Persephone returns, so do spring and summer.

Portina Greek/Roman Goddess who blessed the drinks of children and worked with Cuba, who blessed their sleep, and Edulica, who blessed their food.

Prissy The young servant who must help Scarlett O'Hara act as midwife to Melanie Wilkes in the Margaret Mitchell novel and 1939

Hollywood film *Gone with the Wind*. Prissy claims to know all about birthing babies, but then admits, after the doctor is gone, that she's never even seen a baby being born before. Yet she and Scarlett O'Hara use all their resources and, with no experience, successfully help Melanie bring her baby into the world.

Queen Gertrude   Mother to Hamlet from Shakespeare's famous play. She marries her husband's brother after her husband dies, not knowing the brother himself was her husband's murderer. She watches her kingdom fall apart around her but loves Hamlet unconditionally, even as he acts like he has gone mad. She meets her end by drinking poisoned wine intended for her son, in the ultimate act of sacrifice.

Queen Maya   *See* Maya.

Queen Mother   The Queen Mum and former Queen Elizabeth, mother to Queen Elizabeth II of Great Britain and the consort of George VI of Great Britain, died in 2002 at the sagacious age of 101. As Queen Consort and then Queen Mother, Elizabeth saw and participated in the many changes and challenges for women and motherhood in the twentieth century. From the flood of immigrants from Europe to the United States during the start of the century through two world wars, imagine her perspective on life, family, and what is important to pursue and achieve! Queen Elizabeth became queen quite unexpectedly through Prince Albert's ascension to the throne following King Edward's famous abdication. Queen Elizabeth proceeded to lead the nation in courage during the First World War, while raising her children with a profound commitment.

Rumina   Sister of Cuba and Cunina, this ancient Greek/Roman Goddess protected and blessed infants while nursing.

Sarah   Sarah was an Old Testament character married to Abraham. God visited the elderly couple, then named Abram and Sarai, when Sarai was 90, and told them they would give birth to a son. One year later at the age of 91, when her husband was 100 years old, Sarai gave birth to a son. They named him Isaac, and God told the couple that they would forever after be known as Sarah and Abraham.

Sarai   *See* Sarah.

Sarakka   Sister to Uksakka and Juksakka, she is a Finnish guardian Goddess who placed females in women's wombs, and is the Goddess of spinning and reindeer births. Because reindeer were so crucial for the survival of the Finnish people, families offered food and drink each day for Sarakka upon their hearths. She was also the protector of parents.

Selene Selene was the Goddess of the Moon, also known as Luna, Diana, or Artemis in ancient Greco-Roman culture. Every evening, after her brother Helios tugged the sun across the sky with his chariot, Selene began her journey pulling the moon across the night sky with her chariot pulled by two white horses. As the ancient Greeks watched the moon set into the Mediterranean, they envisioned Selene ending her journey with a rejuvenating bath in the sea. Selene represents the moon at its peak of fullness.

Taouris *See* Taueret.

Tarot Empress The Tarot card of the third Major Arcana is the Empress. The Empress is the Earth Mother representing fertility, growth, generosity, and healing. Her presence in a Tarot reading indicates both fertility and prosperity, once again joining these two creative forces into a single wave of impending abundance and future happiness. The Tarot queen is often depicted on a luxurious chair, holding a scepter and sitting next to a heart-shape shield decorated with the astrological symbol for Venus, the planet and the Goddess of love.

Taueret Taueret, sometimes called Taouris, is the Egyptian Hippopotamus Goddess of fertility and birth. "The Great One" helped to birth the sun from the sky, and pregnant women in ancient Egypt called upon her to assist in their births, keeping them safe and healthy and helping them to care for and nurse their newborns. Represented as a hippo standing on her thick hind legs with large, pendulous breasts, Taueret sports a very pregnant belly. Taueret was quite a popular Goddess in ancient Thebes, so much so that many children were named after her and many families decorated their homes with her image.

The Three Fates The Three Fates have different names in different cultures but are probably best known today in their ancient Greek incarnation as Clotho (the spinner), Lachesis (the apportioner), and Atropos (the cutter). These three sisters spun, measured, and cut the thread of each human's life. They created each life according to their whims, and as Clotho spun each thread, Lachesis measured out its length, and Atropos made the final cut, the Three Fates were, in essence, crafting the birth, life span, and death of each human.

The Triple Goddess The single manifestation of the three stages of women: the Maiden, the Mother, and the Crone, or youth, maturity, and the wisdom of age.

Uksakka Finnish Goddess of household affairs and a Mother and Guardian to families, Uksakka is also called "Door Woman." She dwells underground beneath doorways of tents in Finland and Lapland, and uses her magic to change the genders of fetuses that her sisters place in women's wombs. Uksakka specifically used her magic to protect newborns and toddlers, and women invoked her to help babies take their first steps. In all matters of the private household she stood guard. She is sister to Juksakka and Sarakka.

Uzume   A belly-baring Goddess similar to the Greek Goddess Baubo, Uzume appears in Japanese mythology. Uzume coaxed the Sun Goddess Amaterasu back out of a cave with a skirt-lifting, laughter-filled, vulva-bearing burlesque, rescuing the world from a lethal lack of sunshine.

Venus   The Roman incarnation of the Greek Goddess Aphrodite, Venus was the Goddess of love, beauty, and sex. She bore many children by many different lovers and she reveled in her sexuality and beauty.

Venus of Laussel   A carving of a woman on a limestone wall in the Dordogne Valley in France dating back 21,000 years ago. This carving, discovered in 1911 by physician J. G. Lalanne, which archaeologists refer to as the *Venus of Laussel,* probably decorated a ceremonial shelter. The *Venus of Laussel* cradles a pregnant belly with one hand and in the other, holds a bison horn aloft. The wide hips, the breasts ready for nursing, the curvaceous shape, and the symbolic bison horn reveal this figure as a probable fertility figure, and the curved horn, notched with 13 marks, probably corresponded to the 13 lunar months in the year. Some pre-historians also believe that the horn represents the Universal Vulva, that key to the propagation of the species. The 18-inch bas-relief is displayed in the Musée d'Aquitaine in Bordeaux, France.

Venus of Willendorf   The *Venus of Willendorf* is a small figure of a woman carved out of limestone, found in 1908 by archaeologist Josef Szombathy near Willendorf, Austria. Archaeologists believe that it is among the earliest of all human representations, probably dating from somewhere between 22,000 and 24,000 B.C.E. This symbol of fertility and creation is small but with proportionally huge breasts, stomach, thighs, and hips. You can see the statue in the Naturhistorisches Museum in Vienna, Austria.

Virgin of Juquila   A native Mexican incarnation of the Virgin Mary, the Virgin of Juquila bestows miracles in the form of healing and the granting of wishes for love, money, and material prosperity. In the tiny town of Juquila in Oaxaca, Mexico, stands a shrine to the Virgin of Juquila. For centuries, Mexicans have made sacred pilgrimages to visit this Virgin and to make requests for things they need or want—from money to a spouse to a child recovering from illness.

Vivi   Vivi in Rebecca Wells' novel *The Divine Secrets of the Ya-Ya Sisterhood* is at once tragic, beautiful, kind, cruel, sacrificing, abusive, forgiving, and forgivable as she struggles to make sense of her own life as a girl, a woman, a friend, and a mother to her daughter, Siddha.

Woman with a Balance   In the painting called *Woman with a Balance* by Johannes Vermeer (one of the greatest painters of the Dutch Golden Age in the seventeenth century), a woman, quite possibly pregnant, holds a balance in a dim room. As is typical for Vermeer, this painting is loaded with symbolism. While the table at which she stands is filled with pearls and valuables, she ignores them, and her scales are empty. She stands in front of a painting of the Judgment, during which God judges all humankind. Symbolically, the woman is weighing spiritual virtue—she ignores the material wealth on the table, yet the golden light from the window shines upon her extended belly. The painting, probably painted between 1662 and 1665, hangs in the National Gallery of Art in Washington, D.C.

Woyengi   Mother Woyengi was a Creatrix, according to the Ijo people of Nigeria, who sat at a great table and chair with her feet on the creation stone and shaped all the humans who will ever live. She then let people choose whether they would be a woman or a man, what kind of profession they would have, what kind of life they would choose, and how they would die.

Xi Hou   An ancient Chinese Goddess who gave birth to 10 suns. A Mother Goddess and Guardian Goddess, she is also responsible for the proper workings of daylight. Every morning, Xi Hou bathes her 10 children in a lake at the eastern edge of the world. Then, each day, one of these suns has the important job of traveling across the sky to bring daylight to the world.

Appendix B

Mother Goddess Library

Following is a listing, broken down generally by chapter topic, of other wonderful books, both Goddess based and pregnancy/newborn based, to help you explore your Mother Goddess nature more fully.

Chapter 1: Goddesses, the Creative Force, and You

Douglas, Ann. *The Mother of All Pregnancy Books: The Ultimate Guide to Conception, Birth, and Everything In-Between.* John Wiley & Sons, 2002.

Feldman, Gail Carr, Ph.D., and Katherine A. Gleason. *Releasing the Goddess Within.* Indianapolis: Alpha Books, 2003.

Murkoff, Heidi, Arlene Eisenberg, and Sandee Hathaway. *What to Expect When You're Expecting* (Third Edition). Workman Publishing Company, 2002.

Stone, Merlin. *When God Was a Woman.* San Diego: Harvest Books, 1976.

Chapter 2: Celebrate the Female Cycle

Angier, Natalie. *Woman: An Intimate Geography*. New York: Anchor Books, 2000.

Baring, Anne, and Jules Cashford. *The Myth of the Goddess: Evolution of an Image*. London: Arkana, 1993.

Bonheim, Jalaja, ed. *Goddess: A Celebration in Art and Literature*. New York: Stewart, Tabori, and Chang, 1997.

Chearney, Lee Ann. *Visits: Caring for an Aging Parent*. New York: Three Rivers Press, 1998.

Woolger, Jennifer, and Roger Woolger. *The Goddess Within*. New York: Fawcett Columbine, 1989.

Chapter 3: Fertility and Conception

Nagle, Doreen. *But I Don't Feel Too Old to Be a Mommy: The Complete Sourcebook for Starting (and Restarting) Motherhood Beyond 35 and After 40*. Health Communications, 2002.

Sjoo, Monica, and Barbara Mor. *The Great Cosmic Mother: Rediscovering the Religion of the Earth*. San Francisco: HarperSanFrancisco, 1987.

Stoppard, Miriam. *Conception, Pregnancy, and Birth*. London: DK Publishing, 2000.

Weschler, Toni. *Taking Charge of Your Fertility: The Definitive Guide to Natural Birth Control, Pregnancy Achievement, and Reproductive Health* (revised edition). New York: Quill, 2001.

Chapter 4: Embryonate: Potential Takes Hold

Deming, Lynne M., ed. *The Feminine Mystic*. Cleveland, OH: The Pilgrim Press, 1997.

Romm, Aviva Jill. *The Natural Pregnancy Book: Herbs, Nutrition, and Other Holistic Choices*. Crossing Press, 1997.

Shanahan, M. Kelly. *Your Over-35 Week-by-Week Pregnancy Guide: All the Answers to All Your Questions About Pregnancy, Birth, and Your Developing Baby.* Prima Publishing, 2001.

Tsiaras, Alexander, and Barry Werth. *From Conception to Birth: A Life Unfolds.* New York: Doubleday, 2002.

Chapter 5: The First Trimester: Dreaming, Planning, and a Sense of Wonder

Bolen, Jean Shinoda. *Goddesses in Every Woman.* New York: Harper & Row, 1984.

Cameron, Julia. *The Artist's Way: A Spiritual Path to Higher Creativity.* New York: Jeremy P. Tarcher, 1992.

Iovine, Vicky. *The Girlfriends' Guide to Pregnancy: Or Everything Your Doctor Won't Tell You.* Pocket Books, 1995.

MacDougall, Jane. *Pregnancy Week-by-Week: Everything You Need to Know About Yourself and Your Developing Baby: Plus Essential Weekly Planner.* New York: HarperCollins, 1997.

O'Brien, Paddy. *Yoga for Women: Complete Mind and Body Fitness.* London: Thorsons, 1994.

Chapter 6: The Second Trimester: Feeling Good … Powerful, and Showing It

Baker, Jeannine Parvati. *Prenatal Yoga and Natural Childbirth*, Second Edition. Freestone Publishing, 2001.

Goldberg, Natalie. *Writing Down the Bones: Freeing the Writer Within.* Boston: Shambhala, 1986.

Kindlon, Daniel J., Michael Thompson, Dan Kindlon, and Teresa Barker, cont. *Raising Cain: Protecting the Emotional Life of Boys.* Ballantine Books, 2000.

Pipher, Mary. *Reviving Ophelia: Saving the Selves of Adolescent Girls.* Ballantine Books, 1995.

Weed, Susun, and Janice Novet, illus. *Wise Woman Herbal for the Childbearing Years (Wise Woman Herbal Series, Book 1)*. Woodstock, NY: Ash Tree Publishing, 1985.

Chapter 7: The Third Trimester: Living Large

England, Pam, and Rob Horowitz. *Birthing from Within: An Extra-Ordinary Guide to Childbirth Preparation*. Partera Press, 1998.

Franck, Frederick. *Zen Seeing, Zen Drawing: Meditation in Action*. New York: Bantam Books, 1993.

Lim, Robin. *After the Baby's Birth: A Woman's Way to Wellness: A Complete Guide for Postpartum Women* (revised edition). Celestial Arts, 2001.

Wesson, Nicky. *Natural Mothering: A Guide to Holistic Therapies for Pregnancy, Birth, and Early Childhood*. Inner Traditions International Ltd., 1997.

Chapter 8: Labor: Empowering the Pain of Creation

Balaskas, Janet. *Active Birth: The New Approach to Giving Birth Naturally*. Harvard Common Press, 1992.

Nhat Hanh, Thich. *The Miracle of Mindfulness: A Manual on Meditation*. Boston: Beacon Press, 1987.

Sears, William, M.D., and Martha Sears, R.N. *The Birth Book: Everything You Need to Know to Have a Safe and Satisfying Birth*. Little Brown and Company, 1994.

Simkin, Penny. *The Birth Partner, Second Edition*. Harvard Common Press, 2001.

Chapter 9: Birth: Manifesting Life

Bond, William, and Pamela Suffield. *Gospel of the Goddess: A Return to God the Mother*. Artemis Creations Publishing, 1994.

Knight, Sirona. *Goddess Bless: Divine Affirmations, Prayers, and Blessings.* Red Wheel/Weiser, 2003.

Placksin, Sally. *Mothering the New Mother: Women's Feelings and Needs After Childbirth, a Support and Resource Guide, Second Edition.* New Market Press, 2000.

Sena, Ramaprasada, Clinton Seely, trans., and Leonard Nathan. *Grace and Mercy in Her Wild Hair: Selected Poems to the Mother Goddess, Second Edition.* Hohm Press, 1999.

Chapter 10: Postpartum: One Becomes Two

Adamson, Eve, and Maureen Kays, M.D. *Breastfeeding: A Holistic Handbook.* New York: Berkley Books, 1999.

Spock, Dr. Benjamin. *Baby and Child Care.* New York: Hawthorn Books, Inc., 1976.

Starhawk. *The Spiral Dance: The Rebirth of the Ancient Religion of the Great Goddess* (twentieth anniversary edition). San Francisco: HarperSanFrancisco, 1999.

Chapter 11: New Mom Fulfilled: Nurturing New Life

Coyle, Rena. *Baby Let's Eat!* New York: Workman Publishing, 1987.

Dominguez, Joe, and Vicki Robin. *Your Money or Your Life* (new edition). New York: Penguin Books, 1992.

Komitor, Jodi W., M.A., and Eve Adamson. *The Complete Idiot's Guide to Yoga with Kids.* Indianapolis: Alpha Books, 2000.

Lansky, Vicki. *Feed Me! I'm Yours.* New York: Bantam Books, 1974.

Shelov, Steven P., M.D., F.A.A.P., ed. *American Academy of Pediatrics Caring for Your Baby and Young Child, Birth to Age 5.* New York: Bantam Books, 1994.

Chapter 12: Mother and Child Reunion

Budilovsky, Joan, and Eve Adamson. *The Complete Idiot's Guide to Meditation, Second Edition.* Indianapolis: Alpha Books, 2003.

Johnson, Cait, and Maura D. Shaw. *Celebrating the Great Mother: A Handbook of Earth-Honoring Activities for Parents and Children.* Inner Traditions International Ltd., 1995.

Kuffner, Trish. *The Toddler's Busy Book.* Meadowbrook, 2000.

Lovelock, James. *Healing Gaia: Practical Medicine for the Planet.* New York: Harmony Books, 1991.

St. James, Elaine. *The Simplicity Reader.* New York: Smithmark, 1999.

Starhawk, Diane Baker, and Anne Hill. *Circle Round: Raising Kids in Goddess Traditions.* New York: Bantam, 2000.

Books to Share with Your Children

Brown, Margaret Wise. *Goodnight Moon* (reissue). New York: HarperCollins, 1991.

Curtis, Chara M., and Cynthia Aldrich, illus. *All I See Is Part of Me.* Illumination Arts, 1994.

Frasier, Debra. *On the Day You Were Born.* New York: Harcourt, 1991.

Hamilton, Virginia. *In the Beginning: Creation Stories from Around the World.* New York: Harcourt, 1991.

Root, Phyllis, and Helen Oxenbury, illus. *Big Momma Makes the World.* Candlewick Press: 2002.

Goddess Index

A
Aditi, 162
Armaiti, 21
Artemis, 21
Ashke-tanne-mat, 132
Athena, 127

B
Baubo, 159
Blackfoot First Woman, 49
Bly, Carol, 9

C
Cuba, 185
Cunina, 185

D
Devi, 9, 46
Diana, 35

E–F
Earth, 43-44
Eileithyia, 129
Eingana, 81

Four Meshkents, 181

G
Gaia, 9
Goldberg, Natalie, 9
Grandmother, 92
Great Mother Goddess, 19

H
Haumea, 152
Hecate, 35
Hera, 9, 195

I–J
Inanna, 9
Ishtar, 166
Isis, 43-44

K
Khotun, 66
Kwan Yin, 6-7

L
Lakshmi, 63-64
Lucina, 35
Lunar, 35-36

M
Macha of the Red Tresses, 114-115
Menses, 30

Meshkent, 181
Moon, 77
Mother Woyengi, 59
Mwana Waresa, 9

N–O

Nut, 42

O'Hara, Scarlett, 148
Ogboinba, 97-98

P–Q

Pandora, 24

Queen Mother, 203

R–S

Roman Goddess, 21
Rumina, 185

Selene, 77

T–U

Taueret, 109
Themis, 94

Uksakka, 177

V–W

Virgin Mary, 9

X–Y–Z

Xi Hou, 198

Index

A

Abraham and Sarah, 61
active phase (labor), 128-130
Addie (*As I Lay Dying*), 12
Aditi, 162
Aegean Venus, 75-76
Aegeria, 117
altars (Motherhood), 21-23, 191
anatomy (breasts), 67
announcements (birth), 154-155
Apprortioner, 34
archetypes (mother)
    literature, 10-13
    Tarot cards, 13-17
Armaiti, 21
Arnolfini Wedding Portrait, 94
art
    births, 149-151
    portraits (Mother Goddess), 101
    pregnancy, 94-95
Artemis, 21, 35, 77
Arthurian legend, 12
artistic outlet exercise, 54-55
As I Lay Dying, 12
Ashke-tanne-mat, 132
astronomy
    Big Bang, 143
    embryos, 65-67
Athena, 127
Atropos, 34

B

babies
    birth announcements, 154-155
    breastfeeding, 163-167
    crowning, 135
    feeding, 99, 185
    life paths, 180-183
    naming, 123-124
    naps, 185
    play, 186-188
    rooms, 98-99
    routines, 183-186
    sleeping guardians, 185
    society preparations, 197-199
baby books, 189-191
baby name websites, 123-124
Babylonian Goddess Ishtar, 166
balance, 95
Baubo, 159
beauty, 64
Beecher, Henry Ward, 196
Belly Goddess, 159
Bhagavat Pourana, 62
Big Bang, 143
birth, 143
    announcements, 154-155
    art, 149-151
    Goddess webs, 153
    Mother Goddess comfort, 151-153
    mystical air, 144-146
    unexpected, 147-149
Birth, The, 150
birthing partners, 132
birthing plans, 82, 119-122
Blackfoot First Woman, 49
blastocysts, 57
Bly, Carol, 9
bodhisattva, 6
bodies
    postpartum, 158-160
    third trimester, 107-110

waxing, 76-78
weight, 92-96
body cycles, 28-30
books (baby), 189-191
boxes (Motherhood), 23-25
Brahman, 46
Braxton-Hicks contractions, 117
breaking water, 126
breastfeeding, 163-167
    benefits, 164
    inconveniences, 165
    latching on, 164
breastmilk
    Khotun, 66
    Lakshmi, 63-64
    producing, 67
    sea of milk, 62
breasts
    anatomy, 67
    breastfeeding, 163-167
    breastmilk
        Khotun, 66
        Lakshmi, 63-64
        producing, 67
        sea of milk, 62
    Milky Way project, 69
Buddhist god of mercy, 20
bulbs, planting, 67-68
Burnell, Jocelyn Bell, 66

C

careers, balancing, 96-98
Celestial Vault, 42-45
Celie (*The Color Purple*), 200
Celtic Goddess of War, 114-115
children
    faith, 200-201
    genetics, 58
    individuality, 58
    society preparations, 197-199
    touch-base rituals, 205-206

Chinese Virgin Mary, 6-7
choices, making, 59
Clotho, 34
Color Purple, The, 200
colostrum, 164
conception
    artistic exercise, 54-55
    Celestial Vault, 42-45
    Creatrix exercise, 53-54
    Earth, 51-52
    male/female partnership, 44-45
    mother personalities, 45-47
contractions
    active phase, 128
    Braxton-Hicks, 117
    doctor, calling, 126
    latent phase, 126
    second stage of labor, 133
    transition phase, 131
Cosmic Mother, 4
Creatrix, 4, 53-54
Crones, 37
crowning (baby), 135
Cuba, 185
cultivating Mother Love, 6-9
Cunina, 185
cycles (body), 28-30

D

daily routines, 183-186
daughter-mother relationships, 31-33
decision-making, 59
Demeter and Persephone, 32
depression (postpartum), 160-163
Devi, 9, 46
Diana, 21, 35, 77
Divine Secrets of the Ya-Ya Sisterhood, The, 13
Doll's House, A, 12
downward-pointing triangles, 37

E

Earth, 51-52
Egeria, 117
Egyptian Mother Goddess of Childbirth, 181
Eileithyia, 129
Emain Macha, 114
embryos
    astronomy, 65-67
    bulb-planting exercise, 67-68
    universe, 67
emotions
    guardianship, 176-178
    Mother Love, 6-9
    postpartum depression, 160-163
    weather charts, 171-172
Empress (Tarot deck), 100
Endymion, 77
Ensler, Eve, 68
epidurals, 128
exercises (yoga), 82-85
van Eyck, Jan, 94

F

Fairy Godmothers, 78
faith, 200-201
families
    faith, 200-201
    generations, 202-204
    touch-base rituals, 205-206
Fargo, 111-112
fate, 33-34
le Fay, Morgan, 12
fears, releasing, 80-82
feeding babies, 185
feelings. *See* emotions
female/male partnerships, 44-45
fertility, 42-45
Finnish Goddess of Household Affairs, 177
first stages of labor
    active phase, 128-130
    birthing partners, 132
    epidurals, 128
    latent phase, 126-127
    meditation, 130
    transition phase, 131-133
first trimester
    fears, 80-82
    moment of knowing, 74-75
    tea, 86-87
    waxing body, 76-78
    wishes, 78-80
    yoga, 82-85
flowers, 63
force (Goddess), 4-5
Four Meshkents, 181

G

Gaia, 9, 51
generations, 202-204
genetics (children), 58
ginger, 86
Giorgione, 168
Goddess force, 4-5
Goddess webs, 153
Goddesses
    night, 29
    sun association, 28
    triple, 36-37
Goldberg, Natalie, 9
Gone with the Wind, 147
Grandmother Goddesses, 92
Great Deep, 42-45
Great Mother Goddess, 19
Greek Goddesses
    belly laughter, 159
    childbirth, 129
    Earth, 9
    marriage and children, 9
    Pandora, 24

guardianshi (homes), 176-178
guidance pendulums, 136-138
Gunderson, Marge (*Fargo*), 111-112

H

Hamlet, 12
hands across generations, 40
Haumea, 152
Hawaiian Earth-Mother Goddess, 152
hCG (human chorionic gonadotropin), 57
Hecate, 35
Hera, 9, 195
Hindu Goddess Devi, 46
Hindu trinity, 46
Hippopotamus goddess of fertility and birth, 109
history
    Buddhist god of mercy, 20
    generations, 202-204
    Great Mother Goddess, 19
    patriarchal tribes, 19
    sun association, 28
Hobbes, Miranda, 161
homes
    guardianship, 176-178
    preparing, 98-100
horn of plenty (second trimester), 90-91
human chorionic gonadotropin. *See* hCG

I–J–K

I Don't Know How She Does It, 13
Inanna, 9
Indian Mother Goddess, 9
individuality (children), 58
Isaac, 61
Ishtar, 166
Isis, 43-44
Japanese spider Goddess, 132
Jewish Bride, The, 95
Jocasta (*Oedipus the King*), 11
Juichimen, 20
Jung, Carl, 10
Juno, 9, 21, 195
Jupiter, 195

Kahlo, Frida, 150
Khotun, 66
Kubai-khotun, 66
Kwan Yin, 6-7

L

labor, 125
    birth, 143
        announcements, 154-155
        art, 149-151
        Goddess webs, 153
        Mother Goddess comfort, 151-153
        mystical air, 144-146
        unexpected, 147-149
    crowning, 135
    doctor, calling, 126
    first stage
        active phase, 128-130
        birthing partners, 132
        epidurals, 128
        guidance pendulum, 136-138
        latent phase, 126-127
        meditation, 130
        second stage, 135-136
        transition phase, 131-133
        water meditation, 138-140
    latent phase, 127
    mucus plug, releasing, 126
    second stage, 133-135
    water, breaking, 126

Lady Justice, 94
Lakshmi, 63-64
Lalanne, J. G., 91
latching on (breastfeeding), 164
latent phase (labor), 126-127
life paths (babies), 180-183
life stages
    fate, 33-34
    hands across generations, 40
    lunar Goddesses, 35-36
    personal triangles, 38-40
    triple Goddesses, 36-37
literature
    Arthurian legend, 12
    As I Lay Dying, 12
    books, reading, 188
    Color Purple, The, 200
    Divine Secrets of the Ya-Ya Sisterhood, The, 13
    Doll's House, A, 12
    Hamlet, 12
    I Don't Know How She Does It, 13
    Metamorphoses, 11
    Mother archetypes, 10-13
    Mother Goose, 188
    Oedipus the King, 11
    poems, 172-173
    "Song of Myself," 172
    Woman's Dictionary of Symbols and Sacred Objects, The, 83
Long-fingered woman, 132
lotus flowers, 63
Lucina, 35
luck, 64
Luna, 21, 35, 77
lunar Goddesses, 35-36

M

Macha of the Red Tresses, 114-115
Maidens, 36
male/female partnerships, 44-45
mantle of motherhood, 195-197
Marge (*Fargo*), 111-112
Maya (Queen), 145
meditation, 76, 130
    Meshkent, 181
    water, 138-140
Menses, 30
Meshkent, 181
Metamorphoses, 11
Milky Way, 66-69
moon, 34-36
Mother archetypes
    literature, 10-13
    Tarot cards, 13-17
Mother Earth, 51-52
Mother Eingana, 81
Mother Goddess
    portraits, 101
    qualities, choosing, 207-208
    walks, 101
Mother Goose, 188
Mother Love, 6-9
Mother of the Fruitful Breast, 166
Mother Woyengi, 59
mother-daughter relationships, 31-33
Motherhood altar, 21-23, 191
Motherhood boxes, 23-25
mothers, 36
    balance, 95
    Cosmic Mother, 4
    faith, 200-201
    mantle of motherhood, 195-197
    multi-tasking, 167-170
    personalities, 45-47
    types, 60-62, 193
Mountain Pose, 84
mucus plug, releasing, 126
multi-tasking, 167-170
Mwana Waresa, 9

N–O

naming babies, 123-124
naps, 185
nausea, curing, 86-87
Navaratri, 46
Nigeria (Mother Woyengi), 59
night goddess, 29
Nora (*A Doll's House*), 12
nursing. *See* breastfeeding
Nut Goddess, 42

O'Hara, Scarlett, 148
Oedipus the King, 11
Ogboinba, 97-98
Old Testament, 61
Osiris, 44

P

paintings
   Birth, The, 150
   pregnancy, 94-95
   Tempest, The, 168
Pandora, 24
patriarchal tribes, 19
pendulums (guidance), 136-138
Persephone and Demeter, 32
Persian Goddess Armaiti, 21
personal triangles, 38-40
personalities, 45-47
phases (labor)
   active, 128-130
   latent, 126-127
   transition, 131-133
plans (birthing), 82, 119-122
planting bulbs, 67-68
playing (babies), 186-188
poems, 172-173
portraits, 101
positions (labor), 135

postpartum
   bodies, 158-160
   breastfeeding, 163-167
   depression, 160-163
   poems, 172-173
   Renaissance woman, becoming, 167-170
   sexuality, 167
   weather charts, 171-172
pregnancy
   art, 94-95
   birthing plans, 82, 119-122
   first trimester
      fears, 80-82
      moment of knowing, 74-75
      tea, 86-87
      waxing body, 76-78
      wishes, 78-80
      yoga, 82-85
   labor. *See* labor
   second trimester, 89
      careers, balancing, 96-98
      feeding spaces (baby), 99
      home, preparing, 98-100
      horn of plenty, 90-91
      nursery, 98-99
      salads, 101-102
      weight, 92-96
   third trimester, 105-106
      appearances, 107-110
      birthing plans, 119-122
      Braxton-Hicks contractions, 117
      names, choosing, 123-124
      partners, 118
      slowing down, 113-115
      Tao, 115-116
      workloads, 110-113
preschoolers, 186
prosperity, 64
pushing (labor), 133

Q–R

qualities (Mother Goddess), 207-208
Queens
    Coins, 16
    Cups, 16
    Gertrude, 12
    Maya, 145
    Mother, 203
    Pentacles, 16
    Swords, 15
    Wands, 15
quizzes (Tarot Mother Goddess), 13-17

reading, books, 188
Reddy, Kate, 13
Rembrandt, 95
Renaissance woman, 167-170
rituals (touch-base), 205-206
Roman Goddess Juno, 21
routines, 183-186
Rumina, 185

S

salads, 101-102
Samanta-gambhira-shri-vimala-prabha, 29
Sarah and Abraham, 61
sea of milk, 62
second stage of labor, 133-136
second trimester, 89
    careers, balancing, 96-98
    feeding spaces (baby), 99
    home, preparing, 98-100
    horn of plenty, 90-91
    nursery, 98-99
    salads, 101-102
    weight, 92-96
Selene, 21, 35, 77
Sex and the City, 161
sexuality (postpartum), 167
Shiva, 46

Siddhartha, 145
Simpson, Marge, 194
Simpsons, The, 194
sleeping children, guardians, 185
snake Goddess (Mother Eingana), 81
"Song of Myself," 172
Starry One, 42-45
Sumerian Queen of Heaven, 9
sun, 28
Sun card (Tarot deck), 27
Sun Salutation, 84

T

Taoism, 116
Taouris, 109
Tarot cards
    Empress, 100
    Mother archetypes, 13-17
    Sun card, 27
Tarot Mother Goddess quiz, 13-17
Taueret, 109
tea, 86-87
Tempest, The, 168
Themis, 94
third trimester, 105-106
    appearances, 107-110
    birthing plans, 119-122
    Braxton-Hicks contractions, 117
    names, choosing, 123-124
    partners, 118
    slowing down, 113-115
    Tao, 115-116
    workloads, 110-113
Three Fates, 33-34
touch-base rituals, 205-206
transition phase (labor), 131-133
triangles, 37-40
trimesters
    first
        fears, 80-82
        moment of knowing, 74-75
        tea, 86-87

waxing body, 76-78
wishes, 78-80
yoga, 82-85
second, 89
careers, balancing, 96-98
feeding spaces (baby), 99
home, preparing, 98-100
horn of plenty, 90-91
nursery, 98-99
salads, 101-102
weight, 92-96
third, 105-106
appearances, 107-110
birthing plans, 119-122
Braxton-Hicks contractions, 117
names, choosing, 123-124
partners, 118
slowing down, 113-115
Tao, 115-116
workloads, 110-113
trinity (Hindu), 46
triple Goddesses, 36-37
Tubman, Harriet, 135-136

U–V

Uksakka, 177
unexpected births, 147-149
universe
embryos, 67
fertility, 42

Vagina Monologues, The, 68
Vedic mythology, 62-64
Venus, 11
Venus of Laussel, 91
Venus of Willendorf, 29-30
Virgin Mary, 9
Virgin of Juquila, 79
Vishnu, 46
Vivi (*The Divine Secrets of the Ya-Ya Sisterhood*), 13

W

Walker, Alice, 200
Walker, Barbara G., 83
walks (Mother Goddess), 101
water, breaking, 126
water meditation, 138-140
waxing body, 76-78
weather charts, 171-172
webs (Goddess), 153
weight, 92-96
Whitman, Walt, 172
Wilkes, Melanie, 147
wishes, 78-80
Woman's Dictionary of Symbols and Sacred Objects, The, 83
workloads, balancing, 110-113

X –Y–Z

Xi Hou, 198

yin/yang, 28-30
yoga, 82-85

Zeus, 195
Zulu Sky Goddess, 9
zygotes, 57

Love yourself, know yourself, and be the *Goddess* you are!

Are you a Goddess? Of course you are! *Releasing the Goddess Within* offers a fascinating look at ways you can integrate the Goddess into your daily life. It brings the Goddess up to the twenty-first century by exploring spirituality; the ages and stages of women; and the ways in which food and drink, sleep, exercise, play, sex, and more lend women their strength and creativity. The heart of the book shows how meditation, knowledge, and action can release the Goddess within you. Enjoy the confidence and well-being that come with Goddess discovery and self-awareness.

Available at all retailers.

ISBN: 0-02-864405-0
$16.95 US/$25.99 CAN
6" x 9" • Paperback • 240 pages

ALPHA